CW00383300

COLOUR OF PARADISE

Colour of Paradise

THE EMERALD IN THE AGE OF GUNPOWDER EMPIRES

KRIS LANE

YALE UNIVERSITY PRESS
NEW HAVEN AND LONDON

For information about this and other Yale University Press publications, please contact:
U.S. Office: sales.press@yale.edu   www.yalebooks.com
Europe Office: sales@yaleup.co.uk   www.yaleup.co.uk

Set in Adobe Caslon by IDSUK (DataConnection) Ltd.
Printed in Great Britain by TJ International Ltd, Padstow, Cornwall

Library of Congress Cataloging-in-Publication Data

Lane, Kris E., 1967
    The colour of paradise: the emerald in the age of gunpowder empires/Kris Lane.
      p. cm.
    Includes bibliographical references and index.
    ISBN 978–0–300–16131–1 (ci: alk. paper)
    1.   Emeralds—Spain—Colonies—America—History. 2.   Emeralds—Colombia—
History. 3.   Inquisition—Spain. 4.   Inquisition—Portugal.   I. Title.
    TN997.E5L36 2010
    553.8′609—dc22

                                                                                  2009026512

A catalogue record for this book is available from the British Library.

10 9 8 7 6 5 4 3 2 1

To the memory of A. B. K. Matongo,
son of the Copper Belt

'It's hard to explain what happened to me in Colombia, renowned home of the finest emeralds. They searched one out for me there, discovered it and carved it, and all the poets held it up on their fingertips to offer it to me, and there from the tips of the hands of all the gathered poets my emerald ascended, celestial stone, until it vanished in the air amid a tempest that left us all trembling in fear.'

Pablo Neruda, *Stones of the Sky*

Contents

Illustrations

15. Emerald Centrepiece Inscribed with Shi'i Prayer (Harold and Erica Van Pelt photo)
16. Coscuez Miner Temístocles Reasgos with Gem Rough (author photo)

❖

Preface

A N experiment in global history by way of a luxury commodity, this book examines the mining, exchange and consumption of Colombian emeralds from the early sixteenth to late eighteenth centuries. In this long period, which marked both the beginnings of European overseas expansion and the emergence of Asia's so-called gunpowder empires, emeralds originating in the mines of north-central New Granada – primarily modern Muzo, Colombia – became for the first time a global commodity. Art historians and gemologists have documented consumption of these stones in Latin America, Europe, the Middle East and South Asia, but to date there has been no systematic historical investigation of how they were produced, shipped or exchanged, and in what quantities or forms.

Colombian emeralds, which reached Europe after the Spanish conquest of the Muisca highlands around Bogotá in 1538, were greatly esteemed by Habsburg and other Eurasian princes as gems and objects of scientific curiosity. Throughout Christian Europe, faceted, rounded and tumbled emeralds were incorporated into crowns, rings, religious ornaments and other jewelled artefacts. Some extraordinary crystals were showcased in wonder cabinets alongside Native American featherwork and other marvels. Yet the largest stones produced in early modern Colombia soon found their outlet not in Europe or the Americas – or even China, destination of much New World silver – but in South and southwestern Asia, where they were consumed, hoarded, ritually exchanged and pillaged by the rulers of the Ottoman, Safavid and Mughal empires, and their many tributaries, neighbours and offshoots.

These gems, mined in the hills of northeastern Colombia by Amerindian serfs and enslaved Africans from the sixteenth to nineteenth centuries, remain centrepieces of the crown (now state) jewels of Turkey and Iran. Those of India were largely scattered to private collectors and museums. Combining a wide range of archival and published sources from the sixteenth century onward, this book tracks the extraordinary odyssey of Colombian emeralds from the period of Spanish conquest to the Age of Napoleon and Bolívar. A brief postscript outlines the Colombian emerald industry since independence. Despite new emerald finds in Central Africa, South Asia and Brazil, Colombia remains the world's most significant emerald source.

Those who profited most from the early world trade in emeralds were not the owners of the mines but rather a small number of Spanish, Portuguese, Flemish and other mostly European merchants who managed to survive punishing sea voyages and overland treks to carry exotic stones deep into the kingdoms and principalities of South Asia and the Middle East. Most prominent among these merchants across the entire period covered by this book were clans of Sephardic Jews and so-called New Christians, or Iberian ethnic Jews forced to convert to Catholicism. When living in Spanish and Portuguese territories, including distant Goa, capital of Portuguese India, the Sephardim were forced to ride out waves of persecution by the Inquisition, and many fled to the Netherlands, England, France and Italy. The global gem trade migrated with them.

A common trend by the late seventeenth century was for New Christian merchants living in colonial Colombia's port of Cartagena de Indias, Lisbon or Seville to send emeralds to their openly Jewish relatives living in Amsterdam or London for re-export to India, Turkey or Persia. By 1700, London-based Sephardim regularly sent emeralds to Madras on English East India Company vessels to exchange for diamonds. Land-based Asian traders, including factors for the Ottomans, Mughals and Safavids, must also have profited from the emerald trade through Aleppo, Shiraz and other cities, but surviving sources say little about these alternative routes.

An equally important, practically forgotten, story regards emerald mineworkers, most of them native Andeans, West and West-Central Africans and their descendants. Grubbing for emeralds was deadly. Documents show that landslides were frequent and that mine overseers meted out cruel punishments and kept workers underfed. Still, the greatest danger was disease. The best mines were located in a lowland rain forest where mosquito-borne diseases were endemic by the early seventeenth century. Unsanitary camp conditions also led to outbreaks of dysentery, cholera and other debilitating and often fatal maladies. Under such conditions, labourers were unable to reproduce themselves, forcing replenishment from outside if emeralds were to flow. Documents also show that throughout colonial times mineworkers remained adept at finding, secreting and bartering prime stones, despite the hardships and an alarming death rate.

When possible, this book attempts to convey a sense of the daily life and struggles of the thousands of mineworkers who unearthed the great stones treasured by Eurasian nobles of various religious persuasions. It is interested in the petty smugglers, gem cutters and other socially marginalized individuals drawn into the secretive and specialized world of emeralds. This book also attempts another difficult task: to fathom what emeralds meant in several Asian and mostly Islamic gift-giving economies far removed from the concerns of ordinary folk, at the other end of what some have termed the commodity chain.

This is a story of trade, but also of transformations – of how members of profoundly different societies on opposite sides of the globe assigned value to what in the end were no more than a few thousand pounds of imperfectly shiny but rare green rocks.

❖

Acknowledgements

R OMANCING Colombia's stones has been a shared adventure. I thank the staffs of the several archives and libraries I consulted, especially Dr Mauricio Tovar of the Archivo General de la Nación in Bogotá. I also thank the miners and gem cutters of Muzo, Coscuez, Chivor and Bogotá who patiently explained the complexities of their trades in the course of several visits over the last decade. Special thanks are due to miner and master jeep pilot Hildebrando 'Mataperros' Dotor of Muzo, to mining operations director Héctor Varela of Chivor and to master lapidary Diana Cañón of Bogotá. All gave me a sense of what it means to rely on emeralds for a living. I am also indebted to Dr Daniel de Narváez McAllister, who not only made my unforgettable visit to Chivor possible, but also graciously shared his knowledge of Colombia's emerald business, geology and history.

Others who provided valuable leads and aid include Susan Ramírez, Alfonso Quiroz, Henriette de Bruyn Kops, Robert Ferry, Hermes Tovar Pinzón, Renée Soulodre-La France, Molly Warsh, Tom Cohen, Abdul-Karim and Zahi Rafeq, Jorge Flores, Bradley Naranch, Jos Gommans, Daviken Studnicki-Gizbert, Kim Lynn, Wim Klooster, Aurelio Espinosa, Robert Marx, Hazel Forsyth, Bhaswati Bhattacharya, Benjamin Teensma, Erick Rochette and Bruce Lenman. For image help, I thank Sarah Williams, Sibel Zandi-Hayek, Sinéad Ward, Revinder Chahal, Mike Blum, Vera Hammer, Budour al-Qassar, Alison Miner, Erica Van Pelt, Dylan Kibler, Susan Danforth and Michael Francis. Rick Britton mapped the emerald world. I also thank members of the Rocky Mountain Council of Latin American Studies and members of the Early Modern Studies groups at Catholic, Vanderbilt, Brown, and Penn State universities, and finally my College of William & Mary colleagues for commenting on preliminary findings and prodding further explorations. Professor Maxine Berg of the University of Warwick and my department colleague Paul Mapp both read my wordy draft-in-the-rough and offered sage advice on how to cut and polish. If the result is less than lapidary the fault is mine. At Yale University Press, London, I thank editor Robert Baldock and his wonderful team, in particular Candida Brazil, Tami Halliday, Steve Kent, Rachael Lonsdale, and Patricia Hilton-Johnson.

Although I began collecting material on Colombian emeralds while in graduate school in Minnesota in the early 1990s, the core research for this book was funded by a Fulbright-IIE visiting scholar grant to Colombia (2005), an NEH grant to read at the John Carter Brown Library in Providence, Rhode Island (2006), and a David B. and Carolyn D. Wakefield Distinguished Associate Professorship, which paid for travel to archives in Seville, Madrid, Lisbon and London (2004–7). Color illustrations were made possible by generous support from the College of William & Mary and a gift from Joseph Plumeri. I am most deeply indebted to my wife, Pamela, and my daughter, Ximena, who supported this project despite some hair-raising travels and several extended absences. Finally, I dedicate this book to the memory of A.B.K. Matongo, a great colleague and close friend from my Minnesota years. It was Albert who first piqued my interest in this topic by showing me a *New York Times* article profiling Muzo emerald boss Víctor Carranza.

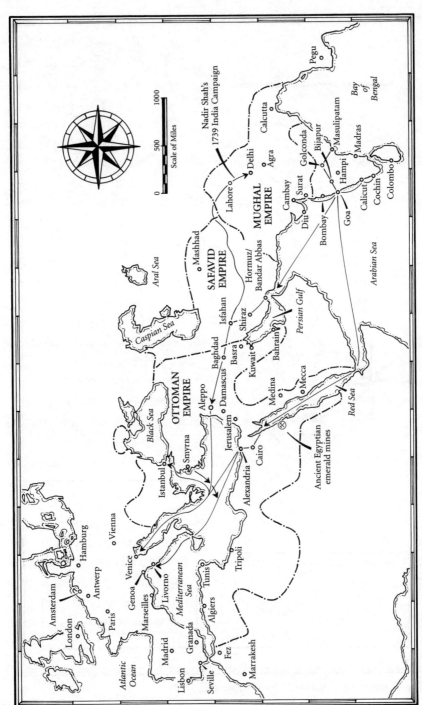

1 European Trade and Gunpowder Empires

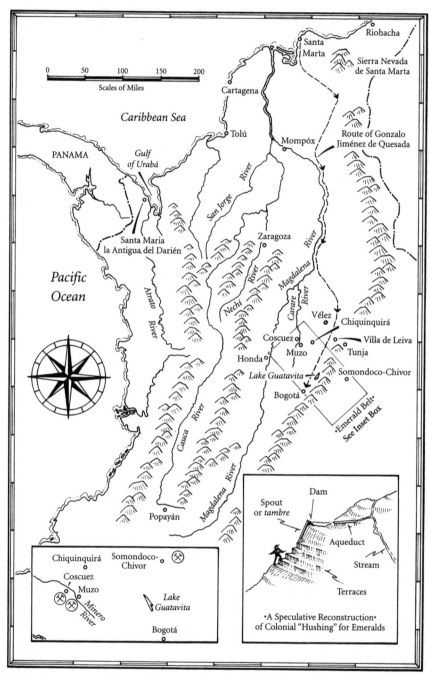

Scales of Miles

0 50 100 150 200

Caribbean Sea

PANAMA

Pacific Ocean

Riohacha

Santa Marta

Sierra Nevada de Santa Marta

Cartagena

Tolú

Mompóx

Route of Gonzalo Jiménez de Quesada

Gulf of Urabá

Santa Maria la Antigua del Darién

Zaragoza

Atrato River

San Jorge River

Nechi River

Cauca River

Magdalena River

Carare River

Vélez

Chiquinquirá

Villa de Leiva

Coscuez

Muzo

Tunja

Honda

Lake Guatavita

Somondoco-Chivor

Bogotá

•Emerald Belt•
See Inset Box

Popayán

Chiquinquirá

Somondoco-Chivor

Coscuez

Muzo

Minero River

Lake Guatavita

Bogotá

Spout or *tambre*

Dam

Aqueduct

Stream

Terraces

•A Speculative Reconstruction•
of Colonial "Hushing" for Emeralds

2 The Conquest of Colombia's Emerald Fields, 1537–87

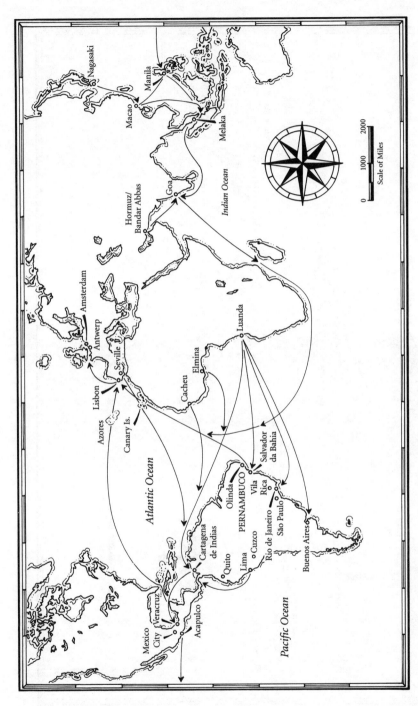

3 Iberia's Global Shipping Routes, Sixteenth to Eighteenth Centuries

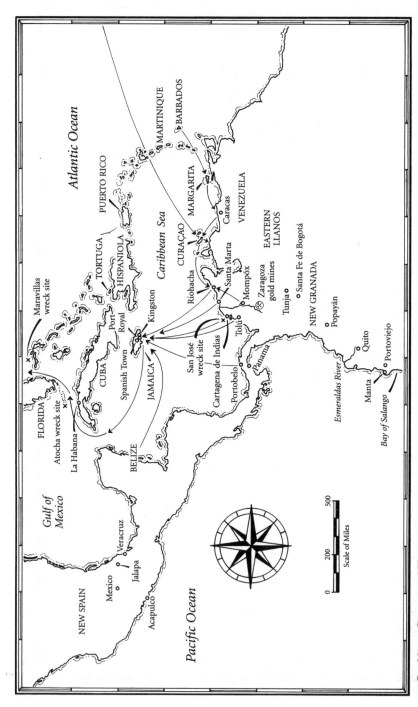

4 Caribbean Contraband Trade Networks, c.1655–1808

Introduction

BY the end of the seventeenth century, Safavid Persia's decline had become painfully obvious. It was in the reign of Shah Sultan Husayn, beginning in 1694, that the most serious threats arose. Neighbours in Georgia mounted the first external challenges, followed by others from Russia inspired by Peter the Great. More worrisome were much older rivals to the west: the Ottomans. Harsh treatment of Sunni subjects on Persia's western frontier encouraged Turkish aggression in the first decades of the eighteenth century. But in the end it was Afghani tribesmen, nominal subjects of the shah, whose rebellions finally brought down the Safavid Dynasty.

Strong as they were, the Afghanis soon lost power to a defender of the Safavids recruited from the ranks of the nomadic Afshar Turkmen of northeast Persia. One of Asia's greatest warriors since Timur, he would call himself Nadir Shah (Plate 1). From his first campaigns in 1726, while still a subaltern, to his assassination in 1747, Nadir terrorized and dominated a considerable portion of South and southwestern Asia.

Nadir's 1739 sack of Delhi stripped the Mughal emperor of both his title and centuries' worth of accumulated treasure. Amongst the booty were the legendary Peacock Throne, the Koh-i-noor diamond and the largest stock of emeralds, mostly of Colombian origin, in the world. The Peacock Throne was parcelled out and the Koh-i-noor diamond found its way into England's crown jewels, but scores of Mughal emeralds remain housed in Iran's Central Bank Museum.

How did this come about? According to contemporaries, the Mughals, like the Safavids, had, by the turn of the eighteenth century, become weak – soft creatures of the harem, or dupes of clever eunuchs. Both dynasties had for generations lacked a charismatic leader bent on terrorizing subjects or conquering neighbours. Such a man was Nadir Shah. By all accounts a brilliant military strategist, he rose to prominence first in the service of a Safavid pretender, then seized the reins of power for himself. Though a provincial commoner by birth – a 'son of the sword', he liked to say – Nadir gladly took up the cause of Persian revival. By the time of his assassination in 1747 he had expanded the empire far beyond the limits set by his Safavid predecessors and laid the foundations for modern Iran.[1]

Squadrons of well-trained musketeers were critical to Nadir's arsenal, as were long-barrelled cannons capable of penetrating metres-thick stone bastions. Although some historians now bristle at the term 'gunpowder empire', coined by Islamist Marshall Hodgson in 1974, they agree that gunpowder was a key ingredient of Nadir Shah's success.[2] Critics are right, however, in that on the battlefield it was not guns or powder, but rather Nadir's more traditionally terrifying blend of audacity and speed that ensured victory. A true warrior in the Central Asian tradition, he was master of both open field and high-country ambush. Nadir's favourite weapons were horses and dromedaries.

After crowning himself emperor in 1736 by placing his jewelled *jiqa*, or turban ornament, on the right rather than left side, Nadir let no one stand in his way. First to pose a challenge were internal enemies, many of them tribal mountaineers like his own ancestors. After suppressing them by force or co-opting their chiefs, he turned to the Uzbeks, then the Ottomans. The Turks were reeling from setbacks in Central Europe, but proved themselves much stronger than Nadir had hoped. According to Armenian eyewitness and historian Abraham of Erevan, they drove him running from Baghdad under heavy fire following what seemed an easy victory.[3]

As war costs soared, the famous jewelled treasures of the Mughals grew more attractive. Spies suggested an easy target in the person of Muhammad Shah, a mere shadow of his grandfather, the great conqueror and 'warrior of the faith', Aurangzeb. It was thus plunder more than desire to rule South Asia that brought Nadir to northern India in January 1739. For propaganda's sake it helped that he was following in the footsteps of Alexander and Timur.

As Nadir and his forces approached the frontier city of Lahore, he was offered money, jewels and elephants as ransom by its governor and citizens. The invader accepted these 'gifts' with proper reluctance then marched on towards the great city of Karnal. Here Nadir and his battle-hardened followers faced off against the Mughal emperor, his generals and a sea of raw recruits. Troops were estimated at more than 100,000 on both sides, and Nadir's forces were said to include some 7,000 armed female captives disguised as men.[4] Nadir's plan, hatched on the spot as usual, worked perfectly. Elite Mughal columns were ripped apart by well-placed musketeers while camels carrying flaming platforms frightened the emperor's war elephants. Retreating forces were cut off and captured. Muhammad Shah abdicated on 26 February 1739.

Nadir and his men rode triumphantly to Delhi, the humiliated Muhammad and his retinue trailing some distance behind. Once in the city, India's newest conquistador was presented with a staggering array of Mughal treasures dating to the time of founding emperor Babur. According to the contemporary Persian chronicler Mirza Mehdi, '. . . all the treasures of the kings of the earth were not equal to the tenth part . . .' of what Muhammad Shah had to offer. Nadir again feigned disinterest for a moment, then had coins struck in Delhi's mint proclaiming: 'The Sultan over the Sultans of the Earth is Nadir the King of Kings, Lord of the Fortunate Conjunction.'[5]

The citizens of Delhi were less acquiescent than their emperor, and soon flowed out in open rebellion. Snipers killed several of Nadir's men, and the reaction of India's newly anointed 'King of

Kings' was swift and ruthless: house-by-house searches for rebels produced piles of bodies. More ransom than before was demanded of the terrified survivors, and Nadir's soldiers were allowed to take what they could. Still, India's humid heat quickly sapped the desert mountaineers' will. Nadir named Muhammad 'King of Hindustan' and packed for Persia. As hoped, he carried with him, along with huge chests of money, one of the world's greatest accumulations of gems and jewelled objects.

It is impossible to calculate the value of the emeralds Nadir Shah took home to Iran, although Mirza Mehdi described the Mughal Emperor's jewels as 'beyond enumeration'. Muhammad Kazim, another chronicler, said of the jewels: 'the mind is incapable of imagining them'.[6] Diamonds, rubies and pearls were numerous, and many large, but emeralds still stood out. So many were taken that a late nineteenth-century shah ordered hundreds of them incorporated into a golden globe to prevent theft. Emeralds so outnumbered all the other loose gems they were set to colour the world's oceans. One stone was engraved with the name of the long-dead Mughal emperor Jahangir.

Before leaving Delhi, Nadir paraded through the city on a fine Iraqi horse, a red cap on his head wrapped in a white cashmere shawl and ornamented with a jewelled *jiqa*. Like a Mughal, he flung fistfuls of rupees to bystanders as an emblem of his generosity. According to eyewitnesses, he counselled the humbled Muhammad not to tolerate challenges from nobles, and to properly centralize power. What Muhammad made of these unsolicited lessons in absolutism we do not know, but neither he nor his successors won back the jewels.

Like so many conquerors, Nadir Shah's fortunes reversed not long after his greatest victory. Indeed, he soon seemed all but cursed by the same Mughal treasures he had imagined would guarantee freedom from war-induced penury. On the march north Nadir ordered that all booty be collected from his own men, including ranking officers, at river crossings and passes. They were told this was to prevent divisive arguments, but arbitrary confiscations in an army motivated by plunder only broke morale.

Once back in Persia, Nadir invested a portion of the wealth of Delhi in the construction of palaces, shrines and mosques in the hope of replicating Mughal splendour. He had brought with him Indian architects and artisans. The great tombs of Mashhad, near his homeland, still stand as mute testament, their imposing scale a reminder of the India campaign. Still more effort was put into fortifying the hilltop town of Kalat, where the bulk of the artistic treasures, including the Peacock Throne and other jewelled items, were to be housed. Furiously jealous of these treasures, Nadir ordered court eunuchs and others close to the Kalat building project killed so as not to reveal their secrets.

Nadir used another portion of the treasure to fund a war on Turkestan, and also to buy a small navy to patrol the Persian Gulf. As before, however, it was the fight with the Ottomans that strained Persian resources. Instead of selling off the precious jewels of the Mughals, Nadir raised taxes on his subjects. Evaders were publicly tortured and executed. The extortions grew worse, and the killings more gruesome. Nadir obsessed over his accounts and raged over the alleged stinginess and ingratitude of his people. Government employees accused of minor theft were blinded, burned and beaten to death. Internal rebellions broke out in every quarter, forcing a treaty with the Turks.

As the once invincible 'Lord of the Fortunate Conjunction' approached total insanity, even close confidants began to plot his murder. To seal the treaty with their volatile neighbour, the Ottomans organized an embassy and commissioned gifts. Among the items carried to the Persian border by Ahmad Pasha Kesrieli and one thousand retainers was an emerald-studded dagger, today the pride of Istanbul's Topkapi Palace Museum (Plate 2).

On the eve of his murder, Nadir sent his own gift ensemble to the Ottoman sultan. It consisted of Gulf pearls, a jewelled Mughal throne and two dancing elephants (also Mughal). All were ceremoniously received in Istanbul. It may have been better in this instance to give than receive, as lavish giving was the surest mirror of power, but this was to be a one-sided exchange. At news of Nadir Shah's assassination, the Ottoman embassy returned home from the frontier with the treasured Topkapi Dagger.

Throughout the Islamic world Nadir Shah's blood-spattered arc provoked ambivalence. On the one hand his audacity and obvious battlefield talent were sources of pride, yet on the other, his seeming descent into madness and murderous greed struck most, Sunni or Shi'a, as irreligious in the extreme. Nadir's attempt to fold Shi'ism into Sunnism as early as his 1736 self-coronation was for many Persians, especially proponents of the old Safavid theocracy, far more serious. While some of his countrymen saw a pragmatic unifier at work, others saw a heretic. For Europeans, Nadir's story was no less awe-inspiring, but quickly came to serve as yet another confirmation of 'oriental despotism'.

Emeralds and Early Modern globalization

Behind Nadir Shah's strange career lies a longer, less personalized, even hidden story: that of emeralds and their role in early modern globalization. Diamonds were greatly prized by Nadir and his fellow Islamic emperors in India and Turkey, as were rubies, pearls and other stones. But emeralds were special for two reasons: what they signified and where they originated.

In Islamic tradition, green is the colour of Paradise; green garments and headgear are reserved for descendants of the Prophet. Thus, among the Mughals, Ottomans and Safavids, emeralds held pride of place among gemstones simply for their sacred colour. Many were set in turban ornaments or inscribed with verses from the Qur'an and sewn into garments for ritual investitures. Others were embedded in the hilts of royal daggers and quivers. Still others were encased in gold, hung with pearls and sent to Mecca and Medina as votive offerings.

Emeralds were also exotic despite persistent claims of Old World origins. Unlike most other gems, including the Koh-i-noor diamond, which came from India's own mines, the emeralds of the shahs did not originate in Asia but rather from the Americas. Most came from a small cluster of diggings located deep in the jungles of Colombia – then a Spanish colony known as New Granada – near the town of Muzo.

How these deep-green gems, still regarded as the world's best, got out of South America and halfway around the world to Asia in the age of sail and gunpowder – who mined them and who traded them – are the main subjects of this book. Theirs, like Nadir Shah's, was a long, strange trip.

Understanding how Colombian emeralds were produced, traded and consumed in pre-industrial times is a curious enough tale, but what insights might this study offer to students of world history? I argue that emeralds, like Spanish America's more famous colonial product, silver, help to reveal slow shifts in a deep current of global political economy. It appears, despite the aims of numerous European merchants and princes, that Colombian emeralds, much like silver, got swept into an Asia-centred world-system that modulated the pulse of key commodity exchanges until at least the mid-eighteenth century. Put another way, emerald flows help clarify how, for a few centuries, Europeans wedded America to Asia.

The shape and pace of post-Columbian globalization are hotly debated, but among historians of commodity exchanges a new consensus is emerging. Until recently, the prevailing world-systems model of global economy placed Europe at the centre of capital accumulation from the late Middle Ages forward. Europe was, after all, the seat of the world's first truly global maritime empires, and fuelled by enterprising banking families these began competing not long after the Black Death to see who could lay claim to the biggest portion of the globe's people and material resources. In some reckonings the mad scramble initiated here has yet to end.

Even those who emphasized early modern consumption rather than production or circulation argued that from the time of Columbus, American, African and Asian commodities, notable among them precious metals and gems, flowed overwhelmingly north, first to southern Europe, then to Paris, Amsterdam and London, where they accumulated and fuelled financial and later industrial growth.

These views have been lately modified by evidence that China, and to a lesser extent India, absorbed the lion's share of American silver, which is to say the world's money supply, until at least 1800. As is true today, the populations of these two regions alone, much less combined, dwarfed not only Europe, but also most of the rest of the world. Since China and India were major and ancient exporters of luxury commodities, any shift in tax or trade policy by the Ming, Qing or Mughal emperors was bound to have global implications despite the absence of overseas ambitions. A string of decrees demanding cash taxes after the mid-sixteenth century helped make China a silver sump.

Silver absorption aside, East and South Asia's precise roles in early globalization remain difficult to quantify or track with precision over time, in part because Asian monetization and credit structures differed from those familiar to Western Europeans (thus yielding a distinct documentary record). Either way, 'reorienting' early modern global trade necessarily relegates European seaborne merchants – even 'merchant empires' – to the role of helpmeets of Asian economic development, pulled into a more powerful gravitational field than their own.

What the Chinese and South Asians had to offer the world – and it really was the world, not just Europe – were inexpensive, high-quality silk and cotton textiles. There were also dyes, drugs, spices, porcelain and sundry other things, including diamonds, rubies, sapphires and pearls, but textiles remained central for centuries. From Mexico City to Moscow, everyone who could afford to do so draped themselves and their things – including horses, windows and furniture – with the most eye-catching, colourful, and richly textured Asian fabrics. Perishable, and often delicate, textiles wore out, rotted, faded or fell from fashion. In need of constant replacement and consumed more according to taste than need, textiles of such infinite variety as Asia produced were a merchant's dream.

Europeans spent most of the early modern period trying to muscle or connive their way into long-established trade circuits linking China, Japan, the Spice Islands, Southeast Asia, the Indian subcontinent, the

Middle East and East Africa. Betwixt and between, Persia served as both merchant crossroads and major silk producer in its own right. As interlopers in an ancient trading world that could use but did not need them, the Portuguese and later Dutch and English (and to a much lesser extent French, Swedish and Danish) became heavily involved in coastal trans-shipment, as, for example, between India and Southeast Asia, mostly swapping textiles for raw commodities such as sandal-wood and benzoin.

This is not to suggest Europeans did nothing new, or wielded only insignificant power. All came to Asia with grand aspirations and highly developed (if to some degree borrowed) technologies. Sound ships, powerful guns, increasingly accurate maps and navigational instruments, these were but some of the tools of the new, seaborne brand of gunpowder empires, and they only improved with time and competition.

Even with technological advantages, however, forcibly entering Asian trade meant stomaching punishing losses. For Portuguese pioneers, conquering ancient entrepots, toppling sultans and extorting formerly free shippers had to be cast as an extension of the crusade against Islam. Otherwise, it would never have won recruits. When dying of fever or stab wounds between monsoons, even Portugal's many criminal exiles, or *degredados*, probably wanted to believe in a higher purpose. Later Europeans abandoned the crusade, but still cast their commercial enterprises as the taking up of moral burdens.

Dominating Asian seaborne trade with guns was easier than winning Asian hearts and minds, although Spain claimed some success. Spain's conquest of the American mainland empires in the 1520s and 1530s, then the Philippines in the 1560s, redrew the global commercial as well as religious map. Linked by a chain of maritime bases, a new trading world began to turn. As early as the 1570s the Spanish shipped Asian textiles across the Pacific Ocean annually to Acapulco in exchange for millions of ounces of silver. Missionaries and a few Asian converts hitched rides. Tenuous as it sometimes was, this Pacific link alone ruptured millenia-old trade patterns.

Most of the textiles packed on to Manila's fabled galleons were trans-shipped through Mexico and sent on to Europe, as the older Eurocentric world-systems model would have predicted. Yet even a cursory look at Spanish American notary books shows how a considerable portion of these textiles, plus sundry spices, drugs and porcelain, was being consumed by fashion-conscious, and not just rich, colonials. Crown and town officials tried to stop it, but by the 1580s, enslaved African and Native American women in Mexico and the Andes wore scarves and skirts made of Chinese silk and shawls of Indian muslin. Meso-American chocolate was soon spiced with Ceylonese cinnamon. Both as consumers of Asian goods and producers of the mineral wealth that paid for them, Spanish Americans were key players in this reoriented trading world.

'Globalized' after 1570, once-provincial Manila became a world-class bazaar, home to thousands of Chinese and other Asian traders, plus dozens of Portuguese factors based in India. The globetrotting Portuguese, many of them New Christians, or forced converts to Catholicism from Judaism, brought Gujarati and Bengalese muslins and calicoes to the Philippines, along with spices and, occasionally, gemstones. Mostly they traded for silver, and sometimes emeralds.

Manila was not unique in its newfound moneychanging, textile-driven cosmopolitanism. Other European merchants, again led by Portuguese New Christians, found new markets for Indian textiles throughout West and West Central Africa, fuel for the burgeoning transatlantic slave trade, another new link in a global chain. Most enslaved Africans went on to the Americas to cut and process sugar cane, but others were destined to extract Colombia's gold, emeralds and pearls.

What did Europe itself have to offer 'the Orient' besides American precious metals and trans-shipped commodities (as well as slaves) that Asians were already consuming? High-quality woollen and linen textiles were pushed at first, but neither gained purchase. Iron and various metalwares, along with a few drugs and pigments, were also offered, but rarely sold at great profit. The same was true of beads, bells and assorted gewgaws of the kind first traded to Amerindians by Columbus.

There were exceptions. Europe's technological wonders, including mechanical clocks, eyeglasses, telescopes and alembics, found a limited, elite, but critically important market – one that also fixed on guns and other explosive devices. For those in power or aspiring to it, among them Mughal, Ottoman and Safavid royalty, European weapons, especially those capable of mass destruction, were most attractive. Soon, Europeans vying for exclusive trade licences at these and other Islamic courts sent gunsmiths and engineers to every rising emperor or petty king worth visiting. Even Jesuit priests found themselves designing and founding guns in exchange for mission fields.

Yet amid the subsequent rise of land-based gunpowder empires, in full swing from North Africa to Southeast Asia by the mid-sixteenth century, textiles remained key. In sheer variety, and in many instances quality, Asians far surpassed Europeans. Recognizing early on their inability to produce comparable fabrics at home at competitive prices, European merchants and monarchs more or less resigned themselves to sending American treasure, mostly Peruvian and Mexican silver, to balance trade with Asia.

The trend continued through the overlapping eras of Iberian, Dutch, French and English maritime dominance, until finally in the late eighteenth century South Asian print fabrics were successfully copied and cheaply produced by mechanization thanks to British engineers and, soon enough, African-American slaves (as mass producers of cotton and indigo). Solving the China problem, increasingly tied to England's addiction to tea rather than silk by the turn of the nineteenth century, required pushing opium so as not to send silver.

Unlike American silver or Asian textiles, both of which steered and regulated early modern global economic trends, Colombian emeralds, like Indian diamonds and other gemstones, seem mostly to have followed them. As commodities they had – despite Nadir Shah's tremendous haul – little global weight. Few people got rich from trading emeralds and although they clearly helped incite conquest with their sparkle, as far as we know they prompted no wars.

So what then might emeralds offer to the world-systems debate beyond another example of a shiny commodity other than silver that flowed from America to Asia? It is my belief that emeralds, really only a few thousand pounds of beautiful but useless stones that happened to find special significance in the Islamic world between about 1550 and 1750, raise questions rarely asked by economic historians. If we follow economic anthropologists and some sociologists and expand 'economy' to include all human relationships mediated by material goods, globe-circling emeralds find new significance.

Recalling Bronislaw Malinowski's Trobriand islanders who travelled great distances but never got rich by trading shells with neighbours, certain emerald-mediated relationships seem to have served primarily to link individuals, clans – even states – and also to cement ties between humans and deities. As will be seen in the case of the Mughals, but also the Safavids and Ottomans until at least Nadir Shah's time, emeralds helped forge alliances and designate heirs. As predicted by Marcel Mauss's famous essay on the gift, many such gem exchanges could not be priced, even when they may have had certain calculable benefits, such as peace.

Thus I argue that as emeralds left European merchant hands they took on new meanings and increasingly defied Western notions of commodity values as straightforward functions of weight, purity and relative scarcity. Imbued with religious significance and increasingly sucked into the realm of royal gift exchange, emeralds departed the world of ordinary commodities to become rarefied objects of sacred art. It was here more than in any other way that they differed from silver.

There are other potentially illuminating cultural wrinkles in the early modern emerald story. Like most commodities, Colombian emeralds were quickly divorced from the context of their production, alienated from their producers' hands, 'fetishized', as Karl Marx famously put it. Buyers had no idea (or desire to know) how much labour each stone had required, how much blood (God forbid!) it had cost in transit. Yet provenance still mattered to many Old World consumers, whether in Lisbon or Kandahar. Emeralds, like diamonds and pearls, were simply *supposed* to come from 'the Orient'.

Trapped by this ancient bias, confirmed by Marco Polo, European traders began almost immediately to divide Colombian emeralds into two categories: 'old', or 'oriental' (best quality), and 'new', or 'Peruvian' (mediocre). They did this almost from the moment of contact as a reflection, I believe (in part since it happened again with Brazilian diamonds in the early eighteenth century), of a generalized Old World perception of the Americas as a false, or at least 'half-baked', Orient.

Mystification of Colombian emeralds thus had to go an extra step – towards fraud. Otherwise, one would have to accept the inconvenient truths explored in this book: that the glorious emeralds of the shahs originated in the unjustly conquered American colonies of Catholic Spain, were mined by forced Native American serfs and African slaves, were carried to Asia by mostly Jewish merchants hounded and tortured by the Inquisition, only to be consumed by the world's most powerful and, frankly, often despotic Muslim rulers. For men like Nadir Shah presumably none of this would have mattered, but for more tenderhearted connoisseurs it was – and still is – much preferred to imagine that glorious gemstones the colour of Paradise could only have originated in 'lost mines'.

Emeralds and Gem Studies

Given the marginal nature of gems and jewels in relation to essential commodities such as grains, lumber, textiles and even precious metals, few economic historians have focused on their production or circulation, especially in the age of sail. Some art historians, among them Manuel Keene, Susan Stronge, Nuno Vassallo e Silva, and Helmut Nickel, have examined consumption. Their archival work has helped trace the likely paths of famous emeralds now held in European, Middle Eastern and South Asian collections. Most of these researchers, however, have tracked the movement of prime stones and jewelled artefacts only within a fairly narrow radius of their endpoint, with a special interest in jewel manufacture and design. To their credit, most respected art historians and gemologists in recent years have argued, based simply on colour and other inherent characteristics, that the emeralds in question must have come from Colombia. These suppositions have recently been confirmed by mineralogical analysis.

Gemologists interested in early modern emerald mining have relied on secondary works to such a degree that many have repeated and even compounded each other's mistakes. The late John Sinkankas's monumental *Emerald and Other Beryls* (1981) is a partial exception.[7] Though some of what Sinkankas had to say about colonial Colombia is entirely incorrect, he did assemble enough published sources to spot contradictions. He even ventured to construct a rough timeline for Colombian emerald mining from the Spanish conquest to the late twentieth century. Considering that Sinkankas did nearly everything short of working in Colombian and Spanish archives, his timeline is not far off, at least for portions of the sixteenth and seventeenth centuries. When it is wrong, however, it is highly misleading.

More wildly misleading are works that have attempted to mix emerald history and lore, such as Diane Morgan's *From Satan's Crown to the Holy Grail: Emeralds in Myth, Magic, and History*.[8] To be fair, the details of mining, labour supply, and long-distance trade fall outside the main concerns of art historians, gemologists and folklorists. My aim is not to criticize them for not doing the work I have attempted here. In fact, this mix of scholarly and popular writings from different disciplinary perspectives has been valuable to this study, not for what it says about early modern gem trade or mining history but rather for how it helps to illuminate worldwide variations in emerald artistry, connoisseurship, myth, geology and chemistry. Thanks to their work I am now convinced that all these factors deeply influenced the many cycles of production, trade and consumption outlined below.

Colombian scholars have written surprisingly little on emerald production in either colonial or modern times. An exception is Gustavo Otero Muñoz and Antonio Barriga Villalba's 1948 *Esmeraldas de Colombia*, published to celebrate the Bank of the Republic's 1947 takeover of the Muzo mines.[9] Otero Muñoz's brief historical overview was drawn entirely from published sources, and as a result says almost nothing about production, labour patterns or the gem trade between conquest and independence. Instead, it resorts to a dubious, if entertaining, indigenist folklore. On the other hand, the other half of the book, Barriga Villalba's more technical discussion of emerald mining and cutting *c.*1948, remains quite useful, and includes valuable maps and diagrams. Rafael Domínguez's 1965 *Historia de las esmeraldas de Colombia* offers a similarly compressed version of colonial events based on a narrow range of published sources (mostly Otero Muñoz), plus a few select documents, but more clearly narrates the post-independence period.[10]

Possibly the most informative study of Colombian emerald mining to date is Martha Rojas's unpublished 1974 licenciate thesis in anthropology.[11] As an archaeologist in training at Bogotá's University of the Andes, Rojas was especially interested in pre-Columbian emeralds. Still, she devoted considerable space in her study to colonial documents, especially those relating to the late eighteenth-century Crown administration period covered in Chapter 8. Rojas ends with a startling ethnographic description of emerald mining in and around Muzo in the early 1970s. The great Colombian historian Juan Friede published a short article on Muzo's mid-colonial demographic decline in 1967, and more recently, in 1995, Luis Enrique Rodríguez Baquero published a licenciate thesis expanding on Friede's work.[12] These studies are both of the highest quality, but have little to say about emerald mining or trade. Most recent scholarly writing on emeralds in Colombia has highlighted connections to drug trafficking and paramilitary violence.

Historians and the Early Modern Gem Trade

'Jewel trading, both amateur and professional, must surely have constituted one of the greatest semi-visible, half-clandestine economic activities of the early modern period.'[13] Despite this generous assessment of its importance by historian George Winius, the history of gem trading is not well developed for any place or period. Winius's own work on Portuguese India, though thoughtful, has been more suggestive than definitive – it is certainly not quantitative – and there have been few followers. As one might imagine, the work that has been done has focused mostly on diamonds.[14] Leaving out so-called conflict diamonds (a distinction Marx might have found humorous), this is as true for the early modern period (*c.*1450–1750) as it is for the modern (*c.*1750–present).

There have been a few exceptions. The late Gedalia Yogev studied the early English diamond trade first in India, then Brazil, and also examined the trade in coral, a gem-like product of the western Mediterranean prized in India, albeit at a lower social level than diamonds, along with emeralds and pearls.[15] Using private merchant papers and records from the English East India Company, Yogev managed to quantify roughly the diamond and coral trades through Fort St George/Madras and other factories for portions of the eighteenth century. In later chapters I examine some East India Company records not consulted by Yogev that add emerald-related details to this established coral-and-diamond circuit for the eighteenth century.

Edgar Samuel's more recent work on the Jewish gem merchants of Lisbon, Amsterdam and London serves as an essential 'prequel' to Yogev, but as is to be expected the focus is again overwhelmingly on diamonds, and to a lesser extent pearls. As Samuel amply demonstrates, these 'white' gems, rather than coloured stones, were generally favoured in England and other northern European countries, especially in the seventeenth century. Samuel's interests include how Jewish merchants gauged fickle consumer markets. Colombian emeralds make a cameo appearance in Bruce Lenman's brief examination of the early seventeenth-century English East India Company trade in gems going in the other direction, but homeward-bound diamonds are again the main topic.[16]

As luck would have it, just as this book was going to press, Francesca Trivellato published a wonderfully detailed history of the Sephardic gem merchants of Livorno. Mining a rich cache of merchant correspondence, among other records, Trivellato takes Yogev's work on coral much farther, and adds many illuminating details on the diamond trade from India into the heart of Europe, as well. Focusing mostly on the eighteenth century, Trivellato stresses the importance of gem merchants' links with 'strangers', or merchant clans outside the Sephardic sphere, a challenge to older, more hermetic trade diaspora models. She gives compelling evidence, for example, of continued trade to Goa long after its heyday via Hindu factors of the Saraswat caste. Emeralds get scant mention, but a second link explored by Trivellato is highly suggestive for the current study. Livorno, or Leghorn, was Britain's key Italian entrepot in the late seventeenth and early eighteenth centuries, and many of the Sephardim of London had close ties to Livornese families. These in turn traded frequently (sometimes via French connections) in Istanbul, Smyrna, Aleppo, and other Ottoman-controlled cities. It could be that these traders were among the key suppliers of Colombian emeralds to Turkey, perhaps even those used to fashion the nonpareil Topkapi Dagger.[17]

Aside from mineralogists only art historians have spent much time looking at the specifics of gem provenance, yet their work has been understandably more focused on setting styles and lapidary techniques than on the mechanics of mining or trade.[18] This type of work, in particular that of art historian Priscilla Müller, has proved essential to understanding how subtle shifts in taste might have affected demand for emeralds in different parts of Europe and its colonies over the course of three centuries.[19] Although there were periodic gluts, the European and colonial American markets were never insignificant, despite what appears to be a fairly steady Asian demand.

An ocean-crossing exception that predates Winius's call for contributors is Enrique Otte's pioneering work on the Venezuelan pearl industry, which peaked in the sixteenth century but continued on a reduced scale throughout colonial times.[20] Otte's main focus was not trade but production, especially problems of labour supply and eventual overworking of delicate oyster beds near the tiny island of Cubagua. He only tentatively explored where New World pearls went once they crossed the Atlantic, what prices they fetched, and how markets changed or moved. As in the case of emeralds, these are not easy matters to sort out. As we now know from the work of Willem Floor and Molly Warsh, the world's best pearls were being fished in the Persian Gulf, near modern Bahrain and the United Arab Emirates, briefly annexed by Nadir Shah in his last years. Good pearls were also taken from the warm waters of southeast India and northwest Sri Lanka, a trade influenced by resident Jesuits as early as the sixteenth century.[21]

According to several sources, including reports by sixteenth- and seventeenth-century gem dealers Jan Huyghen van Linschoten and Jean-Baptiste Tavernier, Venezuelan pearls competed with those of the Persian Gulf and Indian Ocean, but mostly in a second tier, their colour allegedly tending to be more 'leaden'. Still, large, asymmetrical specimens from the Caribbean beds known as *berruecos* in Spanish found eager buyers in Europe by the late sixteenth century, giving name to the so-called Baroque period. Global tastes varied: Asian princes were said to prefer their pearls spherical and white.

What then are the questions to be asked in a study of early modern emeralds? Given the current state of knowledge it may be best to begin with the most basic ones before attempting to assess significance: Where were they found? When? By whom? How were they mined? How many were produced? How were they classified or priced? Did anyone manage to monopolize production, hoard stones above a certain size, or otherwise corner the market? Did royal or religious authorities intervene in the processes of mining, trade or consumption? How did early modern world emerald markets function? How did emeralds differ from other precious stones? Where were the stones cut? How? By whom? Who traded them? Who wanted them most? How did the emerald business change over time, and why? Finally, how important were emeralds in relation to other high-value commodities such as precious metals, spices, drugs and dyes?

As set out within the chapters, some of these questions are easier to answer than others. Some may not be answerable beyond a guess barring discovery of new sources. For Colombian emeralds the documentary record is richest on the side of production, that is, near the mines. It gets considerably thinner as one attempts to track emeralds from American shores to Europe and Asia. I have found only the most fragmentary evidence, for example, of emeralds crossing the Pacific via Spain's annual treasure galleons, yet it stands to reason that some (or many) did, given three centuries of steady traffic and the documented presence of Sephardic, India-based gem traders in Manila. As for the Atlantic, the several thousand emeralds recovered from the 1622 wreck of the Spanish galleon *Nuestra Señora de Atocha*, salvaged in the 1980s off the Florida Keys, seem to hint at a fairly massive unregistered trade going in this direction.

'Stowaway' commodities of a strange, even mystical, sort, Colombian emeralds emerged from the dirt of remote jungle mines and the fog of trader subterfuge to surface on the pallid necks of Europe's princesses and the gnarled fingers of its bishops. A few freakishly large ones showed up in Habsburg wonder cabinets, or in wartime buried treasure. Yet New World emeralds found their sink not in Europe but in Mughal India, Safavid Persia and Ottoman Turkey. Some of these 'gunpowder empire' gems are mentioned in princely memoirs or depicted in finely rendered miniatures, but most are today preserved as museum pieces. Barely understood except by a handful of specialists, they remain beguiling products of natural and human history.

Sources

This book began as a chapter in a larger project comparing gold and gem mining in colonial Colombia and Brazil. As expected, the tale grew in the telling. The much expanded result offered here is based on extensive research in Colombia's National Archive in Bogotá (AGNC), the Regional Archive of Boyacá in Tunja (ARB), the Archivo Central del Cauca in Popayán (ACC), the National Archive of Ecuador in Quito (ANE), Spain's Archive of the Indies (AGI) and National History Archive (AHN), the National Libraries of Spain (BNE), Portugal (BNP), and Great Britain (BL), Portugal's Torre do Tombo National Archive (ANTT), England's Parliamentary Archive

(PA), the John Carter Brown Library in Providence, Rhode Island, USA, and several other repositories. I have also relied heavily on the Interlibrary Loan Offices of the College of William & Mary's E.G. Swem Library and Brown University's J.D. Rockefeller Library.

For the chapter treating emeralds in the pre-Columbian Americas I rely on the work of numerous anthropologists, most importantly archaeologist Warwick Bray, whom I thank deeply for his scholarly generosity. I have also relied on interpretations of ancient crystal symbolism in works by the late Gerardo Reichel-Dolmatoff. For the sections on emerald lore in ancient and medieval Western and Eastern cultures I have been guided by the late John Sinkankas, along with a variety of medieval and early modern 'lapidaries', or mineral-healing catalogues, such as that of Ahmad ibn Yusuf Al Tifaschi, recently translated to English from the original Arabic by Samar Najm Abul Huda. On emerald geology and mineralogy, fields careful readers will quickly see lie far beyond my expertise, I have followed Ali Kazmi, Lawrence Snee, Gaston Giuliani, and many others. I thank Professor Brent Owens of the College of William & Mary's Geology Department, who screened my narrative on emerald formation and deposition for howlers.

The chapter on conquest, although it includes supplementary archival material, was most helped by Professor J. Michael Francis's timely publication of key document translations from the early sixteenth century, along with the venerable works of Franciscan historians Fray Pedro de Aguado and Fray Pedro Simón. Aguado, who finished his great work around 1581, offers a surprisingly thorough account of the conquest of Muzo territory beginning around 1540, as well as the opening of the first mines in the 1560s. A manuscript version of his work was allegedly consulted by the Colombian mining engineer Francisco Restrepo in the 1880s, leading to the rediscovery of the fabled Chivor, or Somondoco, deposits northeast of Bogotá. Simón, whose extensive 1625 work fills in some blanks, also appears to have consulted Aguado. He is sometimes charged with simply elaborating on the magnum opus of New Granada's great epic poet Juan de Castellanos (author of the massive *Elegías de*

Varones Ilustres, which I also cite), but at least regarding emeralds there is much to be gained by reading Simón.

The chapters on mining, labour systems, taxation and fraud rely almost entirely on manuscript documents, mostly lawsuits, royal tax books, worker muster rolls and investigative reports now housed in the Colombian National Archive in Bogotá and the Archive of the Indies in Seville. A few descriptions are drawn from sixteenth- and seventeenth-century historians of greater Spanish South America, including José de Acosta, El Inca Garcilaso de la Vega, and Antonio Vásquez de Espinosa. Only the last of these chroniclers personally visited Colombia's emerald mines. A few key mining references come from Gonzalo Fernández de Oviedo's *Historia General y Natural de las Indias*, only the first part of which was published before the nineteenth century. Fernández de Oviedo, who died in 1557, claimed to have interviewed some of the first Spanish visitors to the mines of Chivor when they stopped on Hispaniola.

The chapters on trade draw from a mix of archival and secondary sources. Archival materials include royal cabinet and treasury inventories, tax records and official correspondence. Most revealing of early gem trading networks, however, were documents produced by the Spanish and Portuguese Inquisitions. Inventories drawn up by the Cartagena, Lisbon, Coimbra and Goa tribunals, in particular, offer insights into the global movement of emeralds and other gemstones. Also useful were published studies of the merchant communities of Cartagena, Lisbon, Seville, Curaçao, Port Royal (Jamaica), Amsterdam, London, Antwerp, Luanda, Goa, Surat and Cairo. In the early Atlantic context, when emeralds were apparently traded in greatest numbers, the superb synthetic work of Daviken Studnicki-Gizbert on what he aptly calls the 'Portuguese Nation' served as compass. James Boyajian's magisterial *Portuguese Trade in Asia under the Habsburgs* played a similar role for eastern shores.[22]

The chapters treating emerald consumption, primarily in South Asia and the Middle East, were most challenging given my training as a Latin Americanist with only a tentative footing in early modern world history. Here I rely almost entirely on published sources, some in Spanish, Portuguese and French, but many in English translation (mostly from the original Persian). Thankfully, there is now available not only a wide range of traveller's reports, several of them containing detailed descriptions of the gem trade in the sixteenth and seventeenth centuries, but also a number of newly translated documents relating to the inner workings of the Mughal, Ottoman and Safavid courts. Best for my purposes here are the Mughal annals, some composed by the emperors themselves, others by court historians. Both frequently mention the exchange, usually by gift rather than sale, of emeralds and jewelled objects.

The chapters treating smuggling, and the Spanish crown's attempts in the late eighteenth century to revive the Muzo mines by way of state management and monopoly, are based almost entirely on documents from the National Archive in Bogotá and the Archive of the Indies in Seville. Only one important document from this period, a 1786 report written by the famed Basque mining specialist Juan José D'Elhuyar, has been published. It belongs to the José Celestino Mutis collection in Bogotá's Royal Observatory Museum. At the end of the crown monopoly period in the mid-1790s, the emerald trail goes cold until just after independence in the 1820s, when the Muzo mines were reopened by associates of Simón Bolívar.

CHAPTER 1

❖

Sacred Origins

COLOMBIA'S emeralds were infused with meaning long before
they went global, yet it is only after the arrival of Europeans
in the Americas that we know much about them. A close reader
of Marco Polo, Christopher Columbus, for whom Colombia was
named, died believing he was close to Çipango, or Japan, 'a huge
island rich in gold, pearls, and precious stones'.[1] Columbus touched
on a small portion of Venezuela's coast in 1498, where he found the
predicted pearls, but it was not until 1499, during the first voyage of
Alonso de Hojeda, that sustained contact with indigenous peoples in
what is today Colombia began.

While trading for pearls, Hojeda met briefly with native inhabitants of the barren Guajira Peninsula, perhaps ancestors of the
modern Wayúu, from whom he received some green stones.[2] These
may have been the first genuine New World emeralds handled by
Europeans, but it is just as likely they were a more common variety
of greenstone beads found by archaeologists in the region today.
Hojeda was not so sure. On returning to Seville in spring 1500, he
handed the beads over to his Spanish and Italian backers. They told
him to follow up on this curious 'discovery'.

Hojeda returned to the peninsula later the same year, but his
attempt to found a town, a Spanish compulsion, failed. Even

before Hojeda's try at settlement, however, his pilot joined fellow merchant-explorer Rodrigo de Bastidas on a trading voyage that touched on much of Colombia's Atlantic coast from the deserts of Guajira to the jungles of Panama. Interactions with native peoples were allegedly friendly and yielded considerable gold. Most was bartered from inhabitants of the picturesque shores surrounding the Gulf of Urabá. In the meantime, Columbus, already out of favour at court and on Hispaniola, reached the gulf independently in 1502. He barely paused in the land that would someday bear his name before moving on to west-central Panama to restart Veragua, his last gold-mining venture.

The next Spanish attempts at permanent settlement were on or next to indigenous villages astride natural harbours: Santa Marta, Cartagena, and in the Gulf of Urabá, Santa María de la Antigua del Darién. Since the Spanish by this time seemed bent on either enslaving native inhabitants or desperately searching for gold, most contact was conflict rather than cooperation. Local Carib speakers responded to Spanish threats and sorties with evasive guerrilla tactics supplemented by poisoned arrows. Wise Spaniards, such as Francisco Pizarro and Diego de Almagro, shifted southward to Pacific shores by crossing the Isthmus of Panama. Inspired after about 1520 by the feats of Hernando Cortés in Mexico, Pizarro and Almagro pooled resources to find golden kingdoms of their own.

Along the way to a still mythical place called Perú, Pizarro's followers found emeralds. They were said to be most abundant near Manta, on the west coast of Ecuador. As El Inca Garcilaso de la Vega later recounted:

Among the objects they worshiped in the valley of Manta, which was as it were the capital of the whole region, was a great emerald, said to be almost as large as an ostrich's egg. It was exhibited in public on their great festivals, and the Indians came from great distances to worship it and sacrifice to it, bringing gifts of smaller emeralds, for their priests and the cacique of Manta put it about that it was a very agreeable offering for their goddess, the great emerald, to be presented with smaller emeralds, which were her daughters. By means of this covetous doctrine they collected a great quantity of emeralds in this place, where they were found by don Pedro de Alvarado and his companions, one of whom was my lord Garcilaso de la Vega [the author's father], when they went to conquer Peru. The Spaniards broke most of the stones on an anvil, thinking, like very unskilled lapidaries, that if they were fine stones they would not break however hard they were struck and that if they broke they were only glass and not fine stones at all. The emerald that was worshiped as a goddess was spirited away by the Indians as soon as the Spaniards entered that kingdom: and it was so carefully hidden that, despite much search and the application of many threats, it has never reappeared.[3]

Although he was writing more than eighty years after the fact, El Inca Garcilaso had a special interest in the emeralds of Manta. As he notes, his father had participated in the first Spanish reconnaissance of the region (*c.*1535), and he had probably heard of the Manteños' great 'emerald goddess' first hand. Earlier sources back him up.

Indeed, the first explicit mention of South American emeralds (as opposed to generic green stones) comes from the early Pacific coast reconnaissance missions of Francisco Pizarro. Having coasted south from Panama in late 1526, Pizarro and a small number of followers put in at what they called the River San Juan, sending their companion and pilot Bartolomé Ruiz further south. Just beyond the equator Ruiz encountered a large, sail-equipped balsa-wood raft, apparently on its way to or from Ecuador's Bay of Salango and loaded with a wide array of luxury goods. Among the items mentioned were shells, fine textiles, gold and silver cups, and emeralds.[4] The Salango trading vessel was the first indication of urban civilization in the South Sea.

Soon after this remarkable encounter, Pizarro and his men reached a bay in northwest Ecuador they named San Mateo, near the mouth of what they dubbed the Río de las Esmeraldas, or 'River of Emeralds'. The river's name was given, it was later said, after getting word – or sign – of emerald mines somewhere along its banks. More concrete evidence came at a nearby town called Coaque, some distance along the coast to the south (perhaps in northern Manabí Province), where the Spaniards allegedly tested potential emeralds in the manner described by El Inca Garcilaso – smashing them with hammers.

When the fragile crystals shattered, according to Pedro de Cieza de León and other chroniclers, the disappointed Spaniards collected the fragments and bartered them back to native traders for cloth and food. Several accounts agree that Dominican friar Reginaldo Pedraza knew a bit more about gems than his companions. He was said to have sewn a large number of the uncut green crystals into his doublet and taken them back to Panama.[5] As if cursed by his greed, the priest soon died of a fever allegedly contracted in Coaque. According to the story, the stones were discovered while preparing the corpse for burial and sent on to Spain, where they excited the interest of the queen. Whether stupidly smashed by gullible conquistadors or hidden away by a doomed friar, New World emeralds were already fuelling moral tales.

Colour of Heaven

In mineral terms, emerald is a variety of beryl (beryllium aluminium silicate) that differs from its many cousins such as aquamarine only in having a tincture of chromium and in some cases vanadium to render it green, preferably deep or, as gemologists and art historians say, 'saturated' green. Substantial emerald deposits and much smaller occurrences have been found in Central and southern Africa, Madagascar, Pakistan, Afghanistan, Russia, Austria, Brazil and the southeastern United States, yet the most esteemed stones still come from Colombia, in particular from about a dozen mines located on either side of a steep-sided wash called the Quebrada de Itoco, or Itoco Creek, a tributary of the Minero River near the town of Muzo. Muzo lies in the hot and rugged hill country just west of the highland Marian shrine town of Chiquinquirá.

The nearby mines of Coscuez have also been important since colonial times, along with the more distant Chivor district, southeast of Tunja where the Department of Boyacá borders Cundinamarca. Smaller mines have been exploited near the towns of Maripí, Peñas Blancas, Yacopí, and a few other mountain pueblos in the vicinity of Muzo. A dozen more occurrences have been mapped in a belt trending northwest of Bogotá about two hundred kilometres to some fifty kilometres to the southeast. Taken together, no other emerald region in the world has been so productive for so long, and none has produced finer stones.

In Old World antiquity, most emeralds originated in Egypt, although surviving specimens suggest their quality was rarely good. Some modern gemologists even say the Egyptian mines' product was not true gem emerald by modern standards, but rather just a greenish, semi-opaque beryl dulled by the presence of iron. In early medieval times, and perhaps before, emeralds were mined in Austria, Pakistan and Afghanistan, although very few outstanding specimens from premodern or precolonial times are known. Some gemologists speculate that sporadic surface collection rather than true mining accounted for seemingly minuscule production of many of these stones. The mines of Central Africa, Madagascar, Brazil and the United States are of recent discovery.[6]

Early European travellers to the Near and Far East occasionally mention emeralds, but it is difficult to know if the stones being described were emeralds or something else, such as green peridot or sapphire. Marco Polo focuses on diamonds and pearls, only mentioning emeralds in passing. The Bolognese traveller Ludovico di Varthema, whose 1510 account mentions numerous precious stones, claimed that a fellow traveller purchased two emeralds in Java, and that the world's best emeralds were found there. No evidence of Javanese or any Southeast Asian emerald mines has surfaced since. When trading for rubies in Burma, Varthema claimed that emeralds were quite scarce, and more valued there than in Italy.[7] The Portuguese traveller Duarte Barbosa's 1518 account of a similar voyage treats the gems circulating in the Indian Ocean in more detail, suggesting that eastern emeralds were instead mined in Babylon, in the vicinity of Baghdad.[8] This was clearly untrue, although Barbosa offers useful information regarding emerald appraisal in medieval India:

> They are green of a fine color and beautiful, and besides are light and soft. Many false ones are made, but by looking through them towards the light the counterfeits show little bubbles such as are seen in glass. This is not so in fine emeralds, the sight of which is pleasing to the eyes. The best give out a ray like the sun, and when touched by the stone leave a brass-colored streak. The emerald which does this is true, and is worth at Calicut as much as a diamond or even more; not so much by weight as by size, by reason that diamond weighs more in proportion than the emerald. There is also found another sort of emerald very green but not of so much value, that all the Indians use them to mix with other precious stones. These do not leave the brass color on the touchstone.[9]

True emerald leaves a clear or whitish streak, so it is hard to know what stones these were. In crystal form, emerald occurs as blunt-ended hexagonal prisms, rarely more than a few centimetres thick, although some extraordinary, almost fist-sized, specimens have been discovered. The 1,384-carat Devonshire Emerald, on display in the British Museum of Natural History, is a prime example. Colombia's Bank of the Republic in Bogotá holds several similar specimens.[10] Crystals of the desired deep green colour range, but without considerable internal fractures, clouds, 'feathers' and mineral or organic inclusions – often collectively called *jardín*, or 'garden' – are exceedingly rare.

The word 'emerald' has either a Persian or Sanskrit root, depending on the authority, but it is its Greek derivative, *smaragdos*, that has given rise to most modern Western renderings, among them *esmeralda*, *emeraude* and *smaragd*. Emerald has always been associated with divinity in Eurasian mythology, and by extension with the highest-ranking elites. The secrets of Hermes Trismegistus of

Alexandria were allegedly inscribed on an emerald tablet, and some medieval writers claimed the Holy Grail was carved from a single emerald crystal. Emeralds were among the first gems to be prized in the ancient Near East, as well, not only for their beauty but also for their presumed healing and divining powers. Emerald was the stone of the immortals, a universal antidote; it revealed unchastity, it was a cure for epilepsy and good for the eyesight and general mood.

Emeralds became a significant luxury commodity in Eurasia when exploited by ancient Egyptians along the margins of the Red Sea, beginning some four thousand years ago. Later associated with Cleopatra, the mines of Djebel Sikeit and Djebel Zabarah were active on and off until early and perhaps even late medieval times.[11] The mines of Djebel Sikeit were then lost until 1818 and those of Djebel Zabarah until 1990. All attempts to revive these mines have failed, and it appears the ancients and their medieval followers exhausted the gem-quality stones. Museum displays of Greek, Roman and Byzantine jewellery incorporating Egyptian emeralds suggest they were only rarely faceted or tumbled; most were bored horizontally through the crystal and strung with other beads.[12] Most of these emeralds are small, and only a few approach modern colour standards.

There is some disagreement among gemologists as to the origin of early modern emerald classifications, but for reasons probably having to do with ancient trade patterns, sixteenth- and seventeenth-century Western writers used the term 'oriental' to refer to a presumably Egyptian standard of greenness. A more recent term from South Asia, much remarked on in the period of British rule, is 'lost mine' (or 'old mine') stones. Scientists have recently shown what the world's most expert gemologists have long suspected: that nearly all so-called oriental or lost-mine emeralds, whether in European or Asian collections, are in fact from Colombia, specifically Muzo.[13]

Mineralogists suggest the peculiar geology of the Muzo deposits, which occur in massive Cretaceous shale beds on either side of Colombia's Eastern Cordillera, made possible the formation of stones not tainted by iron compounds, giving them an unusual lustre and colour some observers describe as yellow-green (in fact a deep blue-green with a subtle yellow tint). This peculiar colouration makes it relatively easy for trained gemologists to identify Colombian, and especially Muzo, emeralds without resorting to complex chemical or spectral analysis. Stones from Chivor, which some connoisseurs prefer to those of Muzo, tend more towards blue, but again of a tint found nowhere else in the world. Only recently discovered Afghani emeralds from the Panjsher region bordering Pakistan have proved to be similar in colour to either Chivor or Muzo stones, although their chemical signature is distinct.

Unlike diamonds, rubies and sapphires, emeralds are relatively soft for gemstones (about 7.5–8.0 on the Mohs scale), friable and never flawless – or even nearly so. Internal fractures and chemical impurities, or 'inclusions', sometimes enhance the play of light in a stone according to connoisseurs, whereas surface flaws are always considered undesirable and are often hidden by oiling and other forms of chemical impregnation. Quality stones above a few carats can exceed the value of the choicest diamonds of the same weight. Attempts to synthesize emeralds have been successful chemically since the mid-twentieth century, but less so aesthetically.[14] Mineralogists speak of a process in which the Muzo emerald crystals were formed with the cooling of super-heated brines, cracked from later heat and stress, and then 'healed' in their original veins by the influx of new fluids, a sequence that has thus far been impossible to duplicate in the laboratory.

Most Colombian stones come from dozens of small opencast and shaft mines located in the rugged mountains and foothills north of Bogotá. As described in the postscript, some mines have been run on a larger scale by the Colombian government and private concerns. All have been worked by small-scale scavengers, or *guaqueros*, as well. Despite their proximity to the national capital, located on a permanently cool plain 2,640 metres above sea level, almost all of Colombia's emerald mines fall in hot, rough and remote low country. The great exception is Chivor, also in rugged terrain but perched high on the east flank of the Andes overlooking the vast Llanos, or

Great Plains, of the Orinoco. Nearby are the more recent discoveries of Gachalá and Macanal. On the west flank of the Eastern Cordillera are the hot country mines of Coscuez, Peñas Blancas, La Pita, Yacopí, and finally Muzo, the world's most productive emerald district since the mid-sixteenth century. Despite several dramatic boom-and-bust cycles, these last mines, historically regarded as home to the world's finest stones, were never lost.

Muzo lies a short distance from colonial Colombia's main Atlantic transport artery, the Magdalena River, or 'Río Grande', as it was known in colonial times. This fact greatly facilitated contraband trade; it was simply easier to go downstream to the Atlantic than up and over the mountains to Bogotá, then back down again to Cartagena de Indias, the colony's official port of call. A visit to the hard-luck town of La Trinidad de los Muzos today would seem to belie any claims of colonial opulence, but it is worth bearing in mind that the town, founded in 1558, was levelled several times by earthquakes and fires. In more recent times, Muzo has been the epicentre of considerable political and criminal violence, including gangland-style massacres carried out by the heavily armed henchmen of rival emerald bosses. The *Erythroxylon coca* bush also flourishes in the region, serving as a kind of insurance when the mines do not yield.

Geology

Geologists and geochemists differ on the particulars of emerald formation in various parts of the world, but most agree as to why they are rare. First, the elements beryllium (part of emerald's structure) and chromium (source of its green colour) are relatively scarce in the earth's crust. Second, and more important, these elements nearly always occur in radically different geological contexts. Finding them together is itself evidence of an unusual sequence of events. For emeralds to form, rocks of very different kinds presumably had to have come together, and under fairly pressing circumstances. Finally, beryllium and chromium are not chemically compatible under normal conditions, making emerald formation even less likely. For these reasons, the natural substitution of a small amount of aluminium by chromium in the formation of beryl crystals, the usual explanation of how emerald came to be, suggests a truly rare episode in earth's natural history.

According to Ali Kazmi and Lawrence Snee, whose work on Pakistani emeralds led them to map and compare world deposits in the 1980s, it is only when the chromium-bearing ultramafic rocks typical of oceanic crust happen to crash into much later-stage igneous rocks containing beryl that emeralds have a chance to form. Most of the later-stage rocks containing beryl are pegmatites, a frequent host rock for a variety of gem minerals. The rare conditions necessary for emerald formation appear to have been obtained in certain so-called suture zones, a prime example being where the Indian subcontinent joined Asia and pushed up the Himalayas. Kazmi and Snee suggest that comparable arguments can be made to explain emerald deposits from nearly every part of the world except one: 'The sole possible exception to our classification is, of course as nature would have it, the most important emerald deposits of the world – those of Colombia. Despite the importance and numerous studies of these deposits, their origin remains unclear.'[15]

In short, the geological setting in which Colombian emeralds are found, that is, extremely thick and twisted Cretaceous shales, suggests much dramatic uplift and folding, but no 'suturing' of continental plates, and therefore no obvious sources for either chromium or beryllium. Geochemists who have studied the many mineral inclusions typical of Colombian emeralds argue that these rare elements must have been present in the shales themselves, and somehow percolated into fracture zones in the midst of folding, mountain building and other transformative episodes. Kazmi and Snee do not find these claims convincing, and leave the matter open, to be resolved in future.

Even though Colombian emeralds are somewhat of a cipher for geochemists, the basic geological context in which they are found can be described with some precision. All of Colombia's significant emerald deposits occur in the country's Eastern Cordillera, which although it is not as high as the towering Central range or the more isolated Sierra Nevada de Santa Marta, includes peaks more than five thousand metres above sea level. Unlike the Western and Central ranges, which are more or less a continuation of the high and often volcanic Ecuadorian Andes, the Eastern range is geologically distinct. It consists of folded sedimentary rocks initially laid down to a depth of more than ten thousand metres. The oldest sedimentary rocks date to the early Cretaceous. Fossils resembling those of other world regions, including parts of Europe and Patagonia, have long aided stratigraphers, many of them sponsored by petroleum companies.

At Muzo, emerald is found amid carbon-rich pyritic shales near the base of the massive Villeta Formation. The Villeta shales, occasionally interspersed with thin layers of sandstone and limestone, and topped by thick blocks of fine-grained sandstone used since colonial times for construction and paving, were laid down in a thick package of sediments along a continental margin. As their types imply, these deposits formed beneath an ancient sea whose depth varied over time. The grey to black host rock in which emeralds occur is said to be of lower Middle Albian age, formed in a sea perhaps six hundred metres deep. Emeralds probably did not appear, however, until these strata were folded and fractured during a much later period, probably the late Miocene Andean orogeny, or uplift, that gave rise to the Eastern Cordillera, the last of Colombia's three ranges to form.[16]

Many of the Muzo mines sit on an anticline named for the famous Cerro, or 'Hill', of Itoco, and several faults criss-cross the zone. An extraordinarily deep thrust fault along the Minero River renders the town of Muzo's geology somewhat distinct from that of its nearby mines. Emeralds are found in folded shale beds known as *capas esmeraldíferas*, or emerald-bearing overlayers. These all but spill, as if poured like coats of tar, over less altered beds of limestone and shale. These deeper layers are, however, interspersed with irregular layers and veins of calcite, quartz, pyrite and other large, crystalized minerals left behind by percolating fluids. Embedded pyrite crystals are not uncommon in Muzo emeralds, and inclusions of halite, or cubic sodium chloride crystals, are frequent. Layers rich in calcite and albite, a feldspar mineral, are topped by a greyish dolomite-like rock called *cenicero*, the Spanish word for ashbin (wood ash being a close approximation of its colour). The *capas esmeraldíferas* lie right on top of the *cenicero*.

The first scientific description of the Muzo deposits comes from a 1786 report written by the Basque mining engineer and mineral-ogist Juan José D'Elhuyar. D'Elhuyar had been sent to New Granada by Spain's Minister of the Indies to revive moribund silver mines, but he visited other sites and collected mineral samples from all over the viceroyalty. D'Elhuyar described the *capas esmeraldíferas* on either side of Muzo's Itoco wash this way:

> The exposed rock of this mountain is a type of schistos, or very carboniferous black shale, divided into coat-like layers of greater and lesser thickness. In this rock there run, in different directions and inclinations, an infinite number of veins of calcite. These vary greatly in thickness, from a quarter of an inch to two feet thick. Such variation frequently occurs within a single vein, such that although in one place it was found quite thick, in another it thins out so much it tends to be lost. The inclination and direction of a given vein is just as variable, with some perpendicular ones soon running horizontal, and so on; its course or direction tends to be of such short extension that as soon as one thinks one has cut into a vein it disappears altogether. In spite of their short extension, experience has shown that the majority of veins, and the most useful ones, tend in an east-west direction. In these calcite veins emeralds are found in greater or lesser abundance and of diverse crystalized qualities, or in tiny pieces with no regular form. Even the crystalized or 'cane-segment' ones (*cañutos*), as they call them, tend to be naturally divided into different pieces, breaking apart at the lightest strike or handling.[17]

D'Elhuyar goes on to say this last fact should correct allegations that the fractured nature of Muzo stones was due to the 'ineptitude and carelessness of the miners'; rather, he says, 'it is Nature'. A visitor to the mines in 1766, crown gem cutter Pedro Puig, had maintained that miners' careless use of hammers and chisels caused many good stones to be damaged.[18]

For now it may be sufficient to stress the almost unpredictable occurrence of Muzo emeralds. Even with great advances in geological understanding and remote sensing, they are not easily found and thus have not been exhausted despite almost 500 years of intensive mining. Mining in pre-Columbian times was less invasive, at least in the Muzo region, but it should be noted that nearly all deposits known today were located by indigenous prospectors many centuries, or even millenia, ago. Most were probably found by chance in streambeds then traced to outcrops. Dams and aqueducts were constructed using wooden implements, and soil and other soft overburden were removed by irrigation. According to documents, hydraulic mining methods established by indigenous miners at some point in the remote past were little altered in colonial times except by replacement of wooden with iron and steel tools, and eventually – only in the late eighteenth century – black-powder blasting and underground tunnelling.

Ancient Emerald Trails

According to the early seventeenth-century Franciscan historian Pedro Simón, Chief Goranchacha was the product of an immaculate conception. His mother, a chief's daughter from the Muisca pueblo of Guachetá, followed the advice of soothsayers who advised her to lie with her legs open atop a hill as the sun rose, exposing herself to its first rays. After doing this several times she became pregnant and in nine months gave birth to a *guacata*, said to be the Chibcha term for a large and beautiful emerald. The emerald was wrapped in cotton and carried back to the village by the young virgin nestled between her breasts. After a few days it turned into an infant, the boy Goranchacha. Spawn of the Devil, according to the Spanish priest, he ruled for many years as a tyrant before disappearing in a cloud of fetid smoke.[19]

As indicated by both archaeological evidence and colonial documents, the Muisca of Colombia's Eastern Cordillera had the most developed and diverse range of beliefs regarding emeralds of any known pre-Columbian group. This makes sense given the fact that emeralds of several distinct varieties were found only in their homeland. Unfortunately, what we know of these beliefs is highly fragmentary, and as with the quote above from Pedro Simón, often distorted by Christian European anxieties. Early post-conquest documents and chronicles mention emeralds being placed in sacred sites, mostly hermitages, lakes and headmen's burial mounds. Several accounts of grave-robbing mention the placing of emeralds in the body cavity of dead chiefs, although we have little idea what this meant beyond what is suggested by stories such as Simón's about Goranchacha. It appears there was some association between the emerald and the power of the sun. Emeralds were clearly understood to be potent, perhaps even alive.

A *c*.1545 chronicle known as *The Epitome of the Conquest of the New Kingdom of Granada*, probably written by conquistador Gonzalo Jiménez de Quesada, mentions a type of Muisca household god in the form of a golden or wooden image. Such images were less clearly linked to chiefly power, but in apparently mimetic fashion they always contained emeralds 'in the belly'. The author states:

> In addition to idols in the temples, every Indian, no matter how poor, has his own idol, or two, or three, or more. These idols are exactly the same as the ones possessed by the gentiles [i.e., non-Christian ancestors] in their time, which were called *lares*. These household idols are made from very fine gold; and in a hole in the idol's belly they place many emeralds, in accordance with the wealth of the idol's owner. If the Indian is too poor to have a gold idol in his house, he has one made out of wood; he also places as much gold and as many emeralds as he is able into the hole in the idol's belly. These domestic idols are small in size; the largest ones are roughly the same length as the distance between the hand and the elbow. And their devotion to these is so strong that they do

not go anywhere, whether it is to work their fields, or to any other place, at any time, without them. They carry their idols in a small basket, which hangs from their arms. And what is most alarming is that they even carry them to war as well; with one arm they fight, and with the other they hold their idol. This is especially true in the Province of Tunja, where the Indians are deeply religious.[20]

The author of the *Epitome* goes on to describe the use of emeralds in Muisca burials:

> In terms of burial practices, the Indians inter the dead in two different ways. They bind the corpses tightly in cloth, having first removed the intestines and the rest of their insides. Then they fill the empty stomachs with gold and emeralds. They also place much gold around the corpse and on top of it, before tightly wrapping the entire corpse in cloth. They build a type of large bed, which sits just above the ground inside certain sanctuaries, which are used only for that purpose, and are dedicated to the deceased. They place the corpses there and leave them on top of those beds, without ever burying them; this practice later proved to be of no small benefit to the Spaniards. . . . The other method they use is to inter the dead in water, in the great lakes. The deceased is placed inside a coffin; they may add gold, depending on the status of the deceased. Then they add as much gold and emeralds they can fit inside the coffin. With all this inside the coffin, together with the body of the deceased, they drop it into the deepest depths of the deepest lakes.[21]

Aside from these references to emeralds being carried in hollow images and placed with the presumably eminent dead, little is known. There are, however, further suggestions of emerald's association with the sun, again complemented by gold. The two Spanish writers of the 1539 'Relación del Nuevo Reino' vaguely mention a ritual practice among the Muiscas, which was to burn emeralds as sacrifice: 'These Indians are idolatrous; they sacrifice small children, as well as parrots and other birds to the sun; and they burn emerald stones. And it is said that the greater the lord, the more precious the stones offered to the sun.'[22] It is perhaps worth noting that emeralds are relatively fire-resistant among gemstones, and I know of no other references to child or parrot sacrifice among the Muiscas.

As if to confirm the legend of El Dorado, however, emeralds were found along with assorted gold items by Spanish treasure hunters in Lake Guatavita, not far from Bogotá, as early as 1577. This was when the first such stones were registered for taxation by a royal contractor, Antonio de Sepúlveda, charged with emptying the lake. A one-fourth duty was paid on these 'grave stones' rather than the standard miner's fifth (see appendices). The first two stones were described as: 'one of 293 ¼ carats, of reasonable green' and the other '40 ¼ carats all plasmatic [i.e., cloudy] and of a very dark green'. Other emeralds were taxed in 1577 after being taken from the 'sanc-tuaries of Fontibón and Bogotá', a reference to Muisca chieftain burials.[23]

In pre-Columbian times, the native peoples of northeastern Colombia traded the emeralds of their homeland widely. The stones appear in grave goods as far afield as Ecuador, Peru and Mexico. One apparently Olmec anthropomorphic carved emerald figure has recently been identified by spectral analysis as likely Colombian emerald, or at least green beryl. Much later, the Aztecs were alleged to have carved pyramids of emerald when Cortés arrived in 1519, although this was probably Guatemalan nephrite. Colombian emer-alds were allegedly known and esteemed by the Incas, although unequivocal early references are rare. The seventeenth-century Peruvian historian Fernando de Montesinos, who likened Spanish America to the legendary Land of Ophir, was especially fond of linking Incas with emeralds.[24]

Before the arrival of Europeans, American emeralds were not faceted but rather carved into beads or left in their natural form as hexagonal crystals, some of remarkable size and colour. A rare exception is a finely polished emerald set in the back of a gold reptilian figure unearthed in 1940 at Sitio Conte, Panama (Plate 3).[25] Emeralds as jewellery tend to appear in ceramics, usually as a bead threaded onto a nose ring attached to clay figurines. Early Spanish accounts suggest emeralds were traded for gold, salt, fine cotton textiles, seashells and feathers. Like most of these items, emeralds seem to have been reserved for powerful chieftains and their families.

Pedro Simón stated that offerings of cotton cloth, gold and emeralds were frequently made to various gods in Muisca country. The god Suchaviva, a rainbow spirit who looked after women in childbirth and those suffering from fever, was said to receive gifts of small emeralds, beads and low-karat gold.[26] Simón also maintained the Muiscas had originally been the lords of both the Somondoco and Muzo, or Itoco, emerald mines, but that the Carib-speaking and allegedly cannibalistic Muzos had taken over the latter in their wars of expansion from the Magdalena valley.[27] He described Somondoco emeralds, adding 'photosynthetic' speculations:

There are found in these mines, as in those of Muzo, two types of veins, some of very clear crystal from which they take many and very fine crystals called by the name 'de roca' ['of the rock'] and very large pieces; and I saw on one occasion a very beautiful piece of crystal that had at its heart and centre a piece of golden marcasite [i.e., pyrite] the size of a large hazelnut that must have been caught in the middle when that crystal started to form. And other veins of emeralds, very green and fine, and others not so green, and others quite clear, and even one that was brought to this city in past years that was no more than a fine piece of crystal with several very strange green branches that extended all through it. This made many of us wonder whether emeralds were in their first generation clear crystals and only later, by the force of the sun, stained from that white crystal colour to green, explaining also the difficult matter of why some were seen to be so green and dark while others were of such a light green that they seemed to be perfecting themselves in their verdure, having been at first clear crystals that, had they been left longer in their encasement, would have been more perfect, and like the others. The speculation reached this point without being resolved.[28]

Some ritual uses of emeralds appear to have survived conquest, at least among the Muisca. Historian J. Michael Francis has discovered in Colombia's National Archive a series of anti-idolatry investigations from 1595 in the vicinity of Tunja, north of Bogotá. Near the village of Iguaque, tortured native subjects led Spanish priests and secular authorities to a number of graves and shrines (locally known as *cucas*) containing emeralds. Although the Spanish record is not much help in illuminating indigenous perspectives, it shows that emeralds were sometimes included in fertility offerings, bundled with maize cobs and other foods and buried in fields.[29] Others were found with skulls and other human remains, similarly bundled and hidden, some in caves. Nearly all the emeralds were classified as poor quality when taxed by the royal treasury in Bogotá, but the fact they were often placed with gold objects suggests their value was appraised in a way unlike the colonizer's. What might these crystals have meant to the Muiscas?

Crystal Connections

In a pioneering 1981 essay, the great Colombian anthropologist Gerardo Reichel-Dolmatoff reported a connection between the use of crystals among contemporary Amazonian (specifically Tukanoan) and north highland Kogi shamans, and beliefs about emeralds among the pre-Columbian Muiscas.[30] Reichel-Dolmatoff observed that crystals, usually of quartz or tourmaline, were prized tools of the shaman's kit. In both the Sierra Nevada and hot lowland contexts crystals were closely associated with male generative power, and were understood to be a kind of fossilized primordial semen. The six-sidedness or hexagonal prismatic form of crystals such as tourmaline (and emerald) is thought, said Reichel-Dolmatoff, to represent 'a cosmic ordering principle'.[31] Offerings of natural, six-sided crystals are still common among the Kogi, and ancient ones left by their ancestors, the Tairona, were similar. The number six is sacred, and for the Kogi the mountain range in which they live is imagined to be a giant, six-sided crystal. The same ordering principle is seen in the arrangement of constellations, and is therefore reproduced in the ordering of sacred sites. The crystal in its natural form thus both represents cosmic form and encapsulates generative power.

Reichel-Dolmatoff felt confident to project these beliefs back in time and across some distance to the pre-conquest Muiscas, who appear to have extended solar and seminal associations to emeralds as just one of several types of rock crystal. He considered the Muiscas's special access to mineral salt a related phenomenon, probably a feminine inverse. Colonial documents, nearly all produced by writers uninterested in native points of view, are not much help in this quest for indigenous meaning. A mid-seventeenth century Muisca, or Chibcha, dictionary calls emerald *chuecuta*, a word with few apparent relations in surviving vocabularies.[32] *Chue* was said to be the word for teat, and also 'adulterous lover'. 'To breastfeed' was *chuez biohotysuca*. *Chuega ychihiza* was a flower the Spanish called 'local saffron', its plant *chuegasuca*. Stone was *hyca*, and crystalline stone, *hyca chuhuza*. It is difficult to say, then, if *chuecuta* had metaphorical associations with the sun, semen or virility. If anything, the *chue* portion suggests breast milk.

Pre-Columbian Emerald Mining

Unlike gold and certain seashell beads, emeralds were not apparently used as currency among Amerindian peoples, and mining appears to have consisted mostly of scavenging surface outcrops or sifting through river detritus near the few places where emeralds occurred. There is, however, mention of what sounds like indigenous hushing or 'booming' – primitive hydraulic mining – attested to by several conquest-era sources. This would not have been terribly unlikely given the relative sophistication of pre-Columbian gold mining not far away, in hills around the lower Cauca River.[33]

The most detailed description of indigenous emerald mining as it might have been practised before the arrival of the Spanish is found in the early post-conquest *Epitome of the Conquest of New Granada*:

> . . . the mines are located in the Province of Tunja, and it is quite something to see where God felt himself served to place those mines. They are in a strange land, at one end of a barren mountain range. This treeless sierra is surrounded by other, densely forested mountains, which form a kind of pathway through which to enter the mining zone. The entire region is made up of extremely rough terrain. From one end of the mines to the other is a distance of just half a league, or even less. In order to extract the emeralds the Indians have constructed certain devices, which consist of large, wide irrigation channels through which water passes in order to wash away the earth and thus expose the veins where the emeralds are located. For that reason they only work the mines at a certain time of year, which is during the rainy season. This enables them to move great quantities of earth, and allows them to follow the exposed veins. The soil at those mines is loose, easily moveable, and very porous, and it remains thus until the Indians come across one of the veins, which is made of a clay-like substance. The Indians then follow the vein and with their wooden tools they remove the emeralds they discover within it. In this practice, as in so many others, the Indians perform all kinds of sorcery to help them find the emeralds. They drink and eat certain herbs, after which they reveal in which veins the miners will unearth the finest stones. The lord of these mines is a cacique named Somondoco, a subject of the great cacique of Tunja.[34]

There are other corroborating accounts from the same period. In Book VII of his mammoth *Historia General y Natural de las Indias*, Gonzalo Fernández de Oviedo included testimonies taken on Hispaniola regarding the discovery and mining of emeralds during the conquest of New Granada. Among his informants were captains Juan de Junco and Gómez de Corral, who in 1541 described the mines as follows:

... they are in the wilds belonging to the lordship of the cacique Somondoco, on a high and barren range, in a space no more than a league [square], whose location, to be precise, is at five degrees this side of the equator. And in climbing that range the first third, or even half, is wooded and fresh, but from there above it is barren and dry, and in terms of bedrock it is not too hard, but can be excavated with *coas* or sharpened hardwood staves, which the Indians use to recover emeralds, these sticks serving in place of [our] wood-handled crowbars (*barretas*). And when it rains they make some pits, or earthen pools, to collect water that they then guide to that which they have moved or excavated with their *coas*, and they then wash the earth. And thus they discover the emeralds just as nature gave birth to them and formed them, some larger than others, and some more fine and cleaner than others, and in diverse quantities in terms of size, and the price and value at which they will be appraised.[35]

Fernández de Oviedo adds that these men showed him some fifty or sixty emerald specimens of many sorts, or *suertes*. A disciple of Pliny, Oviedo concluded: '. . . until our time no one has ever heard of a discovery, by Christians, of such naturally occurring stones, and the value of that land is enormous, so laden as it is with riches. . . .'[36] Oviedo, who had participated in the failed Darién colony of Santa María and had supervised gold collection in Hispaniola's mines, was not far wrong in his assessment. What he might not have predicted was a rapid drop in European emerald prices resulting from this and subsequent finds. Oviedo might also have been surprised to know that with the exception of new metal tools, techniques of emerald mining in New Granada would remain virtually unchanged for centuries. While he was writing, however, the conquest of Colombia's emerald fields was still far from complete.

❖

CHAPTER 2

Conquistadors

JUST as it took firearms global, Europe gave birth to its own gunpowder empires. As in Asia, gunpowder weapons played a key role in state consolidation and expansion beginning about 1450. Partly for this reason, historians use the term 'early modern' to mark off the explosive era to *c.*1750, when new and profound shifts in military technology and strategy began taking shape. De-emphasizing 'medieval' archers and crossbowmen, catapults, rams and knightly contests, early modern warfare required new battlefield configurations, a new defensive architecture – even new livelihoods, such as gunner or engineer.

Spain has been held up as a prime example of an early modern European state consolidated with the aid of cutting-edge gunpowder weapons.[1] These proved most effective against Granada, the last Islamic kingdom in southern Europe, which fell to Ferdinand and Isabella's forces in 1492. Despite promises of tolerance, al-Andalus was henceforth officially Catholic, a fully subjugated province of neo-Roman Hispania. Such was the power of state-sponsored guns in a contiguous landmass. What about the so-called conquistadors Spain flushed overseas beginning that same fateful year? Were they also agents of an emerging gunpowder empire?

The Spanish conquerors of the Americas brought with them a mix of medieval and modern technologies and fighting styles. Surprisingly few had had formal military experience in Europe, yet most were quick to learn how to use handguns and portable cannons. 'Premodern' steel-edge weapons such as lances, pikes and swords arguably did more harm in the American tropics, however, and steel helmets prevented more deaths than well-aimed gunshots. Indeed, careful scholars of the conquest have shown how few Spanish battles with the Aztecs, Incas, Muiscas, or anyone else were decided by gunpowder weapons. Deadly germs were arguably *the* key factor throughout the hemisphere, but there were others.

Critics of Marshall Hodgson's gunpowder model in Asia have emphasized the enduring significance of the horse and the Central Asian tradition of the lightning-fast cavalry raid. Taking advantage of the power of guns without giving up the horse required a new division of martial labour in the sixteenth century. Equestrian glory remained the ideal of Mughal, Safavid and Ottoman nobles, while gun handling, light and heavy, became the preserve of slave armies. Major contests, especially between the Safavids and Ottomans, were ultimately decided by drawn-out sieges of ancient cities such as Baghdad. Some of the guns developed for these standoffs were larger than anything Europeans ever considered using themselves. Over a century later, Persia's Nadir Shah cleverly fused the two concepts in defeating Muhammad Shah and sacking Delhi.

Spanish Christians had inherited a similar light cavalry tradition from their Berber and Arab ancestors, and it proved a powerful weapon against fellow Europeans in Italy in the era of Columbus. In the Americas, the Spanish *jineta* (or *jinete*) proved far more decisive than gunpowder, enabling a height advantage and mobility envied, and soon taken up, by otherwise pedestrian indigenous warriors armed with the proverbial sticks and stones. Horses were by no means invincible against obsidian-studded clubs, pit traps and poisoned arrows, but in general swift mounts were the land equivalent of Columbus's armed caravels. One competent rider in cotton armour and helmet could face down hundreds of indigenous warriors – or flee in a flash. As if to prove the point, when robbed of their horses by impassable terrain, as happened in Muzo, Spanish conquistadors foundered.

Where Spanish Christians in the Americas most resembled the Safavid *qizilbash* and other Islamic frontier warriors was not in their use of gunpowder weapons but in their adherence to a medieval honour code that regarded raiding for mineral wealth, preferably on horseback, as the surest means to win rank. Conquest in this competitive, hyper-masculine, equestrian world was not so much an official project of state as it was the cumulative effect of numerous individual enterprises followed by decades of angling at court. The early modern ruler had only to inspire subjects with a generalized mission (crusade/jihad) and come through on at least some promises of sinecures and titles in exchange for rents or shares in new adventures.

The violent energies of these self-starting, usually poor and there-fore resource-pooling conquistadors, East and West, could be hard to harness, especially if they struck gold – or emeralds. Expanding the realm of the faithful at the expense of infidels was always praise-worthy in militantly pious societies, but getting rich in the process was highly recommended. With enough booty, or better yet a mine, even a petty warlord could amass a personal fortune, arm a following and deal directly with kings.

Spanish conquistadors soon discovered that quick riches in the Americas were best won by capturing and ransoming unsuspecting headmen, or caciques. Most such caciques were tortured to reveal the location of their treasuries or mines before being throttled for alleged heresy or tyranny. Chief Bogotá was no Muhammad Shah, and certainly no Atahuallpa, yet still his ransom included substantial gold and emeralds. Emeralds stood out. Since Bogotá's gold fell well short of that offered by Atahuallpa, it was arguably New Granada's unique green stones that persuaded Charles V to recognize, albeit reluctantly, Old Granada-born conquistador Gonzalo Jiménez de Quesada.

Spain became a different sort of gunpowder empire once the Aztec, Inca and Muisca conquests were consolidated and America's mineral . treasures began flowing worldwide. The ever-envious French, English and Dutch, unlike the 'stone age' Americans, had guns of their own, and also swift ships. Even in the days of Cortés, defence of empire overseas demanded vast expenditure on weapons, fortifications and personnel. To pay for it all, colonists were taxed on trade and production of precious minerals, and subjected to a variety of monopolies. Indians were taxed, like subjects of Asia's gunpowder empires, for their ill luck at having been conquered. Among the earliest tribute items paid by indigenous Colombians were raw emeralds.

Emeralds and Emperors

Although the Spanish conquistadors' fabled emerald mines turned out to be in the Muisca highlands of eastern Colombia rather than somewhere in Inca Peru or coastal Ecuador, it was Francisco Pizarro who sent the first undisputed emeralds to Spain. Pilot Bartolomé Ruiz had come across emerald beads on an Ecuadorian trading raft in 1526, and a few years later Pizarro named a river in Ecuador's Pacific northwest for the emeralds he and his followers encountered among villagers living along its shores. As a result of this and other finds to the south, the belief persisted that emeralds were produced in Ecuador as well as Colombia. It was only after the government geologist Theodor Wolf surveyed the Province of Esmeraldas in the 1870s that it has been generally accepted that Ecuador's emeralds must have been traded southward from the Colombian highlands.[2]

Colombian emeralds had also reached the Inca heartland of Peru before Pizarro's arrival, although apparently in much smaller quantities than those going to Ecuador. Low-quality emerald beads appear in Inca-period Chimu goldwork from the region around Trujillo, and pre-Incaic examples of emerald beads and inlay work of a similar kind have been unearthed in famous sites such as Sicán. Spanish tax ledgers from the conquest era suggest the Inca Atahuallpa's ransom, collected from all over his vast realm between 1532 and 1533, included some emeralds, although they were so overshadowed by more than a million pesos' weight in gold and several hundred pounds of silver that they appear not to have been appraised or even counted.[3]

Following the arrival of Atahuallpa's ransom and other Peruvian treasures in Spain, Doña Isabel, Portuguese wife of Charles V, issued an order in March 1536 stating that if anyone managed to locate the fabled mines of Esmeraldas, they must not be allowed to work them privately but could only extract stones on behalf of 'the Emperor', to whom they should be delivered. The tone softened in a proclamation sent a few months later to the Peruvian governor's brother, Hernando Pizarro, asking only that the choicest emeralds collected in the *quinto*, or royal fifth of all booty or mined treasure, be delivered to the monarch.[4] The point of these proclamations, however fickle, was that the ancient custom of yielding mineral wealth to the sovereign would be as strictly enforced with emeralds as it had been with gold.

'Inca' emeralds were of interest to Spain's jewel-loving monarchs, notably the queen, but royal attention soon turned to the amazing discoveries made elsewhere in South America by the Andalusian lawyer-turned-soldier, Gonzalo Jiménez de Quesada. After trudging through swamps, climbing mountains and dodging poisoned arrows on their long march inland from their Caribbean base at Santa Marta between 1537 and 1538, Jiménez de Quesada and his 178 followers at last reached the eastern Colombian highlands, home of the Muisca paramount chiefs.

Hurried on by news of competing El Dorado seekers soon to arrive from Venezuela and Quito, Jiménez de Quesada and his men began extorting and ransoming their Muisca hosts. In a story eerily reminiscent of the Inca Atahuallpa's captivity in Cajamarca only a few years before, the paramount chiefs of what would later become the cities of Bogotá and Tunja died in Spanish custody after failing to provide sufficient ransoms in gold and emeralds. Bogotá himself was killed for his intransigence, and other victims soon followed. Eyewitnesses described the captivity and death of Chief Bogotá's successor, his nephew Sagipa:

> . . . Jiménez brought [the cacique Sagipa] with him to the camp, gave him a house in which to stay, and placed him under Spanish guard. And he told Sagipa to hand over all his uncle's gold and

emeralds; until then, he would not be permitted to leave. On hearing this, [Sagipa] claimed he would fill the little house next to his with gold and many stones, all within a period of twenty days. . . . The agreed twenty-day period expired, and nothing of what had been promised was delivered. Seeing this, Jiménez let Sagipa know that it was a very bad thing to mock Christians, and that he should not have done that. . . . [Later,] Jiménez began proceedings against the imprisoned cacique, gathering testimony from many of the lords of this land. It was revealed that Sagipa possessed more than just one [house-full] of gold and a great many emerald stones.[5]

Further interrogations revealed the location of the Muiscas' mines at Somondoco, but seeing emeralds at the source only spurred more extortion. Another eyewitness (probably Jiménez de Quesada, despite self-references in the third person) described the subsequent kidnapping and apparent ransoming of the cacique Hunza, here called Tunja:

From the emerald mines Captain Valenzuela returned to camp, bringing with him three or four valuable stones the Indians had presented him. . . . They claimed Tunja possessed three houses filled with gold, and that the support posts on the houses were made of gold. So the Christians decided to go there. . . . Those who had dismounted from their horses rushed the cacique, and all the gold and emerald stones they found, out of harm's way. . . . It took until the early hours of the morning to gather all the gold, emerald stones, beads, and fine *mantas* [cotton textiles]. . . . That night the Christians seized close to 180,000 pesos of fine and low-grade gold, as well as a great number of emeralds.[6]

Although neither Sagipa nor the cacique of Tunja was executed outright according to these and other conquest-era documents, the fact that both died soon after capture, and after having been tortured, led to royal sanctions against Jiménez de Quesada on his return to

Spain. It was nearly a decade before he was allowed to return to the vast Andean territory he had dubbed the New Kingdom of Granada.

The Mines of Somondoco

The emerald mines that drew the conquistadors' interest were located in a remote mountain site called Somondoco. According to various eyewitnesses and chroniclers, Somondoco was a Muisca cacique subject to the great lord Bogotá. The mines, now known by the name of Chivor, were said to be located a short distance from Chief Somondoco's village. Despite their apparent proximity to the new Spanish settlement of Santa Fe de Bogotá, the overland journey was considerable. Two eyewitnesses described the mine in 1539:

> The mines are located some fifteen leagues from the Valley of the Trumpet, in a very high and sparse mountain range. It appears the emeralds are extracted from an area about a league in size. The lord of the mines is a high-ranking Indian chief by the name of Somondoco. He is sovereign over many vassals and settlements, and his private residence is located three leagues' distance from the mines. No other Indians but his subjects work the mines, and only at certain times of the year, always accompanied by many ceremonies. After the emeralds are extracted they are traded and exchanged among the Indians. The main items of barter are the gold beads that are made in this land, as well as clothing, much of which is made from cotton. . . . Those who went on the discovery of the emerald mines said that from the mines they could see in the distance some great plains, so marvelous that nothing like them had ever been seen.[7]

As nearly every colonial commentator exclaimed, the hill on which the main Somondoco diggings were located offers an unexpected view of Colombia's great eastern plains, or Llanos, through a narrow gap in the mountains (Plate 4).

The early writers also universally noted how the mines suffered from a chronic shortage of water for washing away detritus, a partial explanation for Spanish abandonment soon after conquest. According to Pedro Simón: 'These mines are . . . impossible to supply with water from above. . . . For this reason the Indians of Somondoco worked [them only] in the rainy season or right after rainwater had flowed over them, as it was necessary to scour and carry away the earth and leave visible the veins of stones.'[8]

As these various chroniclers state, a group of Spaniards under Captain Pedro Hernández (or Fernández) de Valenzuela was led from the town of Turmequé to the Valley of Somondoco, and from there to the hilltop emerald deposits overlooking the Great Plains. As Simón notes, the stones greatly pleased the conquistadors, but fell far short of 'filling their empty spaces'. With great effort Valenzuela and his indigenous helpers collected samples to take back to Jiménez de Quesada, but the emerald deposits of Somondoco were a disappointment.

Following Valenzuela's brief reconnaissance, Quesada sent a party of conquistadors off to the Llanos in search of El Dorado while another returned to the emerald mines of Somondoco. Even with the best iron tools available, the Spaniards were severely hindered by the lack of water. A frustrated Quesada came to have a look, and immediately agreed the mines would be extremely difficult to work. This may have simply been a matter of a temporary dry spell, but attention quickly shifted to the more pressing search for El Dorado, and to the easier business of extorting caciques and despoiling emerald-rich graves.

Several sources note that following the kidnapping of the cacique of Tunja, Muisca captives led dozens of treasure-starved Spaniards to scattered grave mounds, where more emeralds were unearthed. Others were removed from corpses left above ground on funerary racks. The resulting gems, gold jewellery and 'idols', as Muisca votive objects were labelled, were later divided up and the gold smelted in the new Spanish treasury office at Bogotá. The search for tombs and offerings continued long after the conquest, as attested by periodic entries in Bogotá's tax books of 'esmeraldas de santuarios'.[9]

Even with the mines of Somondoco moribund, Jiménez de Quesada and his conquistadors gathered a substantial hoard of stones. In Santa Marta in 1539 a scribe tallied some 1,815 emeralds 'of many qualities, some large and others small, and of many grades' amid Quesada's great cache of booty. He also registered some 200,000 pesos' worth (about 920 kg) of gold.[10] Several of Colombia's first plundered emeralds travelled to Germany, Bohemia and elsewhere as gifts of Charles V to his Habsburg relatives (Plate 5). While fighting legal challenges to his claims, Jiménez de Quesada managed to have a mountain covered with emeralds incorporated into his coat of arms in 1546 (Figure 1).[11]

1. Gonzalo Jiménez de Quesada's coat of arms. On returning to Spain in late 1539 to defend his claim as conqueror of New Granada, Gonzalo Jiménez de Quesada submitted this sketch in request of a coat of arms. The traditional Spanish lion and castle symbols are joined by a wooded hill strewn with emeralds.

The Conquest of the Muzos

As hopes for the Somondoco mines faded, conquistadors turned their attention to a newly discovered emerald-bearing district. Located some 180 kilometres north of Bogotá near the headwaters of the Carare River was the Province of Los Muzos. Named for its bellicose, Carib-speaking inhabitants, Muzo was much slower to fall to the conquistadors' swords and harquebuses than Somondoco. There were no open plains or unprotected farming villages here, no broad trails for mounted warriors. According to Spanish chroniclers, first attempts to conquer Muzo country began in either 1543 or 1544, when a reconnaissance party entered the district from the highland town of Furatena. This expedition, like many to follow, was intended to punish the Muzos for abducting their highland Muisca neighbours – now reduced to Spanish serfdom – to butcher and consume them 'like so much mutton'.[12]

The more sedentary Muiscas claimed to have been driven out of the upper Carare River basin by the Muzos at some point in the recent past, and early colonial testimonies suggest the Carib invaders were still expanding their reach in the highlands when the Spanish arrived. Although frightened by the ferocity of the Muzos, Spanish invaders were encouraged to return when in the entrails of recently introduced Castilian hens they discovered 'small but fine' emeralds.[13]

Next came the Navarrese conquistador Pedro de Ursúa, famous for later falling victim to the Basque rebel Lope de Aguirre on the Amazon. Here in Muzo country, a decade before his fatal float – in exchange for broad licences to search for El Dorado later on – Ursúa promised to bring the Muzos under the Spanish yoke. The judges of Bogotá's recently established *audiencia*, or royal appeals court, were anxious to punish the Muzos for annihilating a party of conquistadors after promising peace. According to Pedro Simón, Muzo warriors wore shrunken Spanish heads as trophies.[14]

Ursúa assembled 125 Spanish men and entered Muzo territory from the northeast. According to chroniclers, the Muzos were ready. When not attacking, they harried the invaders with incessant shrieks and shows of force. They fought 'with a bravery never seen among Indians', and led the Spanish to believe they were twice as numerous as they really were. Arrows poisoned with a toxin derived from tree frogs left Spanish attackers to die vomiting and 'raging' within twenty-four hours. After trying to found a town, Ursúa gave up and left to search for El Dorado in 1551. No Spaniard or highland Amerindian wished to remain without him, and no trace of emerald mines was found.[15]

Only in 1558 were Spanish conquistadors and prospectors able to establish a firm presence in Muzo territory. They were led by a Bogotá-based *encomendero*, Luis Lanchero, who had briefly passed through in 1543. Motivated by Muzo attacks on Muisca serfs under his charge, Lanchero descended into the hot lowlands under licence from the *audiencia*. He was accompanied by some sixty armed Spanish men, including future emerald miner Benito López de Poveda and an unknown number of indigenous archers, porters and guides. According to Fray Pedro de Aguado, most of the Spaniards, along with several Portuguese and at least one Genoese and one Greek, were unwilling participants compelled by Bogotá judges.

Aside from surprise engagements with shrieking warriors, which often occurred at night, elaborate mantraps and ambushes awaited the invaders at every turn. Poisoned fruit, palm stakes and arrows also took a considerable toll, both physically and psychologically. Aguado tells of a father and son who made it out of the jungle alive after a brief sortie only to die 'raging with the pain of the cruel poison that tormented them and embraced their hearts'.[16]

In classic guerrilla style, the Muzos used time, boisterous night raids and small-scale daytime ambushes to sap the invaders' strength. It was nearly two months before Lanchero's forces got relief from the highlands. By this time, members of the camp were so hungry from living on scrounged maize they were on the point of eating a lone wounded horse. Relief arrived not on horse- or mule-back but on the shoulders of Muisca porters.[17] Now refreshed with powder, biscuit and ham, the invaders pushed on towards the heart of Muzo territory. In a fierce engagement, the expedition's leader took a poisoned arrow to the chest.[18]

In what he thought would be his last act Luis Lanchero followed the conquistador script and founded a town. The lack of a suitable townsite and likely imminent death of the founder were irrelevant; the actual town, dubbed La Trinidad de los Muzos, could wait. To everyone's amazement, Lanchero recovered. Still, the Muzos retained the advantage; all around the camp indigenous warriors taunted, displaying cords and nets 'with which they thought they would tie up and carry off the Spaniards to eat them'.[19] At this point royal officials sent a militia captain from Bogotá along with thirty Spanish men – all forced recruits. It appears these extra exiles made the difference.

In June 1560 Lanchero laid out the town of La Trinidad de los Muzos on a small terrace below a steep range of hills.[20] The plaza-centred grid was carved into blocks and house lots, one given to each European male participant. Proposed grazing lands and orchards were partitioned in the nearby surroundings, and in the process Muzo maize and manioc plantings were discovered and sacked. Despite these aggressive acts, the Spanish appear to have mostly settled in their crude new grass huts to await further relief from the highlands. In the meantime the Muzos planted the area with poisoned stakes and darts, often entering the town at night. Nine settlers died of the venom.

Attacks and reprisals continued, but after a regional headman was captured in a surprise raid many Muzo villages submitted to Spanish rule.[21] No one could fathom the sudden change of heart, but disease may have played a role. The Spanish remained vigilant. Knowing that in such moments of apparent peace mass rebellion might be brewing, Lanchero left instructions with his most trusted soldiers to stay armed and alert as he left for Bogotá to seek rights to distribute *encomiendas*, or quasi-feudal grants of Amerindian tributaries. For the 'conquered' Muzos now subjected to forced labour and tribute payment, the seeds of rebellion were sown.[22]

Perhaps it was the stresses of guerrilla warfare or the delayed effects of the poisoned arrow in the chest, but for some reason Lanchero turned into an insufferable tyrant. Town council members and all but a few favoured soldiers complained of his insults and demands, and soon several groups of concerned citizens made trips to Bogotá to plead for an audit of Lanchero's governance. The Muzos, meanwhile, continued to harass their new (and divided) masters. In retaliation, several warriors were captured and hanged. Lanchero was briefly jailed, then allowed only to return to Tunja. Muzo would not be his, and the district's emerald mines had yet to be found.

Pedro Simón credits the Spanish invaders' unexpected turnaround in Muzo to the combination of fierce war dogs and Lanchero's personal resolve. In truth, the Muzos were probably suffering from the same disease epidemics (smallpox, measles, influenza) as their highland neighbours, many of whom they were still kidnapping and probably adopting to replenish their numbers.[23] For their part, the Spanish remained deeply divided and bitterly contentious, with no sense of how the new town and district of Muzo might make them rich.

After a hearing, Bogotá's judges sent Muzo its first *corregidor*, or royal magistrate. He was generally well received, and his appointment suggested La Trinidad was fated to survive. The turn to optimism was not, according to Aguado, due to the corregidor's effective governance, but rather to the arrival of Spanish women. The Franciscan observed: '. . . it is certain the newly populated towns of the Indies cannot be called permanent or stable until Spanish women arrive and the *encomenderos* and conquistadors get married . . .'[24] Who exactly these women were we do not know, but since most of the men who preceded them were petty criminal exiles it is likely they were not from the upper echelons of highland society. Simón states that by 1566 there were sixty-one household heads in Muzo, suggesting a total European population of about three hundred. Modest Franciscan and Dominican monasteries were soon founded.

Lucky Strike

Sources disagree on details, but it appears Muzo's famous emerald mines were discovered by a local indigenous inhabitant in the mid-

1560s. Simón gives the date as 9 August 1564. As in so many of Simón's stories, animals served as handmaidens of providence. The 1564 strike was made, he says, after a horse kicked up a broken bit of emerald in the town of Muzo itself. This chance revelation prompted an unnamed Spaniard to ask local Indians what stone this was and where more like it might be found. According to Simón, the Muzos referred to emerald as *tapacaz*, in their language 'green stone'.

A Muzo youth led the Spaniards to the steep and shaly banks of Itoco Creek, a little over a league (about 7 km) away, and there on an adjacent hill *encomendero* Alonso Ramírez Gasco staked the first claim.[25] This version of events, minus the horse, seems drawn in part from the 1582 *relación* of one of Muzo's conquistadors, Diego de Poveda. Legal documents from the period now housed in Bogotá describe formal registration of claims only after October 1566.[26]

Aguado offers a more detailed, and for the most part convincing, discovery tale. He says that in the wake of Muzo attacks following Luis Lanchero's exile, the settlers hunkered down in desperation. An *audiencia* judge at last named Alvaro Cepeda de Ayala as the province's new *corregidor*, hoping to turn things around. The *audiencia* also sent more criminals and 'Portuguese undesirables' as auxiliary soldiers.[27]

Aguado says that the La Trinidad citizens had already fallen on such hard times they were wrapping themselves in Indian blankets, having bartered their fine clothing for livestock and ammunition. In the midst of this 'great affliction,' according to the friar, 'God provided':

One day in the middle of Easter week in the year [15]64, while walking through a certain part of town a resident named Gaspar Salgado, native of the county of Monterrey in Galicia, found on the ground a tiny emerald, which he showed to all the other residents, telling them he had found it right there in that ground. This prompted everyone to begin inquiring of the Indians native to that land whom they kept in their houses [as servants] if and where the older ones had formerly gathered such stones, and some heard stories of this, but very tentative and uncertain. . . . [They] went to the village of Itoco . . . [and] an Indian pertaining to the militia leader [Miguel Gómez] found in the ravine where the mines are now worked, a little section [*cañutillo*] of emerald, although not of fine colour. Everyone relaxed with this second sample, since it seemed to confirm the hope of their desire, and with this alone they all returned happily to town.

Human happiness was evanescent, but God's grace prevailed:

Within a few days [*encomendero*] Alonso Ramírez arrived. . . . [He] questioned the Indians of Itoco as to where the emerald mines were, but none wanted to reveal them. So it fell to a little boy named Juan, a native of that village who had spent much time in Ramírez's power and had been made a Christian. This one, in return for the good treatment he had received from his master, promised to take him to where his parents and other Indians of that village used to get emeralds. Ramírez was not at all slothful in this business, but rather, without losing any time, called upon people to join him, along with a magistrate to register the mines. His guide led them to Itoco, about a league away from Muzo toward Ocaso (although a bit twisted in the southern part) and in the ravine where only a few days before Miguel Gómez had been walking around looking for these same mines, they were discovered by the hand of this same Indian [Juan].[28]

Thus, according to Pedro de Aguado, were the luckless, ragtag European settlers of Muzo at last saved. It is an almost archetypal Franciscan tale in that nothing the sinful Spaniards did brought about their abrupt reversal of fortune. Instead, as if scripted by God, it was a Muzo Amerindian youth who had been well treated and baptized who turned the situation around. The many other Muzos who had tried *not* to reveal the mines were obviously the wiser, but for Aguado they appear as the same old skulking, dissimulating, and worst of all, lazy, elders.

Aguado conceded that not all was joy and happiness among the blessed, although that mood prevailed for some time after the first emerald discovery. News of the strike provoked a minor rush. The *audiencia* president quickly named a new favourite to the post of *corregidor*: Juan de Penagos of Bogotá. Since this change came only shortly after the naming of Cepeda de Ayala, quarrels immediately broke out all over town, mostly between householders who had been away during the mine discoveries and those who had been there to examine the first stones.

Despite the bickering, all was not grief and strife, according to Aguado. In his brief time in charge, Cepeda de Ayala played wise King Solomon and parcelled out the mines in a way that struck most as fair. Discoverers got an extra claim, and some lots were set aside for the king. Most of Muzo's European householders, including those of non-Spanish heritage, got a single thirty-by-twenty-yard plot (Figure 2).

Division and Rebellion

One of mining's curses is that it distracts from raising, or otherwise procuring, food. By forcing their indigenous wards to mine for emeralds, Muzo's mine-owning residents soon found themselves starving. Cepeda de Ayala's solution to this predicament was convenient in that it allowed the search for gems to continue. He sent the reliable Benito López de Poveda and followers out to raid outlying Muzo villages for maize, while captives were brought to town to plant more.

Meanwhile, according to Aguado, several Spanish householders attempted to offset their needs by sending more than twenty Muisca subordinates to the Muzos of Itoco to truck for emeralds on their behalf. The Muiscas carried painted cotton garments and although they were allegedly well received, the Muzos, 'using their ancient betrayals and evils', killed all but one, a woman with a baby at the breast, who somehow managed to hide in the forest before making her way back to La Trinidad at night.[29]

2. A Diagram of the Muzo Emerald Diggings at Bustos' Cliff, 1567. This simply sketched *traza*, or grid, with mine owners' names written in each square, marks out the 30 x 20 yard claims of Muzo's first registered emerald diggings along Itoco Creek. The text says this sketch was copied in 1598 from the "old, torn," original notebook.

Penagos, having taken over as *corregidor*, ordered a reprisal, but according to Aguado the recruits managed only to find the dismembered corpses of the Muiscas, who had allegedly been cannibalized. A general rebellion was evidently brewing, and many formerly pacified villages, including the emerald camp at Itoco, openly defied their *encomenderos*. Wanting to see gems despite the danger, Penagos organized an armed mining expedition to Itoco that he maintained would serve the whole community. 'Latinized' Indians, most of them Muiscas, were sent to do the work of digging, protected by twenty-five armed Spaniards. After ten or twelve days' hard grubbing, they returned to La Trinidad to share out stones. As nearly all of what spilled out on the table was of poor quality, quarrels soon erupted among the claimants, along with charges of fraud.

The Muzos rose in rebellion amid the quarrelling, prompting a new round of Spanish reprisals. No matter how hard the invaders attacked, however, the Muzos only fought back harder. The Spanish now responded with what Aguado terms 'another type of civil war'. All plantings and food stores were destroyed for miles around. What followed was an old and by this time illegal conquistador practice, the *montería infernal*, or 'hellish chase' – hunting Amerindians with greyhounds and mastiffs. Despite the dogs and wasting war, the Muzos refused to surrender. They continued to plant poisoned stakes, dig mantraps and threaten the invaders from the surrounding hills.

Why did the Muzos rebel at this juncture? Aguado suggests, perhaps rightly, that the Muzo chiefs hoped to keep the newly discovered emerald mines from producing in order to starve out the Spaniards. Cutting off the diggings was a good strategy, as there was no other source of income to purchase food from the highlands. Even from La Trinidad the mines could not be reached without armed escort. Colonists were soon reduced to scrounging for herbs in the jungle, and those in the vanguard were forced to wear three-inch-thick cotton boots to resist the inevitable poisoned stakes. Meanwhile the Muzos, according to Aguado, had sworn never to be defeated by the Spaniards, 'spitting into a fire according to a ceremony they use'.[30]

Corregidor Penagos returned from a trip to Bogotá with broader powers, but proved unable to halt the rebellion. One sortie led by Miguel Gómez left three soldiers caught in a trap, one a Lisbon native who allegedly ended up 'minced in a cake'. Several others, including the Genoese Pedro de Ormea and even Penagos's trusty lieutenant Francisco Morcillo, died as a result of stepping on poisoned stakes. Such was the price, says Aguado, of setting aside the 'hot and heavy' cotton boots. Broken despite his long experience as an Indian fighter by these clever guerrilla tactics, Penagos decided to retire to Bogotá '. . . no longer wanting to search for emeralds, which seemed to him riches costing more pain than valour'.[31]

Having once been pushed aside, Alvaro Cepeda de Ayala regained the office of *corregidor* and started re-establishing Spanish dominion over the rebel Province of the Muzos. A series of hard-fought night attacks on local villages eventually succeeded.[32] Despite the Spanish suffering occasional arrow wounds, which they had become more adept at curing, they at least temporarily pacified the better part of the Muzo Province. Aguado estimates that from the time of Lanchero's first sortie in 1558 to this point, almost a decade later, about one hundred Spaniards and other Europeans had been killed. Muzo and Muisca casualties were no doubt much higher.

Aftermath

Emerald production was rarely interrupted after 1568, according to royal tax records, but other sources describe renewed Muzo hostilities right up to the end of the sixteenth century. These uprisings, the worst of which erupted in the 1580s, prompted new punitive expeditions. Local mine owners and *encomenderos* participated, but sources suggest these outings were mostly organized by Spanish newcomers to the highlands seeking to make a name for themselves and win *encomiendas*.

One expedition leader from this unsettled period was Captain Bernardo de Vargas Machuca, a neo-conquistador from Old Castile. Vargas Machuca never won an *encomienda* for his efforts, but he did claim emerald mines in Muzo around 1587. His merit files, copies of which survive in Seville and Bogotá, include the testimonies of a half-dozen young militiamen from Muzo, mostly sons of the first conquerors and mine owners, who served under his command.[33] While in Madrid seeking a promotion in 1599, Vargas Machuca published a manual for conquistadors that drew from his experiences in Muzo and other parts of New Granada.[34]

As discussed in the next chapter, even when the conquest of the Muzos was finally over, the hoped-for bonanza failed to materialize. The peculiar geology and difficult location of Muzo's emerald deposits were partly to blame, but many other factors conspired to make emerald mining uncertain. These included a chronic scarcity of workers, high incidence of disease, consistent undervaluing of emeralds by local merchants and gem cutters, periodic Crown interference in both mining and trade and unpredictable fluctuations in overseas demand. Even Muzo's claim-holding conquistadors were astonished to find that so much hardship unearthing the world's finest emeralds was almost more trouble than it was worth.[35]

This brief conquest chronicle makes painfully evident the tremendous human cost of the European 'discovery' of Colombian emeralds. Beginning with conquistador Gonzalo Jiménez de Quesada and his followers, the bloody expansion of Spain's maritime gunpowder empire into Colombia's northern Andes entailed extorting and murdering headmen such as Bogotá and his nephew, Sagipa, then plundering their ancestors' graves. Muisca emeralds were then offered to the Holy Roman Emperor Charles V in exchange for recognition of political rights. These included reducing conquered peoples to serfdom, including mine labour, to support the invaders.

A subsequent generation of conquerors used the highland bases established by Jiménez de Quesada and others to beat down the less tractable Muzos of the neighbouring lowlands. Emeralds were slow to appear as an incentive for this dangerous endeavour, but once they did, the Muzos' days were numbered. Within little more than a century of European arrival in their homeland, the Muzos, for whom the town and greatest mines and stones were named, were entirely extinct. Indeed, there is virtually no trace of them today beyond a few mountain and river names. Even the much more numerous Muiscas, including those of the fabled Somondoco diggings, were nearly wiped out by the demands of the conquistadors and their descendants, largely as a result of the quest for mineral wealth.

If narrating conquest is step one in demystifying, or 'defetishizing', Colombian emeralds, step two requires examining their production.

CHAPTER 3

❖

Emerald City

EVEN as the blood of conquest dried, Colombian emeralds did not come cheaply. In October 1564 the seven aldermen of the new 'city' of La Trinidad de los Muzos wrote to King Philip II in Madrid. They reported that in the five years since the town's founding all but twenty of the original sixty-four conquistadors had been killed. The native inhabitants, described by the councilmen as 'vicious warriors', continued to use poisoned darts and arrows of the type said to kill within twenty-four hours. Most survivors suffered from wounds and disabilities, including paralyzed limbs. The Muzos, though temporarily 'pacified and reduced', were still much feared and deeply despised. They were again described, perhaps unfairly, as 'a nation of butchering Caribs who eat human flesh'.[1]

On a brighter note, the councilmen reported that 'in this time there have been discovered many mines of emeralds of both the common and fine sort, and others so perfect as to be quite *oriental*'. A bona fide emerald rush seemed imminent: 'And likewise we have other mines of emeralds of great perfection that shall be discovered shortly with the aid of God.' Muzo attacks indeed plagued European emerald seekers periodically for another three decades, but within about a year of the councilmen's letter to the king the richest claims on the Cerro de Itoco were mapped, staked and registered.

As this chapter shows, emerald mining in Muzo quickly became a formalized and well-recorded activity, although excavation techniques remained simple. Mining society was headed by a titled class of mine owners, including some women, mostly descended from conquistadors. Most owners employed European overseers, or *mineros*, to manage work gangs comprising indigenous wards or enslaved Africans. Catholic clergymen established small monasteries but apparently no missions. As native workers died from overwork and disease, mine owners called for subsidized slaves. Such calls went unheeded, and the diggings fell into decline. Mine owner demands for lower taxes were similarly ignored, leading the honest to abandon claims and those less so to engage in contraband trade. By the first decades of the seventeenth century, steep population decline, high taxes and exhausted deposits left the Muzo mines on the verge of total collapse. Muzo's first boom-and-bust cycle took about fifty years.

Punishing as this first cycle was, mining and even taxation are reasonably well documented for Muzo's first decades. Predictably less clear is the early traffic in prime stones, although fraud and contraband investigations opened immediately after discovery. Some Muzo emeralds show up in jewellery, usually as part of elite women's dowries, in colonial records from Tunja, Bogotá, Popayán, Quito and other north Andean cities. The Elizabethan corsair Francis Drake, who sacked Cartagena de Indias in 1586, received part of the city's ransom in emeralds offered by prominent townswomen. Merchants also sent emerald-encrusted jewels with factors travelling to the colonies' richest trade hubs: Mexico City, Lima and Potosí. Others went to Manila. Most emeralds were, however, sent to Spain, although only a few ships' manifests list emeralds, mostly those belonging to the royal treasury. Only chance material evidence, such as that recovered from shipwrecks, offers a glimpse at what went unrecorded.

Laying Claim

Information on early Muzo mining is fragmentary, but the documents show that without doubt the central district of today was the same as in the 1560s. Borrowing the standard term for a temporary military outpost, mining camps were called *reales de minas*. Both camps and diggings, or *trazas*, like mountains and rivers, were domesticated with grids, maps and proper names. Some of the first diggings recorded were La Rica (The Rich) and El Peñol de Busto (Busto's Cliff). Individual mine names ran from religious: San Salvador, San Nicolás, Our Lady of Atocha and, of course, La Trinidad, to more descriptive or imaginative: La Carbonera (The charcoal oven), La Bayona (The girl from Bayonne) and La Cañutería, a reference to the joint-like, spiky crystals all miners hoped to encounter.

The tiny 'city' of Muzo, where all self-respecting European mine owners lived and maintained their households, was even more regulated than the camps or mines. The grid of La Trinidad de los Muzos had been laid out in a bowl-shaped terrace overlooking the Minero River at about 740 metres, or 2,400 feet, above sea level (Figure 3). Despite tremendous ups and downs, it survives. The mines themselves lay some seven kilometres away by rough trail, on either side of Itoco Creek and on the adjacent Itoco Hill (Plate 6). Today, Itoco Creek consists of a braided, intermittently rushing wash fed by a few tributaries. Depending on the season, these lesser creeks flow down in torrents or trickles from the surrounding steep and lushly wooded mountains.

Early claim maps suggest most mines were laid out in the form of adjacent rectangles on the lower slopes of the main hill (see Figure 2). Parts of the hill were extremely steep. Itoco's camp, or *real de minas*, complete with a bamboo-walled, thatch-roofed church, was built in the late 1560s beside the wash. The first *cuadrillas*, or squadrons of workers (again the insistence on orderly, military terminology), consisted primarily of Muisca and Muzo men held in *encomienda*, but enslaved Africans were also present in the diggings from the start. Some of the earliest mine claimants owned up to a dozen captive African miners, most of them men, but also a few women.

Mining emeralds was an uncertain business that relied on scale, as well as luck, to be profitable. Much as in placer gold mining, productivity rose more or less exponentially with the number of labourers

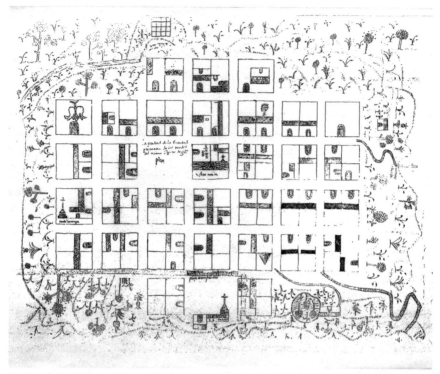

3. La Trinidad de los Muzos Town Grid, *c.*1582. This early town plan, which shows the location of Muzo's main plaza, town hall, parish church, and two monasteries, is virtually identical to the grid of today. The smaller grid to the right is identified as the emerald mines, shown on a hillside beyond the 'Río de Ytoco'.

engaged, but even big outfits could fail. Emerald mining consisted mostly of brute force tasks, with specialized skills concentrated only in prospecting and water management. When executing large or long-term projects, such as dams and canals, mine owners often pooled their enslaved and free labour forces, formalizing these temporary arrangements under the term *compañía*, or 'company'. They later shared out yields according to previously agreed-on fractions calculated from inputs.

Not far from the Itoco mines indigenous women and children engaged in subsistence farming, food preparation and even homespun textile production. Spinning and weaving became important sources of income for Muzo's European overlords, in part because the emerald mines were not reliable rent-producers, and also because not all holders of *encomiendas* in the province had viable mining claims. A substantial textile economy emerged in and around the town of La Trinidad and its satellite communities by the last decades of the sixteenth century, although it fizzled out with demographic decline. Muzo-made textiles disappear from the record by the second quarter of the seventeenth century by which time their weavers had nearly all been wiped out by disease and abuse. Conquistador Diego de Poveda, writing in 1582, said the Muzos numbered about twenty-five thousand, down from some forty thousand in the late 1550s.[2]

Colonial Mining Methods

Muzo's conquest-era emerald diggings are thinly described in lawsuits and a set of 1569 mining codes, but it is clear most work was of the shallow, opencast variety. Forest was cleared with imported axes and machetes, and streams were diverted with mattocks, crowbars and other hand tools. This allowed for the kind of primitive hydraulic mining, or hushing, already described.[3] Washing away mountain surfaces soon necessitated more complex arrangements of wooden or bamboo aqueducts connected to rain-catching reservoirs with their floodgates, known as *tambres*. Controlling water was as important as controlling workers, but even so the search for emeralds was a game of chance. There was no guarantee that even the most extensive or 'well-watered' mines would produce gems.

Writing about 1580, and echoing others' speculations regarding the 'ripening' of emeralds in sunshine, the Franciscan historian Pedro de Aguado described Muzo's early diggings:

The first mine discovered, along with those surrounding it, are called 'de la ruín laya', which is like saying 'imperfect' or 'of a poor greenness'. This is a result of their being in a shady spot, one the sun does not reach except at mid-day. The bed or ridge where these mines are runs North-South. The stones taken from these mines, though they have been many, have been worth little since they are, as already stated, of 'ruín laya', imperfect green. The place where these emerald mines are found consists of a vein of black, volcano-like stone of such type that those who go about working in these mines, thanks to the blackness of the earth, appear to be dusted with charcoal or inked. The stones in the vein are all well placed and ordered just as wise Nature nurtured and arranged them, and in between the emeralds are born, some of them plastered or stuck fast to the live rock.

These were the poor emeralds; soon after the good ones were found:

At the present time these [first] mines are not worked, since soon after these were found Benito López de Poveda discovered others about a half a league away, which they call the 'minas de la buena laya' [roughly, 'mines of good colour']. They run, like the others, North-South, but they are in a spot that the sun, from the time it comes up until it goes down, bathes and heats. The stones they take from here are of many kinds or shades of green, as they have taken extremely fine stones of great perfection and value, and others less so, and still others not at all. The place where these 'buena laya' mines occur are veins of a sort of chalcedony and others of different colours, but with experience it is seen that the vein that has hatched and yielded the best and finest stones is the leonine [*leonada*], which tends a bit towards burnt [*requemada*], and after this the 'wild boar', or bean-coloured chalcedony.

Not all good stones were found in 'leonine' or 'bean-coloured' host rock:

They do not find the exact place where these stones are hatched. What I mean to say is, that not only are the said stones found in the above-mentioned veins, but also amid pebbles, and in live rock, and in piled rubble, and in sand, nor is there the least certainty whether in one vein there have hatched fine stones and in another 'ruinas', because in all these forms and types of veins they find and have found all sorts of stones, good, bad, perfect and imperfect. From the mines Poveda discovered they have taken many and very fine stones, and of great value, among them one that weighed 100½ pesos, which is a pound and four *adarmes* [about 2,310 carats]. This one, being a thing worthy of kings and great lords, was demanded and retained by the king's officials, who, against the will of its owners, who included Cepeda de Ayala [Muzo's *corregidor*, then governor] and Poveda, sent it to Spain, for the king, without assigning it any price, as there was no one who would attempt to perfectly appraise it. Another fine stone was taken out in all perfection that weighed forty-one or forty-two pesos, which is just under half a pound, and another of fourteen or fifteen pesos, of perfect 'laya', which were likewise carried to his majesty. And as for the mines, in the same hill they go on discovering and working new ones each day. The manner of working them is to excavate the earth with the shovel end of the mattock, following the trail of the veins until they reach the main pockets, or places where the emeralds hatch and are found.[4]

Writing about the same time as Aguado, Muzo conquistador and prospector Diego de Poveda, Benito López de Poveda's brother, echoes nearly every detail, adding a few helpful definitions. On rock types: 'Next to the city of La Trinidad in the same caldera and creekbeds and clearings there is a black soil we call "volcano-earth", and it is the same that one finds in the emerald mines; one also finds emeralds in a dark yellow earth and the veins of this colour follow those of a lighter, reddish hue before reaching the volcano type; other veins run in a hard, white to gray stone of a type we call chalcedony, and it is in these rocks that the best emeralds tend to be found.'[5] Colonial 'chalcedony' may correspond to what miners today call 'cenizero'.

These and other descriptions of early colonial emerald mining closely resemble those of primitive gold grubbing, which had been practised all over New Granada since ancient times. The same fire-hardened staves, or *coas*, mentioned in early accounts of the Somondoco emerald mines are noted in various descriptions of conquest-era gold mines, and in both industries the Spanish seem to have introduced few innovations beyond iron and steel tools developed in the Basque Country and possibly Andalusia (Figure 4). Black-powder blasting in the Muzo mines was employed only at the end of the period examined here, beginning around 1771, but even then tunnelling into oreshoots remained generally shallow. Only a few *socavones*, or underground adits, are mentioned in the documents before the end of the colonial period, most dating to the 1650s.[6]

Some environmental consequences of emerald mining were noted by contemporary observers. Antonio Vásquez de Espinosa described Muzo's streams and rivers running black with mine waste in the early seventeenth century:

> The Hill of Itoco, site of the richest mine, is very high; its earth is black like coal, and the veins where emeralds are hatched are

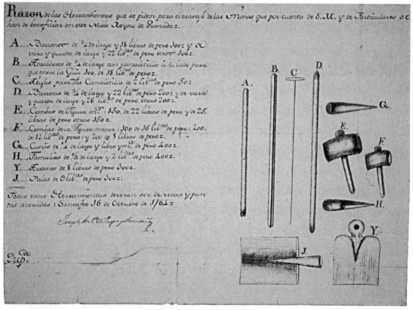

4. Emerald Mining Tools, Muzo, 1764. The tools pictured here, including iron crowbars, sledgehammers, chisels, gads, hoes, and spades, were inventoried by Crown administrators shortly after the royal takeover of the Muzo diggings. Iron and steel tools were mostly imported from the Basque Country or Sweden. The Spanish crown abandoned the diggings in 1792.

usually soft; the means of working them is by excavating all that earth, following the veins in search of emeralds; they have canals coming out from a river that passes near the peak and with them great reservoirs filled with water, with their floodgates, which they call *Tamires* [*tambres*]. The mines being excavated and the veins followed, they open the floodgates, and out flows the retained water with such fury that it carries off all the earth that has been excavated, leaving clean that which has been worked. . . . The water of the river that passes by the city often flows black, both from the colour of the earth and from the work of the mines.[7]

This was only one form of environmental degradation. A lawsuit from 1678 alleged that to develop a mine purchased in 1674 its owner and a partner pooled their indigenous tributary and enslaved African workforces to 'cut the top off Los Peñascos Hill'. A resulting landslide buried the extensive Cascarón diggings below, requiring a major cooperative effort to divert streams to clear out the debris. The project caused two more major landslides by 1702, prompting more suits and an appeal to the regional high court to order a work stoppage.[8]

Although not terribly destructive by modern standards, colonial mining of all kinds speeded up deforestation and led to soil erosion, river silting and groundwater contamination. Still, the massive scarring typical of Spanish American silver and Brazilian gold mines has no equivalent in Muzo or any other emerald district.[9] No mercury or other toxic substances were used to recover or process emeralds, and no heavy metals were apparently released into streams as a result of mining (although pH levels were probably altered). The scale of the work in the emerald mines was also much smaller than that typical of precious metals mines, and rainfall much more abundant. Muzo's chronic wetness exacerbated landslides, but it also prompted a quick return of vegetation in abandoned areas.

Once chipped away with mattocks and adzes, surface detritus was washed downhill, exposing calcite veins that were then pursued with hardened iron and steel bars, hammers and chisels in search of pockets of gem-bearing ore. Open pits and terraces (*bancos*) cut into steep hillsides were preferred to tunnels, as the latter tended to 'drown', as the miners said, or flood. The practice of hushing away surface material with accumulated runoff, called *tirando el tambre*, or 'throwing the floodgate', is still known among older miners in and around Muzo, and was described by foreign mining engineers in the twentieth century. Photographs of mine terraces at both Muzo and Chivor from the 1910s and 1920s probably give a fair idea of how hushing for emeralds was done in colonial times. Only in recent years have the mines gone underground, with dynamite blasting, pneumatic drills and ore carts used as the main means of excavation.

Laying Down the Law

According to Muzo's first mining codes, issued in Bogotá in 1569, mine operators were allowed a maximum of three claims, one currently in operation (*abierta*) and two staked and held in reserve (*estacadas*). Each claim was a rectangle measuring thirty-by-twenty *varas*, or Spanish yards (about 25 × 16.7 m, or approximately 418 square metres). This was about one-fourth the size of a standard placer gold claim in the same period (about sixty-by-forty *varas*). It is likely emerald claims were intentionally much smaller than placer gold claims because they quickly reached bedrock, where gems might be found at any depth. Placer gold claims were usually spread across relatively shallow gravel benches alongside rivers. A 1634 document cites use of a quadrant and survey ropes to reaffirm claim boundaries in disputes, but riverbeds remained an open commons.[10]

According to the codes, non-Spanish foreigners were not allowed to stake or hold emerald claims in Muzo, but names such as Nicolao de Nápoles (Nicholas of Naples), Juan de Candía (John of Crete) and Antonio Flamenco (Anthony the Fleming) on the very first list suggest exceptions. As previously discussed, Muzo was also settled by a number of Portuguese men who arrived against their will from Bogotá, and most who survived conquest staked mining claims. Some claims made by early Portuguese exiles were taken over by others after they had been abandoned for two years. As early as 1568, or a year before the first ordinances were even passed, one Francisco Martín Pavón was recorded as 'reclaiming' such mines by ceremonially digging in them with a mattock in the presence of a magistrate. Others mention ritual tossing of earth in two directions and a verbal statement or oath to formalize a claim. Once staked, claim boundaries were marked with stone cairns supporting posts painted with yellow clay.[11]

It was not unusual in the Spanish Indies for mining rules to be observed in the breach, but there were at least two points where legislation and reality had to mesh: water management and disposal of mining debris. These were the two things over which Muzo's miners sued each other from discovery to the end of the colonial period. The basic problem was that claimants tended to tap into each other's irrigation ditches and then wash their own unwanted rocks and gravel into a neighbour's pit or claim. It was soon discovered that the adjacent, rectangular claims that looked so neat on a map had to accommodate shared canals. To add to the contention, it was often here in the interstices, or easements, where detritus flowed that emeralds were found.

Religious concerns competed with those of the king and his treasurers. In 1599 a number of Muzo mine owners sold choice stones to support their favourite religious sodalities: Our Lady of the Rosary, St Lucy and the Holy Cross. Taxes were paid on stones donated to the Holy Cross brotherhood as early as 1575, and to other sodalities by 1576. The earliest was Our Lady of Muso, offered in 1567, just after the mines opened. In 1583 a number of stones were donated to the cause of redeeming Barbary captives. The practice of donating stones to these brotherhoods and other religious causes was still being regularly documented in tax records in 1644. It is unclear if these gifts boosted production, but Crown officials were certain they reduced royal income.[12] All subsoil wealth technically belonged to the king.

The king was generous to his subjects, even protective. Spanish law required, for example, that he guarantee female ownership of mine claims. Mines owned and operated by women, usually widows of early claimants and conquistadors, but sometimes also their daughters or sisters, were as common in Muzo as in any other Spanish-American mining district within a generation of establishment. Women owned mines and paid taxes on emeralds in 1570 much as they did in 1670. In 1577 Ana de Bobadilla registered some of the finest emeralds produced that year, including a 69-carat plus 'six-sided mirror-stone' (*esmeralda espejuelo sestavado*).[13]

Miners and Mineros

Muzo's European conquerors seem to have imagined mine work in racial terms from the start. There were harsh corporal punishments assigned in the first law codes to 'Indians, blacks, mulattos, and other low persons' for minor infractions such as bartering untaxed gems for food and clothing. Mine owners were usually referred to as 'possessors of Indians' (*dueños de yndios*) or 'lords of blacks' (*señores de negros*), their lordly control over workers presumably more important than possession of rich mining claims. *Encomenderos* and conquistador descendants were at the top of the mining heap.

Mineros, by contrast, were not mineworkers or owners, but hired major-domos, usually low-status Europeans granted a share of yields in exchange for on-site supervision. Most *encomenderos* spent their time in cities, not mines. *Mineros*, as hired administrators, rarely gained much status, although if lucky they could accumulate mines and even labourers. Actual mineworkers, usually described as *indios* or *negros de cuadrilla*, and later *jornaleros* and *peones*, were considered fortunate if they survived for more than a few years. A document from 1567 mentions a mining crew made up of ten enslaved Africans, but it is clear that in the first decades after conquest most of Muzo's mineworkers were indigenous.[14]

Some of the racial language in the early Muzo codes resembles that of the mining laws of contemporary Peru, but there were local variations. Muzo's first ordinances in fact predate those issued by Peru's Viceroy Francisco de Toledo in the early 1570s, but as in the Toledan codes mine labour was calculated in terms of 'blacks'. For example, a mine claim was considered abandoned if not worked for thirty days by 'five work-squadron blacks' (*cinco negros de cuadrilla*). Similarly, enslaved workers only counted for tax or appraisal purposes if they were up to the work of mining; they were classified as so many 'usefuls,' or *útiles*, as opposed to the *chusma*, or 'rabble', made up of children, the sick or wounded and the elderly.[15]

The early Muzo provincial governor, Alvaro Cepeda de Ayala, was ordered by Philip II to put one hundred enslaved Africans to work in the king's own emerald mines in exchange for his post in August 1572, but according to the records he never had access to this many workers, enslaved or otherwise. A 1575 report by a royal inspector noted that Cepeda de Ayala had promised to come up with at least thirty slaves to avoid censure, but failed even to meet this promise. When his estate was seized, only fifteen enslaved African men and six women were counted. It is unclear from the document if women were engaged directly in mine labour or support tasks, but whatever their jobs this small workforce was deemed insufficient to carry out a large excavation project. Five or six of the slaves were said to be ill, besides. Despite the failure of this royal enterprise, tax records show that these few African miners, both male and female, produced some extraordinary emeralds. One was a whopping 495 carats, 'with four [unbroken] sides of reasonable green'.[16] The royal inspector added that there were about twenty-four work gangs active in Muzo in the early 1570s, mostly made up of two hundred *encomienda* Indian men above the age of fifteen.

Fraud, Friendship and Abuse

There are other revealing documents from Muzo's early years. In April 1572 the same Cepeda de Ayala was ensnared in a fraud investigation, although he was apparently acquitted. Here a twenty-year-old woman in his service named Ysabel, whose mother was indigenous and whose father was an African slave, served as an intermediary for her Bogotá-based master. In what she described as more than ten trips to the Muzo mines from the highland capital, Ysabel bartered dry goods for emeralds from indigenous workers, whose language she spoke.[17]

As mentioned above, such bartering went against the 1569 ordinances, as Crown officials rightly imagined that stones traded secretly would not be taxed. A savvy smuggler, Ysabel was said to have stashed emerald rough in a stocking rolled up in a travel mattress, and when she thought this was likely to be searched, she hid the stones in hat ribbons. One may surmise from this document that clever and well-connected gem traders such as Cepeda de Ayala knew right away that it was native American and African mineworkers who found and secreted the best emeralds at the source; one just had to figure out how to trade for them and not get caught. Young Ysabel was a handy go-between, but even Cepeda de Ayala's *minero*, or administrator, Tenerife-born Cristóbal García, was in on the game.

Cross-race alliances or at least peaceful interactions were a recurring theme in Muzo. A 1582 letter to the king from Cepeda de Ayala's successor and relative, Juan Sánchez de Cepeda, offers a surprising challenge to a colony-wide Crown mandate to remove 'blacks' from indigenous villages. Sánchez de Cepeda maintained that not only were there relatively few enslaved Africans in Muzo province, but also those who did live there mostly inhabited Spanish towns and served their masters well. He added: 'those blacks who do go to Indian *pueblos* cause no harm and return to their homes'. Fears of black and Indian workers fraternizing and intermarrying were unfounded, he stated, at least in the emerald zone. As for the potential problem of Africans becoming caciques, here too there was no need for concern. Chieftain succession among the Muzos was decided 'like the Romans', Sánchez de Cepeda said, with the most valiant warrior among them chosen instead of a past chief's son.[18]

Spanish correspondents could just as easily paint a too-rosy picture of labour relations. In a follow-up letter from 1583, Muzo's governor argued against ending indigenous mine work on behalf of their *encomenderos* because 'the functioning of the mines requires so little of their labour; the Indians there work and rest at their leisure as the waterworks do the job'. Problems with Amerindians were of another kind: Sánchez de Cepeda said the recently pacified Muzos were strangely prone to suicide, flight and mutual poisonings.[19] Some recently conquered women fled abusive Spanish masters and found refuge in the distant highlands.[20]

Whether from abuse, disease or despair, indigenous workers grew increasingly scarce. A 1584 *visita*, or official audit, counted only six hundred native residents of the immediate Itoco mine district, women and children included. Also, only a few dozen enslaved Africans were counted, evidence that only one or two mine owners had accumulated enough capital or credit to switch to slavery. If these documents are to be believed, only about one hundred indigenous men were working in the mines for their *encomenderos* in 1584, although there are repeated references throughout the colonial period to uncounted *muchachos*, or boys, working as sifters. Women held in *encomienda* were technically exempted from mining tasks, although some probably engaged in small-scale prospecting.

In 1601, Nuño de Solís Enríquez wrote to the Indies Council from Muzo claiming four hundred native workers were recovering emeralds, but this was only a rough estimate. He also claimed credit for forcing 'lazy' Muzo women and children to spin and weave.[21] Indigenous *encomienda* labour was still central, although groups of ten or twelve enslaved Africans are listed as the core labour force for a few rich miners. Some enslaved work crews were brought in from other districts by newly appointed officials.

Abusive mine owners were probably not rare, if the frequency of flight and rebellion among the Muzos is any indication, but it was the hired *mineros* whose cruelty stood out. Mention of specific mistreatments is rare, often buried in other types of cases. In 1598 a hired mine administrator named Luis Barbosa was accused of secretly trading stones for clothing, knives and other items, mostly to merchant fences in Bogotá, and when exposed for these crimes decided to vent his rage on a number of Indian workers whom he blamed for turning him in. It was said that he kicked one youth in the groin so hard he gagged on his tongue.[22]

Estimating Emerald Production

In 1598, Muzo's town councilmen again wrote to Philip II. First, they asked the king to send them one hundred enslaved African men at reduced prices, to be purchased by mine owners in instalments over five years. Second, they requested that the *quinto real*, or royal fifth, be reduced to one-twentieth, a rate just conceded to several of New Granada's struggling gold districts.[23] Miners' calls for African workers were common throughout Spanish America in the late sixteenth and early seventeenth centuries, but in Muzo as elsewhere there was no chance of the bankrupt Habsburgs subsidizing the transatlantic slave trade.

The Crown's rejection of the lower tax rate on emeralds, by contrast, is surprising. Gold taxes in prosperous regions had been permanently lowered to a tenth by 1598 to stimulate production, and they dropped even more in subsequent years. The pearl beds of Riohacha received repeated breaks between 1595 and 1659 owing to the abduction of enslaved divers by corsairs, beginning with Francis Drake.[24] By contrast, Muzo's emeralds were taxed the full 20 per cent throughout colonial times without exception. This inflexible policy undoubtedly discouraged full reporting and spurred contraband trade.

Imperfect though they may be, the *quinto real* records are the best surviving indicators of production, and they are surprisingly complete, especially up to 1634. When checked against royal audits, ships' manifests and other documents, it is possible at least to glean a sense of secular trends. Figure 5 traces registered production of first- and second-grade stones from discovery to 1634. Quantities given in gold pesos and their fractions have been converted to carats (for numbers and explanations, see appendices).

It is difficult to say how much the Muzo mines ought to have produced in these years, given the number of workers available, quality of deposits and state of technology, but for comparison's sake, records from 1924 to 1927 list 326,956 carats of emeralds excavated using similar, non-mechanized methods.[25] The quality of these

5. Muzo's Registered Emerald Production, 1569–1634. Based on royal tax records for second and third quality stones (AGI Contaduría 1587, 1295). For first quality stones, see appendix 1b.

stones was not stated, but the annual average of just over 80,000 carats fairly matches the low-yield years graphed above. Therefore, although no perfect mirror of production, Muzo's surviving tax records do suggest that the boom years for Colombian emeralds in the colonial period closely coincided with the era of Spanish–Portuguese union (1580–1640). As discussed in subsequent chapters, this was also when the world trade in emeralds became most highly developed.

Death and Decline

The two published studies of colonial Muzo trace the disappearance of the region's indigenous inhabitants. Both are based on late sixteenth- and early seventeenth-century *visitas*, that record, among other things, a marked decline in the tribute-paying population. Since relatively few enslaved Africans were brought to Muzo to make up for the losses, and no major strikes were made, emerald production also declined. Juan Friede (1967) and Luis Enrique Rodríguez Baquero (1995) have detailed Muzo's indigenous demographic collapse (although there are relevant documents from the period they did not cite). What both demonstrate well is that the Muzos themselves were approaching extinction by 1630, and repeated attempts by colonial auditors to revive the mines and simultaneously end abuses were unsuccessful. In their letters and recommendations, Crown officials seem strangely unaware they could not have it both ways; the Muzos and the mines could not be made to 'grow' in tandem.

Drawing from the 1617 and 1629 audits, Friede arrived at the following population figures: 9,127 total, with 2,532 adult male tributaries (aged 17 to 50) in 1617, down to 4,261 total, with 1,486 tributaries in 1629. Interestingly, despite an overall population loss of some 47 per cent in a dozen years, Friede noted that the number of tributaries assigned directly to mine labour barely changed. There were 254 Amerindians distributed among 26 work crews in 1617, and 251 spread among 27 crews in 1629. The number of workers in each 'squadron' varied by mine, but averaged 8 to 10 men. Their labour power was clearly being exhausted. One worker testified in 1617 that he and 'the other Indian miners of his [28-man] crew have continued to serve and work for the *encomenderos* and their overseers in the development of their emerald mines from morning to night with bars, mattocks, and hammers, breaking rocks and excavating under the sun . . . all with excessive labour'.[26]

Friede ascribed the shuffling of the diminishing labour supply to the *encomenderos*' obvious interest in unearthing as many emeralds as possible before they ran out of serfs. He added that Amerindian families inhabiting the immediate mine zone were extremely small (a married couple plus half a dependent on average), and could not have been reproducing the population. Certainly disease and other factors took a toll, but it is difficult to argue against the idea that mining emeralds was killing the Muzos. As early as 1620, proven emerald mines were selling for as little as forty pesos, or about the cost of a fine riding horse. Without workers, the mines themselves were all but worthless.

On enslaved Africans, Friede was less clear. He stated Muzo emeralds were mined 'exclusively by Indians', even as he added in a footnote that one *encomienda* counted only one Amerindian worker and twenty-six black slaves. As previously mentioned, enslaved Africans were critical to the success of Colombia's emerald mines from their discovery to at least the 1640s, and dependence on them grew later on. A sale dispute from 1630 mentions three enslaved Africans working on a small farm near the Itoco emerald diggings and four slaves working in the mines themselves; two of the workers were boys.[27] Child labour was a common feature of mine slavery throughout colonial Colombia, and was one of the reasons slavery was preferred over the more rule-bound *encomienda*.

Life in the nearby town of La Trinidad was apparently no better for the enslaved in these years. In a 1638 appeal, an enslaved black woman named Juana Jacinta testified before the high court in Bogotá of abuses suffered by her and her daughter. The child died after a beating, 'unable to eat or even pass water'.[28] Such examples of physical abuse of the enslaved in both mines and households are hardly uncommon in surviving records for seventeenth-century Colombia. As the Cartagena Jesuit Alonso de Sandoval noted in his 1627 treatise on slavery, New Granada's masters did not treat their chattels well simply because they had an economic interest in doing so.[29]

Whatever the ratio of enslaved Africans to *encomienda* Indians over the years, by 1642 the main Itoco diggings were down to twenty-one mixed work squadrons. Friede maintained that Amerindian workers held in *encomienda* totalled only 117, but other documents suggest about 180 indigenous men in the mines.[30] A 1643 *visita* not cited by Friede estimated the number of enslaved African miners at 42, and *quinto* records from these years suggest five active enslaved *cuadrillas*, the largest made up of 20 workers. One *encomendero* descended from Muzo's first discoverers, Alonso Ramírez Gasco, counted 2 enslaved

African women and several children along with 6 men. The last of the Muzo work gangs counted 6 to 12 men. Owners numbered 26, most of them *encomenderos*, holding fifty-two titled mines. The Franciscans and Dominicans had rights to two indigenous villages next to the Itoco diggings at this time, but it is unclear if emeralds were the designated tribute item.[31]

New rules were issued in 1643 to enforce a shorter workday for *encomienda* Indians, and to outlaw night work, a practice that appears with increasing frequency in documents from the seventeenth century. Workers were even supposed to be left alone to tend maize plantings in the dry months of January, February, July and August, but there is no evidence this was done. Wages of six pesos per year plus extra maize rations were mandated for mine labour and other special tasks, although several commentators wrote that Amerindian labourers went entirely uncompensated. Indigenous workers were drafted without pay, for example, to rebuild 'the bridge over the Great Minero River' in 1640.

Indigenous workers' annual wages were also set to match exactly the yearly tribute obligation (five silver pesos each) – usually collected from *encomenderos* by royal magistrates, and often in arrears – so workers were likely never to see cash unless they managed to sell stones illegally. The elderly and infirm were routinely left to die in the forest, according to the 1643 audit, and young women who had been put in stocks and chains for escaping primitive sweatshops were committing suicide. Other non-mining villagers had been forced to plant tobacco in place of food, and were now starving. Mining emeralds, therefore, was only part of the problem with what the Crown auditor called the 'ferocity of these mine owners'.[32]

Slavery and the search for new diggings were other options. Some enslaved Africans were said to be working the rediscovered mines of faraway Somondoco by 1635, but conflicts over possession of an allegedly 'rich bank', or hillside cut, shut operations in 1643. *Quinto* records offer no hint of production. Slaves were again working in Somondoco in 1672, but without apparent success. Slavery carried on in greater Muzo, meanwhile, but some historians' accounts of a major cave-in closing the mines of Coscuez (about 20 km north of La Trinidad) in the mid-1640s and entombing three hundred workers do not seem to be borne out by the documents. A group of slaves owned by Governor Simón de Sosa had been active in Coscuez in the early 1640s, but overseer Francisco Ovalle asked for indigenous workers from Muzo to be sent in 1646. The request was rejected when other Muzo miners said that the Coscuez diggings were 'cold and wet', and therefore unhealthy (their climate is virtually the same).[33] A special licence to explore the Tunja district for new emerald mines had been granted to a local conquistador's grandson back in 1611, but it is unclear if he found anything.[34]

As if to decisively mark the end of Muzo's precipitous decline, the town of La Trinidad was levelled by an earthquake that rattled much of northeast New Granada in 1646. According to Muzo's governor, Juan Hurtado de Mendoza:

> . . . around one or two in the morning on the third of April this year God was served to send such a terrible earthquake the Dominican church collapsed, and the parish church, the Santa Barbara church, and the one next to the mines were all broken open in many places, and several houses collapsed causing several deaths, and everybody was left smashed to pieces, yet as God dulled the edges of his sword on his temples some of us [taking refuge in churches] escaped alive as if by miracle.[35]

In typical Baroque fashion, the quake, like the decadence of the mines and the loss of Indians to numerous 'illnesses and plagues', was interpreted as payback for Spanish sins. After helping bury the dead, the governor arranged 'exemplary novenas and processions with public penances'.

The earthquake brought other consequences. In 1648, Muzo ceased to be the seat of a governorship and was absorbed by the regional capital of Tunja. The Franciscan and Dominican monasteries were abandoned and several prominent families retreated to the highlands. One observer recounted in a 1648 letter to the king that 'the city of Muzo is so wasted and abandoned, and the output of emeralds so small due to the flight of citizens and lack of Indians to work the mines, and as for the blacks, so few have entered this kingdom [since the Portuguese rebellion of 1640] that hardly a single work squadron can be mustered, and with the earthquakes of past years the city has been ruined, and there are not even fifty householders left'.[36]

Despite the bleak testimonies, all was not lost. As discussed in later chapters, from the ruins of Muzo's quasi-feudal *encomienda* economy there emerged a few clever mine owners who consolidated holdings, bought slaves, searched for new deposits and either kept a low profile or bribed Crown officials to leave them alone. Others diversified assets by investing gains in cattle ranching and small-scale sugar production. Although *quinto* records grow increasingly spotty from the 1630s to the 1670s, mining activity – however diminished – never ceased. Indeed, a handful of powerful mine-owning clans emerged in the 1650s, and some of them used money gained from emerald sales to win local political office. Under their stewardship, emerald mining soon rebounded beyond expectations.

Early Colonial and Hispanic Emerald Markets

Although the best Colombian emeralds soon reached Asia, many also found buyers in Spain and its colonies. Emeralds were frequently and lavishly incorporated into secular and religious jewelled artefacts, and were also a common component of elite women's jewellery, often making up a considerable portion of the all-important dowry. Regarding Renaissance science, a few of the first emeralds discovered made their way to Habsburg curiosity cabinets in Vienna and Dresden, where they are now displayed in museums (see Plate 5). Others landed in Spain's own crown jewel collections.

In 1551, the jewels of the Spanish royal chamber belonging to Charles V's children, María, Juana and Philip, were inventoried. Among them were several faceted emeralds, mostly set in gold.[37] One stone stood out, a 'prolonged', table-cut emerald weighing some seventy carats, set in a gold lizard and valued at ten thousand ducats. This single emerald showpiece accounted for nearly 12 per cent of the value of all the jewels appraised, but this was before the discovery of Muzo, when emeralds were still exceedingly rare. These stones undoubtedly came from Somondoco, and were probably a portion of Jiménez de Quesada's initial conquest plunder.

The 1564 Muzo discovery made truly princely emerald consumption a sudden possibility for the lower orders, including many merchants and moderately wealthy colonists. Following royal example, upwardly mobile families from Potosí to Madrid became avid consumers of Colombian emeralds. The notary records of Tunja, the nearest Spanish town of significance to the emerald mines, show a sudden appearance of emerald jewels in 1568, just after Muzo's discovery.[38] Emerald jewellery quickly became a kind of capital all over the northern Andes, drawing interest from creditors and royal officials alike. Emerald-encrusted jewels held for debts in Cartagena in the early 1570s included 'two chokers with eight emeralds and eight twisted gold bracelets, plus a gold collar and three emerald rings'. Also in hock according to royal officials were 'a common jewel with a red stone and a cross with emeralds' plus three loose emeralds.[39]

This was just the beginning. Notary records from Bogotá to Quito suggest north Andean elite women, in particular, were literally dripping with emeralds within decades of the Muzo discovery. Emerald jewellery abounds in dowries and wills. The citizens of Cartagena even sought to ransom the city from the Elizabethan corsair Francis Drake with emerald jewellery in 1586, as recounted here by an anonymous Englishman:

Alonso Bravo's wife sent unto the general, which he himself presented, a very rich suite of Buttons of gold and pearl, & a very faire jewel set with Emeralds and a ring with an Emerald & another Emerald set in a pendant. The lieutenant general likewise was presented with a fair jewel set with Emerald and a fair ring with an Emerald. All this he presented as from his wife. . . . The Spaniards did most earnestly desire that they might pay the odd 1,000 pesos in Jewells, for they protested and swore they were not able to pay it in plate, but their wives' Jewells must be pawned for it. The general [Francis Drake] was contented to accept so much in Jewells at reasonable prices. So presently they showed their Jewells, which were all Emeralds, saving some pearl, which they held at such prices as the General would not agree with them, at that time offering to rebate them 300 pesos to pay all in plate.[40]

Like most corsairs, Drake preferred gold and silver bars and coins to emerald jewellery. Unfortunately for him, the great Tierra Firme treasure fleet had departed for Spain just before his arrival in Cartagena (Plate 7).

Muzo stones made their way south throughout the Andes. Emerald earrings, necklaces, pendants and finger rings, some quite fanciful, show up frequently in estate inventories and other Quito and Popayán documents by the 1580s, and contracts show that merchants routinely carried emerald-encrusted jewels to the booming silver city of Potosí and elsewhere in Greater Peru. One merchant registered the following emerald jewels with a Quito notary in December 1586 before heading off to 'Pirú' to seek buyers:

a gold jewel in the form of a dragon . . . with twenty-five emeralds and a chain with an emerald pendant; a small gold cross . . . with ten emeralds, three of them dangling; a jewel in the form of a *sortija* [ring or brooch] . . . with nineteen emeralds plus a chain with a pendant; a gold rostrum . . . with twenty-five large, emerald-set sections and twenty-five small ones; another large cross . . . with three pendants with little pumpkins (*calabazitas*) of pearls and seven emeralds; another small gold cross . . . with ten emeralds, three of them pendants; another very large cross . . . set with ten emeralds plus three emerald pendants.[41]

The famous 'Crown of the Andes', a spectacular gold-and-emerald showpiece that wowed U.S. and European connoisseurs in the mid-twentieth century before disappearing from view, was said to have been fashioned in Popayán in the 1590s as a kind of ex-voto. According to the story, the Virgin Mary was credited with saving the town from an epidemic, which led pious citizens to commission the crown.[42] Several waves of epidemic disease indeed struck this part of the northern Andes in the 1580s, but I have found no record of a contract for this object in Popayán's notary records. Whenever and for whatever reason it was made, the 'Crown of the Andes' certainly absorbed a lot of emeralds, a reminder that they could also be valued in colonial Colombia itself.

Cartagena de Indias and the Wreck of the Atocha

As many economic historians have shown, whether for the king or private merchants, shipments of American gold and silver were counted and weighed at every point of transfer, making it possible to track them – and presumably measure 'leakage' – from mines to markets.[43] At the very least, the tremendous scale of precious metals flows becomes clear from these documents. For emeralds, unfortunately, the transport record is less helpful. Of the 1,812 emeralds allegedly collected in Santa Marta and sent to Spain by the conquerors of New Granada in 1539, only 562 were counted by the officers of Seville's House of Trade.[44] More than half, in other words, had disappeared before reaching the customs house. Contraband trade, especially in the vicinity of Cartagena de Indias, was increasingly to blame for such disparities.

The importance of Cartagena was twofold: it was the first major stop for Spain's incoming Tierra Firme fleet, as well as the main port of entry for enslaved Africans. By the 1580 union of the Spanish and Portuguese crowns, merchants trading slaves and European merchandise in Cartagena routinely exchanged emeralds, gold and pearls, along with other commodities in high demand overseas, including indigo, hides, tobacco and cocoa. In the case of emeralds, there was a direct link to the mines: sales tax and other records from seventeenth-century Muzo show that mine owners sent emeralds to Cartagena with factors who then purchased slaves, along with tools and luxury goods.

In the first decades after the Muzo discovery most Colombian emeralds were shipped to Spain on the annual fleets, legally formalized in 1564. Using royal treasury records housed in both Seville and Simancas, Eufemio Lorenzo Sanz has suggested that an average of one thousand pesos' weight of emeralds arrived in the Crown's coffers from Cartagena annually between 1558 and 1600 (he found records for twenty-one of these forty-two years).[45] Of the emeralds described, about 60 per cent were 'third class'. Thirty-eight and one-half per cent were graded *segunda*, and only 1.5 per cent *primera*.

An example of this kind of record is a bill of lading from the treasure galleon *Santa María Juncal*, which docked in Seville in July 1597. On board were the following emeralds belonging to the royal treasury: six *primera suerte* stones together weighing 72 pesos (1,656 carats), 881 pesos' (20,263 carats') worth of *segunda suerte* stones, and 5,000 pesos (115,000 carats) *tercera suerte*.[46] These numbers nearly match Muzo's total recorded *quintos* for 1596: 72 pesos *primera*, 701 pesos *segunda* and 4,400 *tercera*, plus 66 gold pesos in cash (see Appendix 1). The slightly higher numbers of second- and third-grade stones recorded in Seville may have derived from emerald taxes collected in Cartagena (a fragmentary account for that city from 1569 to 1576 notes *quintos* paid on small amounts of emeralds and pearls).[47]

Many of the Crown's stones were sent directly to Madrid from Seville, and records left by Philip II's jewel-keeper, or *guardajoyas*, Bartolomé de Sanctoyo, include some of the same emeralds noted by Sanz. Between 1583 and 1597 an annual average of about five hundred pesos' worth of second-grade stones and twice as much in third-grade stones arrived at the Escorial Palace in small boxes and linen pouches. A few large first-class emeralds were also recorded. The 1597 records above match exactly; all these stones were sent to Philip II on the eve of his death.[48]

The Seville record is far from complete, but both the overall *quinto* numbers and quality proportions for the known years nearly match Bogotá and Muzo records. Much harder to gauge is the number of emeralds being produced and exported in the tumultuous decades after 1600. Clarence Haring noted that as early as 1605 Dutch traders living near Puerto Cabellos, Venezuela, were exchanging slaves and cloth for emeralds, pearls and precious metals. Smuggling to Spain was already just as serious a problem, and by 1618 officials seized more than 400,000 ducats' worth of contraband silver – this from the official fleet.[49] Contraband was not new in the first years after Philip II's passing, but its scale seems to have grown exponentially.

One unusually tangible record of contraband emerald trading from about this time has come to light thanks to marine archaeologists and treasure hunters. The 1622 wreck of the galleon *Nuestra Señora de Atocha* off the southwesternmost Florida Keys is best known. It was unusual for its largely New Granadan – which is to say Colombian, rather than Mexican or Peruvian – treasure cargo. Beginning in 1985, salvage divers working for treasure hunter Mel Fisher discovered masses of emeralds not listed on the *Atocha's* manifest, a copy of which survived on another ship that made it to Spain (Plate 8).[50]

Of the approximately six thousand *Atocha* emeralds recovered to date, only a small number were faceted, and even fewer were mounted or set in jewellery. Two fine gold crosses and a large finger ring, all set with large, deep-green emeralds were among the show-pieces of the *Atocha* treasure. They closely resemble the kinds of jewelled artefacts described by notaries. The vast majority of the emeralds found by divers, however, were Muzo rough, including some very large crystals in their original, hexagonal form.

Both raw and polished emeralds have been found in Spanish wrecks off Bermuda, as well, including a fine *c.*1595 emerald-studded gold cross.[51] Several astonishing emerald-studded gold items, along with some 1,500 rough stones, were found in yet another wreck identified as the *Nuestra Señora de las Maravillas*, sunk off the Bahamas in January 1656. Treasure salvager and archaeologist Robert Marx has periodically worked this wreck site since he discovered it in

1974. A dive in 1993 turned up a gold cross studded with sixty-seven emeralds.[52] Though fragmentary and occasionally misleading, this cumulative material evidence from the ocean floor affirms that emeralds, like diamonds and other gemstones, were mostly traded on the side, kept secret from – or by – royal authorities.

Where were these 'stowaway' gems headed, and who was keeping them secret?

❖

CHAPTER 4

Empires and Inquisitors

As the 1622 wreck of the *Atocha* strongly hints, gem trading in the age of gunpowder empires was often carried out in secret, its full dimensions only partially revealed by criminal investigations or chance discoveries. Trade monopolies and high taxes encouraged subterfuge, but there were other, more natural, incentives. Gemstones such as emeralds, diamonds and pearls – compact, durable and extremely valuable – were everywhere ideal stowaways, a kind of second-tier commodity that could be hidden in the secret compartment of a sea chest, sewn into one's clothes or even swallowed, both for security against thieves and to avoid paying customs and other duties. In an era when money was heavy metal, not paper or plastic, gems packed remarkably well.

In terms of gain, gems were a kind of top-off. Adding stowaway stones to an officially registered cargo of, say, sugar or hides could turn a marginally profitable trip into a windfall. Given the many reasons for moving gemstones on the sly, it is certain that Spanish and Portuguese commercial agents, conquistadors, government officials and clergymen took advantage of political connections, physical mobility and imperial protection within a globe-spanning network to carry Colombian emeralds across oceans to Seville, Manila and even Goa. Most would have thought it foolish not to do so.

Important as this incidental, 'anthill' trafficking by well-placed bureaucrats, factors, priests and soldiers may have been, however, surviving evidence strongly suggests that most early modern inter-continental gem trading was carried out in a far more organized and routine fashion by a few dozen Sephardic merchant families. These families operated – always at great personal and communal danger – both inside and outside the far-flung Luso-Hispanic sphere. Already by the time of Muzo's discovery in 1564, the Sephardim had formed a transglobal merchant community uniquely capable of profiting from such a risky trade over the long term. The early modern global gem business was special. As historian Edgar Samuel has noted (emphasizing diamonds):

> Large gemstones cannot be sold by sample and take considerable time to sell to advantage. The trade therefore calls for much mutual trust and long-term credit. It is essential for a wholesale diamond merchant to know whom it is unsafe to trust. Not only must he be able to appraise the reliability of each man in the trade but, if he is to survive, he must be aware of any decline in reliability or solvency as it occurs. This can only be done efficiently with the close social contact and ample gossip which characterize village society. Yet the diamond trade and industry cannot function in a village. They require a trained urban labour force, good financial and insurance facilities, a just and efficient judicial system and regular and reliable postal and transport services. . . . The ideal unit for the conduct of the international gemstone trade is an ethnic minority living within a major trading city and connected by language and kinship with similar communities in other major cities.[1]

Who were the major players in the early modern world gem trade, and how did their networks and connections change over time? Although the bulk of surviving evidence is anecdotal rather than quan-titative, it is clear that many, perhaps even most, Colombian emeralds moved east across the Atlantic and Indian Oceans through Sephardic Jewish and so-called New Christian family webs, initially based in

Seville, Lisbon and Antwerp. After 1600, the centre of Sephardic gem trading shifted to Amsterdam, then to London following Cromwell's 1655 invitation to resettle.

By the mid-seventeenth century, Ashkenazi families also entered the competition, pulling Hamburg and other northern-tier cities into the same 'southern', or tropical, orbit that had long linked Cartagena, Goa and even Luanda.[2] Other important hubs with less direct ties to the Caribbean included Mediterranean ports: Venice, Alexandria, Iskenderun and, increasingly, Livorno. In addition, some stones were handled by Sephardim living in Fez, Marrakesh, Salé, Tangier and other Moroccan cities, and likely others based in the Ottoman regencies of Algiers and Tunis. The case of globetrotter and gem trader Samuel Pallache (*c.*1550–1616), part-time ambassador for the Moroccan sultan Muley Zaydan in Lisbon and Amsterdam, is instructive. It is highly likely he took Colombian emeralds to Morocco, which in his time qualified as a minor gunpowder empire.[3]

In the simplest scenario, Sephardic and later Ashkenazi gem merchants travelled to India from European and Mediterranean cities by land or sea. They carried Colombian emeralds along with Caribbean pearls, Mediterranean coral, Baltic amber and Peruvian or Mexican silver. In exchange, they purchased diamonds, rubies, sapphires, spices and luxury fabrics. In Portuguese Goa, New Christians, or *cristãos novos*, were the most important dealers in precious gems by 1550, and they remained so for at least another century and a half.[4]

In the decades leading up to 1700, Sephardic clan members increasingly shifted to the more tolerant English ports of Madras (Chennai), Bombay (Mumbai) and Bengal. Venetian and Genoese jewel traders were active in Goa, too, as were Armenians, Punjabi Banias (often Jains), Muslim Gujaratis and probably also several clans of Sikhs and Parsis. The Armenians, who thrived under Safavid protection in Persia, were exceptionally well connected in the Burmese ruby trade. Historian Bhaswati Bhattacharya has discovered emeralds in the wills of several Armenian merchants with ties to Madras, as well as ports farther east.[5]

Further research will reveal more about these other, mostly non-European, gem-trading communities. For now, the evidence suggests none enjoyed the ultra-long distance connections and other advantages possessed by the Sephardim under Hispano-Portuguese rule up to the mid-seventeenth century – this despite the fact that the Portuguese and Spanish Inquisitions persecuted them with frightening regularity. The Sephardim proved resilient, and when the political upheavals and accompanying religious hysteria of the mid-seventeenth century died down, Goa's gem market revived.

Almost miraculously, Goa appears to have remained central to the world gem and jewel trade long after its predicted demise, particularly with the rise of English Madras in the late seventeenth century. Among its advantages, Goa was a heavily fortified viceregal capital and its long-established markets, low taxes and relative stability allowed a wide range of merchants to shop for bargains, find and extend credit and commission finished jewels from among the city's many goldsmiths and stonecutters. Goa, in short, had stuck in people's minds as India's 'natural' gem bourse. Even in hard times Lusophone New Christians, as bona fide Portuguese subjects, could make use of both the official fleet system, or *carreira* (Samuel's 'regular and reliable postal and transport services') and the legal apparatus of the colonial *Estado da Índia* (Samuel's 'just and efficient judicial system').[6]

The security and reliability of Portuguese fleets and courts were at best relative, but there were other factors in Goa's favour until at least 1640. Although Northern European competitors established trading forts all along India's eastern and western coasts, beginning in the 1610s, non-Iberian merchants in this period, for example French Huguenots and English and Dutch East India Company factors, had less direct access to much-needed American treasure, including emeralds and pearls but far more important, silver bars and 'pieces of eight'. Greater India, a mass exporter of cotton textiles with a population near 100 million in 1600, vied with China to absorb as much American silver as Europeans and other foreign traders could pump into its vast, far-flung markets and humming tributary regimes.[7]

Gold from southeast Africa and occasionally Indonesia was equally welcome, but its flow was never as reliable as that of American silver.

India's appetite for precious metals only grew with time, spurring European competition. Eventually, the shifting balance of sea power in favour of the English and Dutch left Goa in the shadows and put Madras and later Bengal and Bombay in the limelight, but this slow if dramatic transition required a number of costly investments – and great patience. Despite military gains, the English, Dutch and French still had to compete with the Portuguese to win trading post concessions from the Ottoman, Safavid and Mughal courts. Although they did so with notable speed after 1600, perhaps most critically with the seizure of Hurmuz in 1622, these overtures for recognition only began to translate into sound bases for commercial growth towards the end of the seventeenth century.

Faced with potentially shattering losses, the stewards of the fiercely Catholic Hispano-Portuguese Empire searched for the infiltrators whom they felt had betrayed them. With almost generational predictability after 1600, official rage was directed at the very same enterprising New Christians who had made the gem trade, pepper trade and other global commodity exchanges profitable. Flemings and other 'foreigners' were also persecuted, albeit typically with less rigour. Some individuals proved wily or at least highly flexible in response to the Inquisition, but as historian Edgar Samuel suggests in the quote above, among New Christians kin ties had substituted for legal and financial institutions in such a way that very long-distance commerce and other risky activities could make money for patient and persistent 'non-state actors'.

As James Boyajian, Anthony Disney and others have shown, although the mostly Portuguese Sephardim lived scattered throughout Iberia's global gunpowder empire by the late sixteenth century and remained highly mobile, they proved relatively easy scapegoats in tough political times. This was largely the result of Spanish and Portuguese crown ambivalence amid periodic financial distress. New Christians who had been allowed to buy immunity from persecution by the Inquisition in the 1620s thanks to Philip IV's pragmatic favourite, the

Count-Duke of Olivares, suddenly found themselves facing not only confiscation of their estates but also permanent exile and even public execution by the late 1630s.[8] The reversal was so sudden and total it helped spark a profound religious revival among many exiles.

The sudden scapegoating, though clearly a surprise to many of its victims at the time, was hardly unprecedented. Inquisition 'crack-downs' on alleged Jewish heresy beginning in the late fifteenth century had driven Iberian New Christians and practising Jews to seek many havens, mostly in countries and territories hostile to the Spanish, and later the Portuguese. Many exiles from the first wave of expulsions settled in Morocco, as well as Ottoman Greece, Turkey and Palestine. Later refugees favoured various parts of Italy and France, then the Netherlands and England, as well as their overseas colonies. With the rise of the Dutch after 1600, Sephardic merchants resident in Amsterdam, Rotterdam, The Hague and other Dutch ports took their long experience in foreign trading back to familiar entrepots as well as to new ones. Many of these merchants' last stop had been Lisbon, where gems from all over the world had long been cut, drilled, polished and traded.

The Lisbon Gem Market

Soon after the conquest of Goa in 1510 and the subsequent tapping of India's vibrant diamond, pearl and coloured stone markets, Lisbon became one of Europe's great centres for gem trading and the lapidary arts. For a time it was closely connected to Antwerp, capital – by the time of Charles V – of the Spanish-claimed Netherlands. Inquisition and other documents describe a thriving and diverse community of diamond polishers, stonecutters, pearl-drillers, goldsmiths and gem merchants in Lisbon. Many resided near the quay in lower downtown on the Rua dos Ourives, or 'Goldsmiths' Street'. Here lived Flemish tradesmen such as Cristoforo Radanac and Cornelis Jangolete, both accused of Protestant heresy by Lisbon's Inquisition tribunal in 1567.[9] The investigation revealed a web of connections among resident Belgians, Germans, Frenchmen and Englishmen, most of them simple gem cutters and polishers but some also working as druggists and physicians.

Many of Lisbon's gem cutters, mostly single young men, worked in shops belonging to New Christian jewellers and merchants, and alongside young New Christian artisans as well. One such artisan, Ruy Gomes, was charged with practising Judaism in 1563.[10] Gomes had been overheard saying that the Protestant Reformation was a sure sign the messiah was due. A number of small-time stonecutters, including a few foreigners, came to Gomes's aid, testifying that he consistently observed Catholic feasts, and counted many Old Christian friends. His boss was the wealthy New Christian merchant Luis Mendes, a heavy investor in the India trade with relatives in Goa. Like most of his peers, young Gomes was not hanged or burned, but rather sentenced to long penitence and what amounted to a Catholic re-education.

As Daniel Swetschinski has shown for seventeenth-century Amsterdam, apprenticeship in gem cutting was standard among many Portuguese Jews, and often absorbed both orphans and resettled kin.[11] A New Christian *lapidario* tried by the Lisbon Inquisition in 1614 was Luis Lopes, the eighteen-year-old son, nephew and grandson of jewellers. Lopes said he cut diamonds as a worker (*obreiro*) in his father's shop on the Rua dos Ourives after being sent as a boy to Antwerp to learn his trade. It was during his apprenticeship there, which began about age nine, that Lopes's life took a turn that would later run him foul of the Inquisition. According to his own testimony, after burning the eyes of a fellow apprentice with gunpowder in some sort of prank, he fled to avoid prosecution and landed in Amsterdam.

Here, in what inquisitors labelled 'the city of heretics', Lopes said he had looked for a ship home but instead stayed five years, mostly in the household of an openly Jewish couple, Simão Lopes Rosa and his wife, Raphaela. While in Amsterdam, Lopes was circumcised (although he said he was tricked and drugged before the ceremony, and even sued his hosts over the whole affair). He eventually boarded a Venetian ship for Lisbon, where he resumed his trade. According to the case file, it was immediately after being reconciled by the Inquisition that Lopes sought licence to ship out for the colonies. At first denied an exit visa 'for having slim understanding [of the Catholic faith], with which he could easily turn and pervert himself through commerce with the Jews who ordinarily reside in those conquests', Lopes left for an unknown colonial destination in 1615.[12]

These cases represent only the plebeian level of gem trading and cutting in Golden Age Lisbon. Among the most prominent New Christian bankers active in both Portugal and Spain in the second half of the sixteenth century were the Gomes and Rodrigues d'Evora e Veiga families. Their commercial correspondence, now housed in Simancas and extensively published by José Gentil da Silva, reveals a vast, pan-European credit web, with bullion and occasionally gem and jewellery exchanges from Lisbon or Madrid to Antwerp, Hamburg, Paris, Lyons, Florence, Venice and Naples.[13] In 1576 Manuel Gomes, whose main business at the time was shipping South Asian indigo to Antwerp, sent a prized sapphire to a factor in France. He claimed demand was up for such stones. Later the same year he mentioned the same 'emerald, I mean, sapphire . . . take care, as it is a very fine piece'.[14] The Rodrigues d'Evora family was best known for trading Indian pepper to Antwerp, but diamonds were often sent on the side.

In 1577 Antonio Gomes complained that prices for small diamonds and rubies, then costly in India, were down in the Low Countries and ought to be temporarily withheld from the market. A year later he suggested diamond prices were so unpredictable that one was better off dealing in textiles.[15] Not everyone agreed, as the merchant Simão Ruis was said to be searching the Lisbon market for good rubies and diamonds in 1578. In the same year Pedro Godines and Fernando Morales were busy sending hundreds of pearls to New Christian and Italian factors in Paris.[16] None of these men, long known to be among early modern Europe's biggest bankers and arbitrageurs, specialized in gem trading; it was simply one of several luxury trades that topped off profits. Their correspondence also confirms Samuel's assertions above regarding the current price knowledge and 'gossip' needed to succeed in this fickle business.

Even sending emeralds to India was apparently no sure thing in these early years, and had its ups and downs. An anonymous mid-sixteenth-century Portuguese appraiser's manual, the hand-written *Cousas de Pedraria*, echoes Samuel on trust, but adds a few twists and helpful details:

> In the business of emeralds it is essential that whoever buys and sells them is most expert as there are many false ones; those who wish to buy them but lack knowledge of them should probe one facet with the tip of a tempered steel knife blade as one does with rubies; if it enters the emerald it is false, and if it does not enter but leaves a mark, it is good. To tell by sight if it is good and fine it must be of a brilliant green, without lines, webs, or fractures, and being perfect it would be worth as much as a diamond. One would have to wait a long time, however, to see a perfect emerald.[17]

The anonymous author seems to suggest emeralds were at this time holding their value against diamonds, although the date of the document is uncertain and may even predate the Muzo bonanza. The author's recommendation with the knife, on the other hand, would have horrified most sellers; emerald is naturally fragile and much softer than ruby. The claim of rampant fakery suggests healthy demand, at least in certain markets. The author goes on:

> There are emeralds that in India if they are *oriental* and fine and of good birth, and of a dense greenness and wholeness, are worth half the price of perfect ones; thus is the price of stones of the second grade and cleanness. There are other emeralds called Peruvian ones that have a clear greenness that many men take from Portugal to India as merchandise, and thus have many been purchased only to [have their owners] return with them to this kingdom well deceived. It is better not to buy and sell such emeralds unless one is an expert, or it will not be a profitable business.

Splitting Colombian emeralds into two categories, 'oriental' and 'Peruvian', was standardized by Spanish jewellers by 1572, to the extent that different price scales were published (see appendices).

'Peruvian' or 'New World' emeralds of the sort the author of *Cousas de Pedraria* suggests would not easily sell in India were already synonymous with grade-three or *tercera suerte* stones. Colombia's finest grade-two and grade-one emeralds simply had to be sold as *oriental*; this was what the Indian market demanded.

There is scant mention of emeralds in the early Lisbon documents outside the *Cousas de Pedraria* manuscript. Yet when they do show up with greater frequency in the seventeenth century it is clear they had simply been slotted into an established global gem-trading network built around diamonds and pearls, but always open to coloured stones, including Mediterranean coral and Baltic amber. The principals of this trade emerge mostly from Inquisition inventories and similar documents.

The Luso-Indian Diamond Circuit

James Boyajian has done most to determine which Lisbon families dominated the Goa gem trade during the Spanish-Portuguese union. During what he calls the 'zenith of the *carreira* trade', roughly 1599 to 1619, New Christians such as the Tinoco, Paz, Fernandes, Silveira, Dias, Sousa and Rodrigues clans, who often intermarried, periodically sent junior kinsmen – and women – to Goa to establish footholds or maintain ties. The trade continued at a brisk pace until the late 1630s, when Inquisition persecution and the 1640 Portuguese rebellion interrupted Lisbon's gem-trading heyday.

The business of *pedraria*, or gemstones, was as secretive in the Portuguese East Indies as it was in the Spanish West Indies, and surviving official registries rarely match the evidence gleaned from occasional inspections and shipwrecks. When some three hundred bulses of diamonds washed ashore after a 1615 wreck in the Azores, for example, the sum 'was more . . . than any of the officials of the Casa da Índia recalled in their collective memories or could find in written records, and [was] far more than the carracks were supposed to carry in a single year'.[18] The stones may have been worth as much as 2.25 million *cruzados*, or some 2.5 million silver pesos of eight *reales*. In

Table 1, Boyajian offers the following official record of private diamond shipments sent from India to Lisbon between 1586 and 1631:

Table 1 Registered *Carreira* Diamonds Shipped from Goa to Lisbon, 1586–1631

Year + No. of Ships	Number of Bulses	Estimated Value, *cruzados*/pesos
1586 (3 carracks)	64	480,000/533,333
1592 (1 carrack)	114	855,000/950,000
1596 (1 carrack)	68	510,000/566,667
1598 (3 carracks)	74	555,000/616,667
1600 (6 carracks + galleons)	3	22,500/25,000
1608 (1 carrack)	114	855,000/950,000
1615 (1 carrack)	125	937,500/1,041,667
1616 (2 carracks)	190	1,425,000/1,583,333
1618 (1 carrack, 1 galleon)	71	532,500/591,667
1631 (1 carrack)	44	330,000/366,667

Boyajian extracted these figures from surviving ships' manifests, or *listas das fazendas*, but as with similar emerald registries sent to Seville from Cartagena de Indias, there are problems. Contraband was rife according to virtually everyone who wrote or testified, and this left thousands of stones – especially large ones – unaccounted for. Even if we were to trust the figures, the value of the diamond bulse, or *bizalho*, was not standard. (There was really no reason to standardize it since the Portuguese did not tax the diamond trade as the Spanish did emeralds.)

Boyajian nevertheless estimates the *bizalho*, a small sealed box, held up to a pound of stones, or some 2,240 carats. 'If the average stone was just 1 carat, the bizalho would have been worth about 12,000 *cruzados* in Lisbon.'[19] This assumes an unlikely uniformity of stone size and quality, but Boyajian gives some scattered appraisals, which suggests his lower, 7,500-*cruzado* average value per bulse is not unreasonable. Of emeralds handled by Lisbon's New Christian gem merchants almost nothing is known. Boyajian cites a rare instance of a contraband emerald shipment seized by officials and sent to Madrid in 1627.[20]

Gem trade values in the *carreira da Índia* may never be determined, but Inquisition records do at least reveal some of the many and far-flung links in this glittering chain. In 1617 the Lisbon Inquisition tried a German goldsmith living in Olinda, a picturesque and thriving sugar port on Brazil's northeast coast, for owning Protestant literature. Thirty-five-year-old Cristovão Raus described himself as a jeweller and lapidary, and said he had come to Brazil with Governor Francisco de Sousa to visit the southern captaincies 'in order to get to know the stones found in those parts' (see appendices).

When Raus's goods were confiscated by church officials they included a variety of half-finished jewels and reliquaries, raw gems and substantial gold and silver. It appears one of Raus's specialties was religious articles fashioned from gilt silver. Along with 'an emerald cross of St Vincent' and 'a gold ring set with four emeralds' were a number of chokers, pendants and other jewels, some of them enamelled and decorated with seed pearls and baroques, and also coral beads. Loose stones included several large and small amethysts and topazes, some 'of good heart', many pieces of clear rock crystal, nine emeralds, one ruby, one 'white sapphire', eleven faceted and twenty-five unfaceted garnets and forty-two unnamed stones 'of low colour'.[21]

Raus also owned a lapidary wheel, or *torcegruos de diamantes*, but what got him in trouble were his books, several in Flemish and one of which he said he had traded with a visiting Englishman. Raus had given up his copy of *The English Schism* for what suspicious officials took to be a Latin Bible. While awaiting deportation to Lisbon, Raus asked that his tools be left him so that he might continue to earn his keep. Although it is tempting to think the German's emeralds were Brazilian, it is far more likely they came, like the pearls and other exotic stones he possessed, from abroad. As Boyajian notes, at least one New Christian factor with ties to Caribbean smuggling rings known to trade in precious stones was based in Olinda at precisely this time.[22]

In the intercontinental emerald business, ties to Seville were most critical, and a thriving gem market had existed there at least since the era of Columbus. New Christians in Lisbon, Évora, Elvas,

Estremoz and even Porto maintained close ties to Seville from about this time, and several interlinked diasporic communities maintained far-flung overseas networks. Boyajian has mapped the Seville-based families most clearly, and also linked them to Cartagena de Indias.[23]

As always, wealthy *conversos* and their descendants attracted predators during periodic bursts of intolerance. The Inquisition was worst, but as Ruth Pike has shown, Seville's merchant and banking elite was so interlaced with *converso* lineages that there emerged a special class of 'Jew hunters' known as *linajudos*, lawyers and town councilmen who specialized in discovering Hebrew genealogies to extort or otherwise persecute social climbers.[24] The power of the *linajudos* did not decline until the late seventeenth century.

In the midst of this poisonous atmosphere one finds cases such as that of Bartolomeu Martins de Moura, a Lisbon native and New Christian diamond merchant denounced for practising Judaism and committing sodomy in 1655. Martins was one of several goldsmiths with business ties to Seville maintained through family members living in the Estremaduran border town of Elvas, near Badajoz.[25] A 1657 inventory of Martins's possessions included four bulses of uncut diamonds said to be worth about two thousand *cruzados* (about 833 silver pesos) plus a small box containing a few cut ones worth two hundred *milreis* (about 333 pesos). Martins's son was found to be in possession of four more bulses, and his wife was accused of hiding still more.

It is in Martins's debt papers that one finds extensive ties to gem dealers in Seville, as well as Rio de Janeiro and Goa. Also among the papers are contracts to send small parcels of emeralds and baroque pearls to factors in India. Martins said he got diamonds in return for these consignments, which he then farmed out to a number of Lisbon lapidaries for cutting, polishing and setting. He did not say who his customers were, but admitted having lived for two years in Mexico City and Veracruz, then half a year in Seville, where he mostly collected debts. Martins was convicted and sentenced to three years as a *degredado*, or penal exile, in some unnamed part of Africa. His appeal was still pending in Easter 1663.

The Portuguese in Cartagena de Indias

Even more important than Seville for emerald traders was Colombia's Caribbean port of Cartagena de Indias. Unfortunately, Cartagena's notary records fell victim to pirates and fires centuries ago, so fragments on emerald exports come only from letters and official materials sent to Bogotá or Spain from Muzo or Cartagena. Among these are the records of Cartagena's Inquisition tribunal, established in 1610 (Plate 9). Although the documents are far shallower than those for Lisbon, Mexico City or Lima, they are nevertheless revealing, especially those detailing confiscations of so-called New Christian or crypto-Jewish merchant estates.

Historian Alfonso Quiroz, in a path-breaking study of estate seizures in Mexico, Lima and Cartagena during the so-called Great Conspiracy years from 1635 to 1649, when Portuguese Jews and New Christians were most harshly and systematically persecuted throughout the Iberian world, found that several Cartagena merchants charged with practising Judaism had dealt extensively in pearls and emeralds.[26] Most were also involved in the more nefarious African slave trade, Cartagena's mainstay.

Among the confirmed emerald dealers reconciled to the Cartagena Inquisition in 1638 was Lisbon-born Manuel de Fonseca Enríquez (using the Spanish spelling found in the documents). In addition to the loss of his emeralds, he also suffered confiscation of a quantity of rubies, diamonds, worked silver and indigo, along with twenty-five enslaved Africans, fifteen of whom belonged to him. Quiroz reports that Fonseca Enríquez had trade ties with factors and other associates in Mexico, Panama, Peru and Spain, all of which would have been standard links had he been a typical Spanish Old Christian rather than a Portuguese New Christian merchant. Transglobal ties to factors – usually nephews or in-laws as far afield as Manila – were common among Basque and Andalusian Old Christian merchant clans. Few of these other clans, or trading 'nations', however, dealt in gems as well as slaves, and none passed as easily between Spanish and Portuguese colonies.[27]

Fonseca Enríquez maintained direct trade ties to Luanda, capital of Portuguese Angola, and he also made considerable investments in the Caribbean pearl trade, said to amount to more than thirty-five thousand pesos. When added to the Angola connections, emerald holdings and pearl business, the mention of diamonds and rubies is unsurprising. In 1638, these gems would have almost certainly come from Portuguese outposts in India, Burma and Sri Lanka. Notary records show that some such stones were finding their way into Spanish American religious art at about this time, and into private jewels, as well. Although the situation would change within two years, Portugal's far-flung *Estado da Índia* was still technically under Spanish control when Fonseca Enríquez was interrogated. His timing could not have been worse.

Although he may have had ties to Dutch Curaçao, established in 1634, Fonseca Enríquez was most likely sending New Granadan pearls and emeralds to Lisbon, where they would have been sorted and packaged for the India run or perhaps, as will be shown below, sold to factors in Amsterdam. Other Cartagena New Christians with relatives in the *carreira da Índia* trade included Antonio Nunes Gramaxo, a major Riohacha pearl dealer from at least the 1620s.[28] Returns on these exchanges were reinvested in textiles, metal wares, wines and other items to be taken to Upper Guinea or Angola and traded for captive Africans sent back to Cartagena. This was one Atlantic circuit. Meanwhile, in and around Goa, in the distant Indian Ocean, emeralds and pearls from the Spanish Main, or 'Peru', were traded for diamonds, rubies and fine eastern pearls, gems in high demand in the West.

Another long-established Cartagena merchant of considerable capital, Juan Rodrigues Mesa, had his goods embargoed by the Inquisition in 1636. Among substantial shipments of precious metals sent to Seville to cancel the debts of his Lisbon-based brother, Andrés Rodrigues de Estremoz, were emeralds and pearls. He sent 1,200 pesos' worth in 1628 alone. Andrés was a contractor in the Angolan slave trade, among many other enterprises. He wrote to his brother in Cartagena in 1635 advising him not to bother purchasing anything but grade-one emeralds, as these alone were profitable in India. 'For *primera suerte* they give 300–400 *milreis* a mark depending on how they are, but for *segunda suerte* they barely pay half a real.'[29] He was presumably referring to the Goa bourse, but may have been giving prices paid in Lisbon before export. Cryptic as it is on prices, the document is key for directly linking a prominent Cartagena-based New Christian merchant to the emerald trade to India via Seville and Lisbon. Enslaved Africans were the main reinvestment avenue for emerald profits.

In their exhaustive study of the early Portuguese slave trade from Upper Guinea (specifically modern Guinea-Bissau) to Lima in the years leading up to the 1640 Portuguese rebellion, Linda Newson and Susie Minchin confirm Rodrigues Mesa's central role as a reseller of enslaved Africans in Cartagena. Newson and Minchin also document Portuguese attempts to find West African markets for Mediterranean coral, Baltic amber and other semi-precious stones.[30] Some slaves traded for gems undoubtedly became miners of gems.

A Cartagena Sephardim with broad Mediterranean connections was Baltasar de Araujo, who in a 1625 testimony described his family's escape from Iberia after being hounded by both the Spanish and Portuguese inquisitions. They went from Galicia via Porto to Salonika, then spent several months in Venice, where Araujo was counselled by rabbis and circumcised before setting out with his brother to trade for pearls in Cairo. Araujo testified that since coming to New Granada he had encountered other crypto-Jewish merchants not only in Cartagena but also in the gold mining town of Zaragoza, several hundred miles inland on the Nechí River. One was Luis Franco Rodrigues, who before his arrest in 1624 allegedly asked a shoemaker friend to hold on to gold and emerald jewellery to prevent its confiscation by the Holy Office. Franco Rodrigues denied accusations of 'judaizing', despite several rounds of torment by what were euphemistically called the 'cord' and 'pony'.[31]

Torture and Trade

In a multi-volume study and transcription of Cartagena Inquisition records from 1610 to 1660, Colombian historian Anna María

Splendiani and her colleagues recorded several cases involving likely and known emerald dealers, including Manuel de Fonseca Enríquez and Juan Rodrigues Mesa. Because the thrust of their work was religious rather than economic persecution, the transcriptions do not include inventories of sequestered goods (now available online thanks to Spain's Ministry of Culture).[32] Still, Sephardic victims' testimonies on matters of faith add salient details regarding these men's far-flung trade networks. They also record in excruciating detail the great dangers faced by Sephardic gem merchants hoping to get as close as possible to the source of Colombian emeralds and pearls.

According to the records transcribed by Splendiani, Manuel de Fonseca Enríquez was first incarcerated in a secret Inquisition cell in July 1636, betrayed, according to the scribe, by his fellow emerald trader, Juan Rodrigues Mesa. Both were among seventeen Portuguese New Christians, nearly all of them wholesale merchants, accused of 'judaizing', or observing Jewish rites and festivals. They allegedly met to fast and worship on Friday afternoons under the guise of playing cards. As soon as they were denounced and jailed, their highly valuable estates were embargoed pending the outcome of what was in fact a much larger – indeed worldwide – investigation.[33]

The houses of Fonseca Enríquez and Rodrigues Mesa were among three routinely named by witnesses as meeting points for what came to be called 'The Brotherhood of Holland' (*La cofradía de Holanda*). Members of this alleged fraternity seem to have ranged widely in terms of the depth of their understanding, or even interest, in Judaic beliefs and practices. As might be expected in a charged atmosphere, however, this range of interests did not stop zealous inquisitors from terrorizing suspected members in roughly equal measure. Most, including Fonseca Enríquez and Rodrigues Mesa, were tortured on the *potro*, or 'pony', a type of hand-cranked stretching rack that often broke toes and sometimes dislocated shoulders (for a modern replica, see plate 9). None of the victims mentioned here appears to have been subjected to 'waterboarding', although this simulated drowning technique was commonly employed in other American tribunals. Despite tight regulations and the presence of physicians, tortures ordered by the Inquisition could be cause death.

Something of a hard case, apparently, Fonseca Enríquez was among the last of his cohorts to crack. Only in the course of the second round of torture in September 1637 did he finally admit to participating in Jewish rites. The dutiful Inquisition scribe recorded his exclamations verbatim: 'Ay! God of my soul, I will tell the truth! I am a judaizing Jew three years now, and have kept the Law of Moses and performed the fasts of Queen Esther [i.e., Purim], some-times in the month of June, other times in August, and others in September.' Fonseca added that he did not eat pork and kept the Sabbath by not working and by putting clean linens on his body, bed and table. He did not believe the messiah had yet come and other-wise observed the 'Law of Moses'. He said he understood all this was contrary to the 'Law of Jesus Christ', but still he believed Moses's Law 'better than that of the Christians'.[34]

More important here, Fonseca Enríquez testified that he had held out in the vain hope of freeing himself and his 'friends', the seven-teen-odd members of the Brotherhood of Holland. It was his fellow gem dealer Juan Rodrigues Mesa who was said to have kept a book at his house containing the signatures of all members. Fonseca Enríquez said he had given three hundred pesos to Rodrigues Mesa to join, with the understanding that the money would go to fund the 'Dutch navy' (*armada holandés*) in its exploits against the king of Spain. Rodrigues Mesa was treasurer, and others had given similar sums, most likely for investment in Dutch West India Company shares (there is explicit mention of *asentistas*, or shareholders – used here differently than when referring to merchant lenders or holders of the slave trade contract, or *asiento*).

Fonseca Enríquez insisted he did not know the name of Rodrigues Mesa's contact, but a certain 'Jew residing in Holland' was said to have been receiving the brotherhood's funds, three hundred pesos per member per annum, since 1632. The donors knew they were funding naval expeditions that would come to 'this port' (i.e., Cartagena) as well as Brazil, where the Dutch had been established since seizing

Pernambuco in 1630. If true, it is possible these contributions, like shipments of emeralds, were being sent to Amsterdam through Curaçao, but the island is never mentioned in the Inquisition testimonies relating to these men. This is not in fact surprising because, as discussed below, the island's famous Jewish community did not thrive until after the Dutch expulsion from Brazil in 1654.[35]

Unlike Fonseca Enríquez, who maintained to the very end to be a recent convert to Judaism, Juan Rodrigues Mesa started right after his arrest in 1636 by confessing at length his various Jewish devotions and deep distaste for Christianity, or at least Catholicism. According to the documents, he admitted without torture routinely fantasizing about 'tearing down and offending' crosses whenever he saw them. On closer examination, if the Inquisition scribe is to be believed, he said he wanted to dump the contents of chamber pots on them.[36] He also offered detailed testimony regarding his avoidance of pork, scaleless fish and other forbidden foods, as well as his consistent performance of various rites and observances, including Passover, Yom Kippur (*lo que llaman del perdón*) and Purim, for almost a decade. Rodrigues Mesa also said he raised and lowered his head at sunrise on some occasions (apparently a form of *Shacharit*, or morning prayers).

Testimonies from the other jailed members of the brotherhood cited connections to observant Jewish merchants in Morocco, the Canary Islands, Holland and Angola. Duarte Lopes Mesa of Portalegre claimed to have renewed his faith in a synagogue in Ceuta (opposite Gibraltar), and to have spent time in Amsterdam with West India Company investors, many of them Portuguese Jews. In later testimony he denounced a number of practising Jews in Angola, presumably fellow factors in the slave trade.[37] Truth could, of course, also be a victim of torture, but Cartagena's inquisitors sniffed doggedly for corroborating testimony, often chasing leads through correspondence with other tribunals.

A Luanda-based New Christian from Elvas prosecuted by the Lisbon Inquisition in 1627 was the slave trader Gonzalo Rois (or Rodrigues) Meneses. Known locally by the nickname 'The Pig'

(*O Porco*), the obese and allegedly fun-loving Rodrigues Meneses was directly involved in procuring slaves from the Angolan interior for the Cartagena and Veracruz markets; he outfitted armed slaving expeditions, or *entradas*, staffed with 'black warriors' (*negros da guerra*). According to his own confession Rodrigues Meneses had first come to Luanda as a young man to participate in an *entrada* around 1598 after abandoning the trade for which he had been apprenticed. He had trained as a jeweller under New Christian masters in Lisbon and Madrid. Among those who testified against him were several Basque slavers, one of them from the Venezuelan town of Mérida.[38]

According to his inventory, Rodrigues Meneses was in debt to at least one member of the Cartagena brotherhood, Francisco Rodrigues Carneiro. Several witnesses called by the Cartagena Inquisition testified that Rodrigues Carneiro had taught many others how to observe the 'Law of Moses' in Luanda before coming to Cartagena. Carneiro chose to plead ignorance to the end.[39]

Yet another member of the brotherhood with direct ties to Central Africa was Manuel Alvares Prieto, whose testimony, along with that of gem dealer Juan Rodrigues Mesa, sealed the fate of several others, including the official holder of the Cartagena slave trade *asiento*, Fernando (or Fernão) Lopes de Acosta. Lopes de Acosta, a sixty-year-old Lisbon native, admitted his 'Hebrew' heritage but stressed that his family had been publicly regarded as Old Christians. He denied all charges. His twenty-one-year-old son, Antonio de Acosta, did the same, but others testified that the Brotherhood of Holland sometimes met at the elder Acosta's home.[40]

Perhaps the most tragic figure of all was Blas de Paz Pinto of Évora, who said he renewed his Jewish faith in Lisbon before travelling to Luanda. Trained as a surgeon, he had come to Cartagena in 1622 with a small number of enslaved Africans whom he hoped to sell. As Newson and Minchin note, nearly all of Paz Pinto's slaves died of smallpox en route, but he soon made a small fortune in Cartagena by purchasing sick slaves from other dealers and nursing them back to health for resale.[41]

After a round of torture that left him with bruised arms and a mangled toe, Paz Pinto revealed the names of all the members of the Brotherhood of Holland. He tried to mitigate the value of this confession by saying they were all personal enemies, but the inquisitors denied the technicality. (The Inquisition was not supposed to accept depositions driven by personal animus.) Paz Pinto died soon after of what appears to have been tetanus; he was unable to open his mouth to receive what would have been a forced communion following the amputation of his damaged toe.[42]

Presumably hoping for a return to the days when New Christians could buy some kind of reprieve, several of the most prominent members of Cartagena's so-called Holland Fraternity appealed to the Inquisition's Supreme Tribunal in Spain. It was not until 1651 that a decision was handed down, and it ended with the permanent expulsion of all remaining suspects. In the meantime, arrests and persecution of other suspected Jews continued apace, with jailings, tortures, confiscations and a host of public and private humiliations.

In 1651, merchants Rodrigo Tellez of Bogotá and his cousin Manuel de Olivera of Quito were arrested after it was discovered they had sent money to a brother, Antonio Mendes Tellez of Amsterdam, and an aunt, Isabel de Olivera, of Bordeaux. A cousin, Lorena Mendes, was allegedly married to one Abraham Henriques of Amsterdam.[43] What all this suggests, despite scant mention of emeralds, is that New Christian merchant connections between New Granada and the Low Countries, though under threat, remained important well after Portuguese independence was achieved in 1640. Emeralds, and the intimate knowledge of their sources and likely values, were presumably also transferred.

Another notable case arose in 1648, when one Luis Mendes de Chaves was jailed and interrogated in Cartagena after the English ship on which he sailed was captured while trading enslaved Africans along the Venezuelan coast near Nueva Barcelona. In his possession were a number of Judaic books, including the writings of Menasseh ben Israel, whose pamphlets and later 1655 visit to London convinced Cromwell to allow Jewish resettlement. More important, Mendes de

Chaves named a half dozen Amsterdam-based Sephardic investors in this particular slaving voyage, among them the diamond and pearl merchant David Gabay. As discussed below, Gabay soon after moved to London to report on English market trends for gems in the first years of the Restoration. Mendes de Chaves was sentenced to exile in 1652, but his exact fate remains unclear from the Cartagena documents.[44]

The Curaçao Connection

Dutch intrusion into the Spanish Caribbean was a long and bloody affair. The initial aim was not settlement and plantations but freer trade. As early as 1594 Dutch vessels, some with Portuguese New Christians aboard, put in along the coast of Venezuela and nearby islands in search of tobacco, salt, hides and other products. By 1600 a thriving contraband trade, mostly in enslaved Africans and European cloth, was underway; Caribbean pearls were but icing on the cake.[45] Spanish reaction consisted of harsh reprisals against both the foreigners and their colonial partners, but this only hardened Dutch resolve. By 1624, when the Dutch West India Company was chartered, several Caribbean outposts were being staunchly defended with guns and powder.

One new base, the town of Willemstad on the island of Curaçao, founded in 1634, lay within a few days' sail of the long and mostly unguarded Colombian coast. Historians Isaac Emmanuel, Jonathan Israel, Willem Klooster and others have described the development of Curaçao's significant Jewish merchant community, the largest in the Americas until the nineteenth century.[46] Documents suggest Spanish colonial ships frequently called at Willemstad, especially after the mid-1650s, with cargoes of contraband tobacco, cocoa, hides and dyestuffs. Such goods, quite valuable despite their bulk, found ready markets throughout northern Europe. For Sephardic merchants with ties to India and other parts east, however, it was Spanish America's other famed commodities, silver, gold, pearls and emeralds, that were most esteemed.

In exchange for Spanish-American treasure, Curaçao merchants offered a range of European textiles, wines, spices and, most importantly, enslaved Africans. Jonathan Israel cites a 1661 Spanish ambassador's report from The Hague that stated that contraband business was typically carried out on Curaçao by night, and that a ship had just arrived in Amsterdam from there loaded with dyewood, silver, pearls and emeralds.[47] The next year, 1662, the Spanish slave trade monopoly was partly supplied by Italian factors residing in Willemstad. As merchants and officials on both sides knew, access to the slave trade monopoly only increased the flow of other goods, most of them illegal. The slave trade monopoly had in fact long been a commercial Trojan horse, a point later driven home *in pleno* by the English.

As the Curaçao connection suggests, Europe's main gem trading hub by the early 1600s was Amsterdam. It had displaced the more traditional north European bourse of Antwerp in the midst of the long Spanish war in the Netherlands. As Miriam Bodian and Daniel Swetschinski have shown, Amsterdam's Jewish and New Christian exile communities were thriving by the first quarter of the seventeenth century, and many merchant families retained close ties with relatives who served as factors throughout the Luso-Hispanic world.[48] Some members were more interested in reviving their Jewish faith than others, but with few exceptions the Cartagena merchants persecuted by the Inquisition really were part of the Brotherhood of Holland.

From Amsterdam to London

That Portuguese New Christians and crypto-Jews were at the centre of the global gem trade long before the seventeenth century has been most clearly documented by Edgar Samuel. For example, Samuel cites a set of rules for Lisbon's craft guilds from 1572 that details New Christian dominance of the jewel-making and lapidary arts in that city.[49] As mentioned above, the records of the Lisbon and Coimbra inquisitions, most thoroughly mined by James Boyajian, amply support this argument. The subsequent bursts of activity in

Amsterdam and London are somewhat easier to trace to their origins.

In reconstructing Amsterdam's seventeenth-century gem-trading networks, Samuel used the city's rich municipal archives along with private letters to establish genealogies and track commerce among Sephardic refugees. One Amsterdam gem dealer active in the second half of the seventeenth century with connections to Curaçao was Manuel Levy Duarte; his brother David was resident in Willemstad by 1660.[50] Like most of his contemporaries, Levy was primarily a diamond dealer, in his case a wholesaler, which meant his most important ties were not to the Americas but to India. Levy and a business partner, Jacob Athias, married sisters Gracia and Constantia Duarte, heirs to a jewellery business linked to the biggest dealers and customers of Antwerp, Paris and London. The factor and brother in Curaçao was but one link in a great chain extending halfway around the world. In exchange for emeralds, pearls and precious metals, along with Venezuelan cocoa, Levy helped subsidize the dowries of his brother's daughters in Willemstad.

According to the documents studied by Samuel, there was considerable money to be made in London after 1660 by sending pearls, polished gems (particularly diamonds) and even finished jewellery from Amsterdam. In London, stones cut, drilled, sorted or set in Amsterdam were exchanged for diamond rough, much of it initially smuggled from Madras by English East India Company factors, ship captains and hangers-on. Other diamonds reached Levy from Goa via New Christians who had managed to evade the Portuguese Inquisition, and still others arrived through contacts with the Dutch East India Company, which collected and shipped diamonds from its early post at Surat. Most of the traders linked to the Dutch factory were openly practising Sephardic Jews. Their correspondence, like Levy's, was in Portuguese.

England's sudden demand for pearls, according to a 1660 letter cited by Samuel, was driven by noblewomen visiting the newly restored English court. The letter was sent to Levy in Amsterdam by none other than David Gabay, the investor in the 1648 Caribbean slaving voyage mentioned in Luis Mendes de Chaves's Cartagena Inquisition testimony above.[51] According to Gabay, wealthy English commoners – unlike contemporary bourgeois Dutch women – clung to a quasi-puritan austerity. It would be a generation or so before they changed their ways, although England eventually caught up with the rest of Europe in embracing Baroque splendour.

As in India and other prime jewellery markets, it made good business sense to keep up with and accommodate local tastes that were themselves reflections of changing political, religious and commercial fortunes (sometimes glossed as the rise of bourgeoisies). Sorting out supply and demand in such capricious circumstances was never easy, as Levy's ledgers suggest, but the gem trade could prove highly profitable with the right mix of luck and salesmanship. The best customers, though hardest to reach, were not snobbish bourgeois arrivistes but rather kings, queens, sultans and shahs. Sales of the highest unit value would always be the Holy Grail (or its Jewish equivalent) of the global gem trade.

Relations between European states shifted almost daily in the late seventeenth century, yet distances kept imperial communications agonizingly slow. Abrupt political reversals, about which news was scarce or contradictory, tested the reflexes of far-flung Sephardic merchants in particular because they had set foot and even put down roots in so many quarters. In 1665, for example, trade between Surat and Goa was legalized, sparking a sudden flow of gems, or rather, a sudden flow of *registered* gems. Many diamonds sent to Surat did not go to Amsterdam but rather to London, further complicating the picture. The English East India Company was involved in these deals, and in 1668 sent more than £11,000 worth of silver, coral and emeralds to factors now residing in Goa. According to Samuel, the return cargo for 1669 was more than £17,000 worth of diamonds, some 40 per cent 'consigned to Jewish merchants'.[52] As discussed in Chapter 7, this registered trade expanded in the early eighteenth century to include the East India Company's forts at Madras, Bombay and Bengal.

The Anglo-Dutch-Portuguese gem trade circuit established in the 1660s continued to operate at a brisk pace for several years, with

English ships apparently now the key suppliers of Colombian emeralds to Portuguese diamond dealers. Intervening wars do not seem to have changed this pattern much. Gedalia Yogev cites the 1675 will of London-based merchant Diego Rodrigues Marques that listed a number of pending shipments from 1673, including a consignment of £4,000-worth of emeralds sent to Goa by a factor in Livorno, Gabriel de Medina.[53]

Fearful of losing out, the Portuguese Crown in 1674 tried to shut down the private trade that was breathing new life into Goa. Like the Inquisition, early modern monarchs could be capricious, and their whims often led to wild swings in supply and demand for all sorts of commodities. The monarchs of the Near East and South Asia were no different. In 1688, the inter-oceanic diamond business suffered a sharp blow when Mughal Emperor Aurangzeb's forces invaded the Golconda mining district of south-central India. A strictly observant Muslim and thus an austere teetotaller, Aurangzeb in fact had little of the notorious interest in gems and other forms of ostentation shared by his father, Shah Jahan, and grandfather, Jahangir.

Making it in the Amsterdam Gem Trade

The Amsterdam documents cited by Edgar Samuel refer with some frequency to precious stones, but only rarely mention emeralds. Only in the Athias–Levy partnership ledgers for the period 1675 to 1685 are emeralds specifically named. Unlike pearls, which were accounted for separately, emeralds and other coloured stones were bundled together with purchase-and-sale totals created for diamonds. Some emeralds were presumably incorporated into finished pieces assembled by artisan subcontractors, as well, but their individual value was not listed. It is therefore impossible to know how profitable these men's trade in emeralds was, or even how exactly the trade functioned other than to imagine that the stones were coming from the family partner in Curaçao. In truth, as discussed in later chapters, they could have come through friends or relations in Jamaica, London, Lisbon or Cádiz. Samuel suggests the overall gem trade yielded Manuel Levy and his partner about 10 per cent per annum in the 1670s and 1680s.

The gem cutters hired by these Amsterdam business partners, including one paid to 'mend some emeralds', were mostly non-Jews (as in Lisbon a century earlier), at least according to their surnames.[54] Most were Dutch and French, and some women were employed for select tasks. Finished jewels were by law made only by Dutch guild members, a surviving medieval brake on vertical integration of the jewellery business by Sephardic and other merchants. In a more modern vein, Levy and Athias took full advantage of Amsterdam's sound banking system and thriving stock market to 'grow' their business. They were nevertheless quite conservative in their investments, according to Samuel, and even sought to recoup insurance fees by insuring others.

Samuel adds that Levy and Athias were involved in several cartels, or strategic partnerships, to buy up large portions of arriving rough diamonds, but it is unclear how effective they were at manipulating prices. They did send finished jewels, for which unfortunately we have no detailed descriptions, to India for sale in the court of Emperor Aurangzeb.[55] Whether or not they were sold we do not know, but as mentioned above, Aurangzeb was no Shah Jahan. Given these merchants' direct connections to Curaçao, and also several France-based Sephardim trading regularly for silver from the Spanish West Indies, it seems highly likely that such exports to India contained emeralds. Once again, the evidence suggests that much more so than even diamonds and pearls, emeralds remained a mysterious, stowaway commodity – more likely to be found in shipwrecks than shipping records.

In part because of this reticence of the records, Samuel reduces the Amsterdam wholesalers' exports to India to what was listed and most important in terms of volume, namely Spanish 'pieces of eight'. Silver was certainly the most critical export of all, for the trading companies as well as their consignment merchants. Indian textiles, the Dutch and English East India companies' main object of desire, could not be purchased any other way.

For gem dealers, returns from India were expected in rough diamonds purchased through resident Sephardic traders. Some of these traders were relatives who periodically left the Dutch and English factories of Surat and Madras to buy directly from the Golconda mines. Seizing their own opportunities, Bania and other Indian merchants with licence from the emperor served as intermediaries between miners and foreign buyers, and some became tremendously wealthy as a result.

By the late seventeenth century, English, Dutch and (belatedly) French company officials, like their Portuguese predecessors and contemporaries, sometimes interfered in the Sephardic and inland gem trades for their own benefit. Elihu Yale, president of Madras's Fort St George from 1687 to 1692, was one example, although he proved more a nuisance than a true barrier to trade in the long run. Levy and Athias lost money to Yale, who had been entrusted with some of their investments, but despite their status as resident aliens they were able to use the English legal system to recoup.

Yale had apparently been so attracted to the diamond business that he became a de facto member of the greater Sephardic trading community. A diamond factor's widow, Jeronima de Paiva, became Yale's mistress and together they had a son. Years later, Yale's considerable estate, auctioned in London in several blocks between 1722 and 1723, included numerous emeralds. To fund a small college in Connecticut, however, he gave only books.[56]

The Enigma of the Cheapside Hoard

The famous Cheapside Hoard, a gem-and-jewel trove (most of which is in the Museum of London) thought to date to about Shakespeare's time, includes a massive Colombian emerald set with a Swiss watch (Plate 10). Other emerald pieces from the hoard include a carved bird reminiscent of fanciful Mughal stones, along with grape clusters mounted on earrings. A number of emerald rings and loose, faceted stones were also unearthed. If the great emerald market of the day was India, what were these stones doing in London?

A roll of testimonies taken in 1641 and now housed in London's Parliamentary Archives may relate to some items found in the hoard, including the great emerald watch.[57] The case regards one Gerard Polman (anglicized Pullman in the documents), a Dutchman who boarded the English East India Company ship *Discovery* in 1631 in Gombroon (Bandar Abbas), the Safavid Dynasty's recently established Persian Gulf port near Hurmuz. After a long struggle with the Portuguese, representatives of both the English and Dutch East India companies (founded in 1600 and 1602, respectively) had helped the Safavids muscle their way into these waters in exchange for trade concessions in 1622.[58] According to various testimonies, Polman, allegedly a jeweller or gem trader in the East Indies for nearly thirty years, offered either £100 or £200 to captain and crew for safe passage of himself and his goods to Europe, presumably to go home to Westphalia.

Luck would not be on Polman's side. When the *Discovery* stopped at the Comoro Islands for water on the way to the Cape of Good Hope he died, either of illness or poisoning. The crew, in particular the carpenter's mate, one Christopher Adams, took the dead man's goods. We know nothing of the remaining trip, but near Gravesend, well before the mouth of the Thames, Adams jumped ship one night and rowed ashore with his booty, said to consist of a half-bushel size 'black boxe' filled to the brim with gems and jewels, plus several chests of Persian silks. These he hid in the houses and barns of various relatives, including that of his wife Elizabeth, whose testimony is the first recorded. She stated that the black box was 'pakt with iowells so shiny that they thought the cabin was afire'. Other deponents who had seen the jewels on board ship said they could read by their brilliance.

The Adams's house appears to have been located in a village somewhere in Southampton (apparently Bashleye, Minton Parish, although I find no modern correspondence). His stashes and safehouses established, Adams then made several trips to jewellers in London, including one Nicholas Pope of Fleet Street, to whose wife he sold many pearls and gems – though far too cheaply, according to his sworn testimony. Meanwhile, word of the Dutchman's booty reached Robert

Bertie, Earl of Lindsey, then treasurer of the East India Company and king's chamberlain. Outraged, the Earl sent his agents after Adams and other *Discovery* shipmates thought to be disposing of his and the company's goods for personal gain.

Eventually, Adams was captured and jailed, in custody for most of three years. After some bargaining he agreed to hand over Polman's 'black boxe' to Lindsey, although he kept one of the keys. According to Adams and other witnesses the chest contained a wide array of diamonds, rubies, emeralds, sapphires and pearls, as well as substantial bags of turquoise (mostly rough), agates, chalcedonies, garnets, carnelians, topazes, heliotropes, bezoar stones and some fine cut rubies, spinels and garnets described generically as carbuncles.

Can this treasure be linked to the Cheapside Hoard? It is difficult to say for certain, but Adams maintained in item twenty-seven of his testimony that among the stones he gave to Rawlinson and Pennycoate, the Earl of Lindsey's detective-henchmen, was a 'greene rough stone or emerald three inches long and three inches in compass'. He said he 'heard it was afterward pawned at Cheapside but to whom he knoweth not'.

Possibly this unusually large emerald had nothing to do with the famous Cheapside watch whose Swiss mechanism has been dated by experts to about 1600 – roughly thirty years before the Polman windfall. Still, a likely scenario is that the emerald mentioned by Adams was the raw material for the watch housing, and that the same unnamed jeweller who fashioned it bought other items from either Lindsey's men, Adams or someone else from the *Discovery*. This person could easily have had a stock of older jewels in progress plus miscellaneous items on hand, such as the many rough turquoises and rubies found in the hoard. Turquoises were a Persian specialty and many of the other Cheapside stones and rings appear tantalizingly similar to those mentioned in the Polman depositions.

As for a reason to bury such treasures, most obvious was the man-and-jewel hunt put on by Lindsey in the mid-1630s, followed by a suit filed by one of Polman's heirs in Holland. Soon after came the English Civil War, which broke out just before these testimonies were taken in September 1641. By October 1642 Lindsey was killed while leading royalist forces at Edgehill.[59]

Whatever its origins or precise date, the Cheapside Hoard and other evidence suggest a continued demand for Colombian emeralds in Elizabethan and Jacobean London, if not in England more broadly.[60] The Polman emeralds are perhaps just as important for what they may say about early Dutch emerald traders operating in Safavid Persia. The emeralds carried by Polman, and there were many others besides the huge rough mentioned by Adams, were almost certainly of Colombian origin. One witness described a parcel of two hundred emeralds, polished and rough, sold to a goldsmith named Jacob Arthur. Others mention a half-peck bag of emeralds plus 'fower greate ruffe emerlds eache of them the bignes of a greate wallnutt', all worth at least £200. Finally, witness Herman Marshall said he saw an emerald two inches across and two fingers' width thick.

So how did Polman get these stones, and why would he risk his life bringing them back to Western Europe, that is, in the direction of their source? As mentioned above, Spanish and Portuguese traders understood early on that some emeralds were 'oriental' and others 'occidental', even though virtually all came from the same Colombian mines. It is entirely likely that someone with as many gems and as many years' experience as Polman would have known how to play this game. Even if he did not find 'eastern' buyers for his 'oriental' stones, he could likely count on re-exporting them to Europe, where they could then be described – and truly – as having come from the Orient.

Bruce Lenman has shown that private traders using the vessels of the English East India Company began sending emeralds to eastern markets on the advice of ambassador Sir Thomas Roe, who personally visited both India's Mughal emperor Jahangir and the Safavid ruler of Persia, Shah Abbas I. In 1624 a parcel of jewels and loose stones was sold by company representatives in Surat on the account of one Morris Abbot. It included three emeralds that together sold for 3,000 rupees, or an average of about £130 sterling each, plus another five stones, three of them weighing more than one hundred carats, that sold for 2,910 rupees.[61] The trade was not large, but it was evidently lucrative. Most emeralds sent east did not come back home.

Tracing these early trans-oceanic commodity chains back and forth may seem an exercise in confusion, yet there is probably no better way to gain a sense of emerald movements from Colombia's port of Cartagena de Indias to the various gem bourses and markets of Europe and Asia. Emerald dealing appears to have been a highly uncertain business, one best carried on in addition to commerce in bulkier commodities such as tobacco, cocoa, hides or textiles. As a largely smuggling or 'stowaway' business, the emerald trade was also clearly linked to the nefarious transatlantic slave trade, and therefore to the famous sugar plantation complex. Like the trade in African captives, links in this chain extended around the Cape to the Persian Gulf, India and Southeast Asia from an early date. The principal agents of these early global trading ventures were polyglot globetrotters of uncertain loyalty.

❖

CHAPTER 5

Globetrotters

IN the year 2000, an international team of mineralogists led by Gaston Giuliani reported its comparisons of oxygen isotope ratios in one of the emeralds recovered from the 1622 *Atocha* shipwreck with those of some famous Mughal stones long thought to be either Egyptian or South Asian in origin. The mineralogists confirmed what historians and gemologists had long suspected: that most of the quality emeralds circulating in Eurasia after the time of Columbus were of New World origin, including those still touted as 'oriental' or 'lost mine' stones.[1] Nearly all the emeralds tested could be traced not only to Colombia's Muzo, Coscuez and Chivor districts, but also to specific outcrops.

There was, however, one surprise. Although three of four stones belonging to the Nizam of Hyderabad said to be of Old World origin proved to be Colombian, a fourth, apparently cut and set in the eighteenth century, had an isotope signature close to that of emeralds from Afghanistan's Panjsher Valley. The colour of Panjsher emeralds is generally distinguishable from those of Muzo, but sometimes approximates to the bluish tones of Chivor. Because there is no historical record of mining in this part of Afghanistan before the 1990s, the mineralogists were left to guess that a few stones found by chance amid surface detritus had entered the Indian market centuries ago.

Further scientific analysis will likely prove the extent of inter-oceanic circulation of Colombian emeralds, but the historical record has plenty of stories to tell. Only documents and published accounts can tell us with any degree of certainty in whose hands and by what mechanisms these stones reached such distant customers as the Mughal Emperor in early modern times. As discussed in previous chapters, most American emeralds began the voyage by doing as the crew of the *Atocha* had hoped: to sail safely across the Atlantic from Cartagena to Seville. This voyage alone, lasting up to six months, broken up with stops in Havana and sometimes the Azores, was long and rife with dangers.

Getting to Seville was an accomplishment, but reaching the East Indies was extraordinary. Giuliani and his colleagues were not wrong to suggest New World stones went to the Near East and South Asia via Seville and eastern Mediterranean overland trade networks, on the one hand, and via the Pacific trade of the so-called Manila galleons, on the other. These latter ships left the Mexican port of Acapulco annually for the approximately four-month voyage to the Philippines, where trade with China, Japan, Southeast Asia and even India was brisk after 1570.

As James Boyajian and others have shown, Portuguese merchants, including prominent New Christians, came to Manila regularly from as far away as Goa, mostly to trade pepper and textiles for Spanish silver, which they then took on to Macao. South and Southeast Asian gemstones were also traded in Manila, and at least one Spanish official writing in 1609 noted Portuguese merchants taking New World emeralds brought via the Pacific to Melaka. Jade-rich China apparently had no need for Colombia's rich green stones, but did apparently consume some Indian diamonds and Burmese rubies.[2]

What Giuliani and his colleagues failed to mention was the standard Portuguese sea route from Lisbon to Goa described in previous chapters. This was by far the most likely avenue linking New World emeralds to Asian customers. Some stones must have leaked to Portuguese merchants in the Azores, where many ships of the Spanish Tierra Firme fleet put in for water and victuals on their way to Sanlúcar de Barrameda and Seville. Others probably reached

Lisbon directly, when the fleets were driven there by wind or news of pirates lurking around the mouth of the Guadalquivir. As previously discussed, Portuguese slavers based in Cartagena de Indias traded for emeralds directly after 1580, as well, and through them and other intermediaries stones were later diverted to the Dutch on Curaçao and the English in Jamaica.

Still, it was the official Portuguese 'India Run', or *carreira da Índia*, spanning the Atlantic and Indian Oceans, that fed most Colombian emeralds to South Asian and possibly Persian consumers until at least 1700. This voyage, often an epic journey lasting up to a year, linked Portugal to its main Asian outpost: Goa. Brazil would become the jewel of the Portuguese Crown following discovery of gold and diamonds there after 1695, but up to the early eighteenth century Portuguese overseas interests centred on the fortified island and viceregal capital of Goa, on India's central west coast.

Colombian Emeralds in 'Golden Goa'

'Into Goa . . . come [diamonds] in considerable quantity and quality. Anyone who knows about them and who might have cash, gold [tinsel] cloth from Europe, or occidental jewels, especially emeralds and red coral, could make some very good investments. They particularly esteem emeralds.'[3]—Venetian traveller Ambrosio Bembo, c.1675

As historian George Winius and others have noted, the Portuguese hardly ever taxed the colonial gem trade. This was true even in Lisbon, long home to a thriving, cosmopolitan stone-cutting and gem-dealing community. Portugal's open policy, so unlike the draconian Spanish one that taxed emeralds steeply at every step, had the twin effects of stimulating commerce and leaving almost no record of it. As a result of this policy plus the great 1755 Lisbon earthquake and subsequent fires, which destroyed countless documents, little is known about volume, price or anything else needed for a sound economic analysis.

As mentioned in the last chapter there are, however, some suggestive fragmentary records of Portuguese exports of diamonds from India contained in governors' reports, ships' manifests, Inquisition papers and other ephemera. Reports of incoming emeralds are, unfortunately, much rarer. Only in odd incidents such as one reported by the Count of Sarzedas, Viceroy of Portugal's *Estado da Índia* in the mid-1650s, is information this specific. In the count's case a large emerald was allegedly required to ransom a Portuguese merchant held by Adil Shah of Bijapur, Goa's powerful neighbour.[4] The famous document collections known as the *Livros das Monções*, or 'Monsoon books', contain decrees regarding the surreptitious trade in gemstones under the generic term *pedraria*, but to my knowledge they make no specific mention of emeralds.[5]

Given the paucity of treasury records and other official sources similar to those found in Colombia and Spain, historians have relied heavily on accounts written by non-Portuguese European merchants, and to a lesser extent, missionaries active in the Portuguese maritime world. For the late sixteenth century a primary authority is the Dutch trader Jan Huyghen van Linschoten, whose two-volume *Voyage* or *Intinerario* was widely read and translated in his lifetime. Englishman Ralph Fitch, who crossed paths with Linschoten in the 1580s, is also useful. Far less well known was a young Florentine merchant and globetrotter, Francesco Carletti, who also left behind a memoir. He resided in Goa from 1599 to 1601, and provided a few interesting details on the Asian gem trade as he understood it.

For the early seventeenth century, Winius, Benjamin Teensma and others have turned to the recently discovered manuscript of Flemish gem merchant Jacques de Coutre, who lived for many years in Goa beginning in 1592. English East India Company merchant Robert Coverte passed through Goa in 1609 and even went overland to visit Jahangir in Agra in 1610. He sold unspecified jewels and stones to princes along the way. A French visitor, François Pyrard of Laval, also offers some useful descriptions of Goa around 1610.[6] For the mid-to-late seventeenth century, the published account of French Huguenot jewel trader Jean-Baptiste Tavernier, who lived mostly at the Dutch and English trading posts of Surat and Madras but knew the Goa trade well, has long been consulted, and remains invaluable. Several key references are also found in the multivolume *Storia do Mogor* of Niccolao Manucci, who lived in Goa for a time but eventually settled in English Madras.

A number of other European travellers such as the Venetian cavalier Ambrosio Bembo, cited above, mention gem dealing in their accounts of commerce in South Asia, Persia, and the former Ottoman Empire. Still, Linschoten, Coutre and Tavernier stand out since they dealt primarily in stones. For the mechanics of the Indian Ocean entrepôt, or re-export trade, I have relied mostly on their works in combination with fragments from Portuguese and other archives. To understand the still more mysterious subject of early modern gem trading and consumption patterns within South Asia and the Near East, I have used European merchants' and diplomats' accounts, which offer helpful hints and observations. Because, however, they were outsiders prone to misunderstanding what drove local tastes and price determinations, it is necessary to turn to sources produced by Mughal, Safavid and Ottoman writers. What survives, in addition to a wide array of paintings and jewelled artefacts, are courtly chronicles and royal memoirs.

Travellers' Tales

The wealth and variety of gems and jewels exchanged from Hurmuz to Melaka had stunned European visitors since Marco Polo. Linschoten described the gem trade in India and Burma in some detail following a residence of several years in Goa and other Indian Ocean ports in the 1580s. On emeralds, he had this to say:

> [Of] the Emeralds which the Indians call *pache*, and the Arabians *samarrut*, there are none throughout all India, yet it is reported that some have been found there, but very few and not often: but they are much brought thither from Cairo in Egypt, and are likewise called Oriental: they are much esteemed in India, because

there are but few of them. There are many also brought from the Spanish Indies, and carried into the land of Pegù [Burma], where they are much worn, and esteemed of, whereby many Venetians (that have travelled thither with Emeralds and bartered them for Rubies) are become very rich, because among them men had rather have Emeralds than Rubies.[7]

Linschoten's reference to Cairo is noteworthy, as it suggests continued use of the ancient Red Sea and Levantine routes for New World emeralds to reach India. This and other overland passages to India from the Mediterranean were in fact well travelled in the era of the Portuguese *carreira da Índia*, as Frederic Lane and other historians have pointed out. Ralph Fitch and his partner John Newberry, who met Linschoten in Goa after being jailed in Hurmuz in 1583, mentioned buying emerald jewellery in Aleppo to trade for diamonds, pearls and rubies in Goa.[8] The Cairo path also had the unwitting advantage of making New World stones seem 'Egyptian'.

The decades on either side of the year 1600 marked an era of intense and often violent competition in the eastern Mediterranean and Near East, with Venice in the eye of the storm. Yet even as the Ottomans expanded their reach into the Arabian Peninsula, Mesopotamia and a portion of the Indian Ocean, Venetian, Armenian, Jewish, Gujarati and Bania merchants continued to move gemstones, precious metals, spices, silk fabrics and other valuable commodities across established routes. Old habits of trade died hard.

A sea change did occur, but it came about gradually, beginning with the English and Dutch alliance with the Safavid ruler Abbas I in the 1620s. Before this, the dangerously overloaded Portuguese carracks that came all the way from Lisbon via the Cape of Good Hope each year ended the old Levantine monopoly on Eastern goods, but never replaced it. As late as 1616 the king of Portugal tried to outlaw foreign merchants and *homens da nação*, or Sephardim, using Goa as their point of entry to buy gems in the Indian interior, which they then sent overland to 'Venice, Turkey, France, Italy, and other parts'.[9] As mentioned in the previous chapter, at least one Cartagena Sephardic merchant with ties to Venice and Salonika had traded directly for Gulf pearls in Egypt.

Linschoten's other reference, to a thriving consumer market for emeralds in Buddhist Burma, famous for its rubies, remains a mystery, perhaps to be solved when new documents come to light. I have only seen a few small cabochon emeralds incorporated into early modern Burmese jewellery (of which little apparently survives).

Presumably referring to Goa, where gem trading was most concentrated and where he spent considerable time, Linschoten describes appraisal practices and relative values for most gemstones. His baseline was what he called a perfect diamond of one carat. A truly flawless diamond of clearest water that size could fetch fifty ducats, or about sixty ounces of silver, according to Linschoten, but so few circulated that what the market regarded as 'perfect' stones were actually mildly flawed ones that sold for a bit less, about forty ducats. This was still good money, as prime slaves from Mozambique sold for as much in contemporary Goa. Noting that 'real' Egyptian emeralds were virtually always poor in quality, Linschoten then applied the following scale of appraisal to stones from the 'Spanish Indies':

> The old Jewellers say that if a man can find an Emerald perfect in all points, as in colour, clearness, fashion, and thickness, that such an Emerald is worth three Diamonds, which according to our account should be 120 ducats, and I believe verily that it is most true, but as yet there was never any found, either little or great that had all those perfections; there are some found that are perfect in colour and fashion, but of clearness and cleanness not one, for they always have some fattiness within them like green herbs and such like, wherefore to make our reckoning, we will say that an Emerald of common sort, estimation, and perfection, is worth 80 ducats, being of the bigness, as that he may compare with a Diamond of one Quilate [carat]. . .[10]

Bearing in mind the appraisal tables compiled by the Spanish court jeweller Arfe y Villafañe reproduced in Appendix 2b, in 1580s Goa a prime, one-carat emerald could bring almost one-hundred ounces of silver, if not more – twice what it might have fetched in Madrid in 1572, and as much as twenty-five times what it might have yielded there by 1598, whether 'new' or 'old'.

Although even in sale records, inventories and tax assessments emeralds were never so clearly and carefully appraised in sixteenth- or seventeenth-century Colombia, records of occasional auctions of the largest and best raw stones show that values in India were exponentially higher than at the source. That even a fine cut stone of one carat would sell for the equivalent of *ten* ducats, much less one hundred, in 1580s Bogotá seems impossible. Even when prime emeralds were still rare in Muzo, the difference was vast. A 1572 fraud case notes the sale either in Muzo or Bogotá of a choice stone weighing some *four hundred carats* for just over two hundred gold pesos, or four hundred ounces of silver, about the going price of a healthy enslaved African adult.[11]

Linschoten does not take into account the exponential rise in price, carat by carat, so carefully laid out by Arfe in his Spanish appraisal tables, a notable omission given the massive size of so many Indian emeralds of American origin now seen in museums. Linschoten also discusses the introduction of Caribbean pearls to India, but states they were virtually all of lesser quality than those already available from various 'Oriental' beds, such as those of the Persian Gulf and southeast India.[12]

Another intriguing account of the gem business in the Portuguese East Indies is Francesco Carletti's *c*.1606 memoir of circumnavigation. Carletti was a Florentine merchant with connections in Livorno who got permission in 1594 to travel from Seville to Cartagena de Indias, then on to Lima, Acapulco, Manila, Nagasaki, Macao, Melaka and Goa. He returned to Europe in 1602 via Mozambique and northeast Brazil.

Carletti's first business was purchasing enslaved Africans in the Cape Verde Islands for sale in Cartagena. He does not mention trading for emeralds in Cartagena, although he notes that enslaved Africans were sent inland to mine them. Along the way from

Melaka to Goa he purchased pearls from Cape Comorin and rubies and sapphires from Ceylon.[13] Remaining in Goa between 1599 and 1601, Carletti participated in the diamond trade, and had this to say about Portuguese profit margins:

> On the [silver] *reales* that come solely from Lisbon they earn more than fifty percent, it happening that the [peso] of eight *reales*, which is worth 320 *reis* in Portugal, is worth 480 and 484 *reis* in India. And thus similarly with other things brought from there to India, such as wines, oil, coral, glass, cats'-eyes, balas rubies, emeralds, large pearls, and various other goods. And on those items incredible profits were and still are made by means of the merchandise that they send from Goa to Portugal on the carracks, which ordinarily leave in the month of December, as also in that of January.[14]

On his way home via the Cape of Good Hope on such a carrack, the typically overloaded *São Tiago*, Carletti and his Portuguese companions were robbed by Zeelanders encountered by chance on the South Atlantic island of St. Helena. Carletti stated there were 300,000 *scudi* worth of jewellery alone on board the damaged carrack, leaving aside the hundreds of bales of fine cloth and a massive cargo of pepper, but perhaps more interestingly, he tells how he and other desperate passengers tried to hide their loot. The Dutch, who were on their way to the Moluccas, preferred jewels to spices by way of ransom, and many were offered in exchange for salvation from the sinking *São Tiago*.

After reaching the island of Fernão de Noronha off Brazil's northeast shore around Easter 1602, the passengers were examined one last time before being released. According to Carletti:

> They were landed all naked, carrying with them only one shirt and a pair of white pants. And they were searched to discover if they had any jewels, which many of them had swallowed, especially pearls, and some diamonds and rubies. Many made little bunches

of them and hid them in their lowest organs. As there were female slaves, their owners had them hide their jewels inside themselves, which perhaps was more convenient, but also was less secure. For one of them, as she came down from the ship to enter the boat that was to carry her ashore, stretched out her legs more than was convenient on that occasion, and dropped – or, to say it better, there came out from underneath – a bunch of diamonds, which quickly was recovered by one of those sailors.[15]

On reaching Middleburg, Carletti lamented having been unable to swallow some of his own pearls due to 'the dryness of my throat'.[16]

The Amazing Jacques de Coutre: Emerald Entrepreneur

Important work by George Winius and Benjamin Teensma on the Portuguese gem trade at Goa has largely been based on a recently discovered, or rather newly appreciated, manuscript autobiography from about 1640 housed in Spain's National Library. The document, published and extensively annotated in 1991 under the title *Andanzas Asiáticas*, was composed in a heavily Portuguese-accented Spanish by a Fleming named Jacob van de Couteren, or 'Jacques de Coutre'. The manuscript was deposited in Madrid soon after the author died there while serving as a court jeweller to Philip IV.[17]

Appended to Coutre's picaresque narrative, perhaps to convince Inquisition censors of his sincere Catholicism and loyalty to the Spanish cause, are detailed recommendations regarding Dutch activity in South Asia and the Far East. As Eddy Stols and his colleagues noted in their research on Coutre's manuscript, the roving Fleming *was* being watched. He shows up in Inquisition records and other Spanish and Portuguese documents for at least two reasons: his close dealings with Portuguese New Christians in Goa and his own 'almost Dutch' origins. Like many Belgians living in the Luso-Hispanic world at this time, Coutre and his brother were jailed and interrogated following a 1605 royal decree requiring all Flemings to submit to questioning.[18] The Bruges-born brothers were helped by the fact that they had married Goan women from respected, Old Christian, Portuguese families.

To judge from his narrative, Coutre took such challenges in his stride and instead focused his considerable energies on locating and buying up as many of India's celebrated diamonds as he could find. To cut out the middleman, he headed straight for the legendary mines of Golconda and Ramalikota, at this time located just outside Mughal territory. The Ramalikota diggings in fact lay near the ruins of the recently fallen Brahmanic empire of Vijayanagar, with its great capital at Hampi. Having sent Indian diamonds through his brother and other factors to Lisbon, Coutre records that he imported New World pearls and emeralds. He also dealt in Ceylonese sapphires and Burmese rubies, but how he obtained them he does not say.

Echoing Linschoten, Coutre notes that emeralds, being so rare in India, were especially prized. Of a 1604 visit to the shah of the Muslim kingdom of Bijapur, whose capital of the same name was located about 250 kilometres northeast of Goa, Coutre recalled the following:

> The king knew I was carrying some large emeralds; one of them weighed three hundred carats, and another two hundred; a third was of drop type, of over one hundred. I sold him all three for two thousand *pagodes* in gold – so it is known, *pagodes* are gold coins the size of an almond bud with a sculptured elephant on them; each one is worth twenty *reales* of our money.[19]

Coutre does not say how he came into possession of these emeralds or how much he paid for them, but he offers extremely rare and detailed evidence of emerald prices in the Indian interior at a fairly early date. By Coutre's reckoning, these three large stones sold for the equivalent of approximately five thousand silver pesos of eight *reales*.

Again echoing Linschoten, it appears from this sale that the price per carat for the emeralds, just over eight pesos, had not risen exponentially. Perhaps large stones were at this time not so rare as they had been in the sixteenth century, or local customs of appraisal did not permit doubling, tripling and so forth in values of very large stones, as was common in Europe. Or perhaps the quality of these particular stones was subprime.

We have reason in any case to think Coutre, no amateur, knew what he was doing. He calls the Armenian merchant accompanying him on this trip, known in the Portuguese community at Goa as Francisco Gonsalves, an able translator, so misunderstanding seems unlikely. There is some question here as in other incidents related by Coutre regarding the risks and resulting price 'distortions' that came with selling luxury goods directly to Indian royalty, but the impression one gets in this case is of a fair and uncontested exchange.

In 1612, Coutre again passed through Bijapur, this time continuing east to visit the diamond mines of Poli, Nandial and Marmur, in the modern state of Andhra Pradesh. He says he carried with him 'rubies, emeralds, pearls, and other precious things to sell to the kings of the Orient. At this time I had great favour among those kings, and as they too trade in stones, they esteemed and honoured greatly those who also exchanged them, and still more so the foreign Christians.' In Bijapur, Coutre says he sold the former prince, Idalcán, now known as Ibrahim Adil Shah, 'some pearls and jewels I carried, and some other merchandise'.[20] This gave him the money he needed to go on to the diamond mines.

Coutre recounts various stops along the way, and says he sold 'some jewels' to royal figures such as Gopal Raya of the fort-city of Malaveli. The wandering Belgian makes no specific mention of emeralds in this case, but presumably his earlier listing of them among the stones he carried meant that some were sold here and elsewhere. (This raises the question as to whether Hindu, or for that matter Sikh, princes were as fond of emeralds as their Muslim neighbours. Later paintings and other evidence suggest they were, but when this began we do not know.) Next, Coutre describes buying chunks of host rock embedded with diamonds from the miners of Poli, the old supplier of Vijayanagar. These he sent to his brother in Goa, so they could be sent to 'friends in Europe'. Coutre claimed to be the first person to venture inland in search of stones, since the Goan Portuguese had not even bothered to learn 'where diamonds are born'.[21]

Coutre makes no more mention of selling stones on this journey, but he offers a memorable account of his descent into the diamond mines of Poli. He says he stripped down to his linen underpants and followed a similarly dressed miner as guide. Ducking and following the miner's lamp, Coutre made his way through an extremely narrow tunnel 'more than two musket shots long', before entering a huge gallery he estimated would accommodate a thousand men. In a heat he says was so tremendous it made the rocks sweat, Coutre saw 'many people working with lamps and great iron instruments'.[22] Here, at last, is an image of the Indian diamond mines to match the strange horrors of Muzo's emerald mines, halfway around the world.

This brief glimpse of Indian gem mining is also justified by Coutre's mention of an aborted diamond purchase. He says: 'in the same cave I bought a diamond from a miner that weighed thirty carats for 700 *pagodes*'. Presumably this was an excellent price, or Coutre would not have bothered (although one doubts he had the 700 *pagodes* on hand given that he was 'naked' and 'totally soaked and covered with mud like the miners themselves').[23] If, using Coutre's earlier conversion rate, a thirty-carat diamond was worth the equivalent of 1,750 pesos of eight *reales* underground, one presumes it was worth double that above, or more.

Unfortunately for Coutre, and even less fortunately for the miner who sold him the day's big rock, the local rajah was soon after informed of this underground exchange. The rajah called Coutre before him and told him that it was only because he was a 'Frank' (i.e., European) that his goods would not be confiscated and all his property burned. Instead, the lucky Belgian was allowed to send word to his brother in Goa to return the stone. (Here and elsewhere Coutre shows how much he trusted presumably Indian intermediaries to ferry money, gems and letters – and how quickly he dispatched valuables to the safety of Goa.) Once the gem arrived, according to Coutre, the rajah thanked him for his cooperation and returned his 700 *pagodes*. These had been extracted from the hapless miner, who, 'as the prize for having found the stone and sold it to me, was beaten so badly they left him for dead'.[24]

Why the punishment? Because, as Linschoten also noted in his earlier discussion of the Indian diamond trade, many local princes, shahs and other royalty reserved access to all stones above a certain size to themselves. Linschoten wrote that in his experience all diamonds above seven carats went to the monarch. Coutre's host simply said: '. . . you knew that stones of that weight are mine'.[25] What this meant for exporters of diamonds, even those as adventurous as Coutre, was extremely limited access to large stones, and thus instant and massive inflation of their value compared to smaller ones of even the best water.

By contrast, only very occasionally were large emeralds from what is today Colombia set aside for the king of Spain, and there had never been a policy requiring such withholding. Colombian emeralds of all sizes and qualities circulated freely from the start, taxed by Spanish kings in the same, gross-volume way as precious metals. If anything, large and exceptionally beautiful stones were precisely the ones most likely to escape Spanish controls and thus drive down prices. In the world of early modern gemstones, it seems, 'Oriental despotism' could be as profitable as it was dangerous, a lesson obviously lost on the metals-obsessed Spanish.

Emerald prices in India were also influenced, one might say distorted, by regal buyers who could exert considerable pressure on foreigners such as Coutre. A subsequent incident in a different prince's court affirms this. In 1614 Coutre travelled on horseback with a few servants armed with harquebuses and bows from Goa to the city of Bagnagar (probably Ahmadnagar, north of Bijapur). On the way, Coutre stopped in the friendly kingdom of Prince Idalcán, where he sold some unnamed jewels and was received with honour, draped in fine cloth and given betel to chew. While continuing on to Bagnagar, Coutre and his servants witnessed an incident in which alleged representatives of the Mughals were harassed for not wishing to pay a duty on some elephants they were transporting from Golconda to Bijapur for sale. The dispute resulted in four deaths, and Coutre delayed his journey, apparently out of sheer curiosity, until the matter was resolved. Soon, representatives of Idalcán's court arrived, freed the men from Golconda, and beheaded the local governor and twenty-five of his subalterns. The corpses of twelve civilians presumably involved in some way with this misunderstanding were placed on pikes.[26]

In relating this gruesome incident, Coutre clearly magnifies the boldness of his own exploits by revealing how risky and uncertain cross-border trade was in India's interior. His turn with powerful buyers for precious stones was just around the corner. Once in Bagnagar, in the court of a prince named Catabusa, Coutre successfully sold two thousand *pagodes*' worth of emeralds, but got ensnared in a dispute over a large suite of pearls. He asked four thousand *pagodes* for the lot, but was told the 'king' would pay only three thousand. Coutre held firm, meanwhile buying up two boxes of bezoar stones, uncut rubies, and 'other things'.[27] In the interim he was forbidden from leaving, and in secret he crated up and sent off with his servants all but the pearls and some cash he held in trust for several Goa merchants. Rajah Catabusa found out about this and had the crates seized and brought to him. Not wishing to take his chances in a land where price disputes could cost a head, Coutre entrusted the pearls and money to a Portuguese friar who served in Bagnagar as ambassador and made his escape on horseback 'like a desperate man'.

As if this were not enough evidence of the fickle tendency of princes to jam the wheels of commerce, Coutre returned to Goa to find his brother, Joseph, imprisoned by the Portuguese viceroy for being a foreigner. Jacques soon joined him. The Dutch had seized Surat in the midst of the so-called Twelve Year Truce with Spain (1609–1621), and now all Flemings living in Habsburg possessions were suspect by association. The foreigner scare in fact went back to a 1605 royal decree, but was now heightened by the perception in India of acute danger.

The pearls and money held by the Portuguese priest were eventually returned to Goa, but the Coutre brothers could not accept them because they had been deprived of their gem business. Not wishing to be sent on the next ship to Lisbon, no doubt in part because of the *carreira da Índia*'s dismal safety record, both Coutres escaped from Goa for some other corner of the Indian Ocean, perhaps as nearby as Surat. Jacques de Coutre simply says he spent the next year trading gems 'among the Moors'.[28]

Apparently unconcerned with having lost his legal ties to Goa, Coutre freely travelled in the subcontinent in the year 1616 trading 'a good quantity of gold, pearls, and emeralds for diamonds, garnets, amethysts, sapphires, aquamarines, hyacinths, and many other stones of various colours'.[29] His brother Joseph was apparently allowed to return to Goa to reopen his shop, as Jacques mentions sending him a letter there. Eventually, both gained permission or pardon from Goa's viceroy, and Jacques also returned.

Meanwhile, a chance to buy some large diamonds from Rajah Gopal of Malaveli again revealed how power could play havoc with price. In this case, the rajah had purchased pearls and unspecified jewels from Coutre and offered to sell him several diamonds weighing between ten and thirty carats in return. Despite his obvious interest, Coutre declined, saying the price offered was double their value in Europe. He then adds, more or less as a maxim: 'It is a certain thing that one may not buy stones and jewels from the hand of a prince unless it be out of pure necessity.'[30]

In 1619, Coutre reached the capital of Agra and paid a visit to the 'Great Mogul' himself, Jahangir. It was no social visit, as he was there to collect payment for stones he and his brother and another Fleming, Fernando Cron, had previously sent.[31] The splendour of the shah's court was almost too much for Coutre, and may serve as a fitting end to his portion of the emerald story:

Well, in the matter of riches it is wisely said that there is no monarch in the world who has such a great treasure, or so many subjects, as the Mogul. And I do not doubt it, because I have walked through and seen a bit of the world, and I am here to say that of what I have seen, the Mogul has more treasure in precious stones, gold, and silver than all the kings of Europe together. . . .

It is a very certain thing that from all parts of the world are sent pearls, emeralds, rubies, and jewels of great price to the India of the East, and we know that all of it ends up with the Mogul.[32]

Coutre's impressions were not unique, and echo statements by various Jesuit visitors and also the English ambassador Sir Thomas Roe. Roe advised English merchants to bring the following gems to Surat to trade with Mughal middlemen in 1617: 'Pearles: anni great well bought; chaines of pearles, between three carrats and ten, the greatest the best. Rubies give the best proffitt, from three carrats upwardes of all sizes, so high in collour and faire. Ballasses: faire and greate, of 60 carrats upwardes. Cattes eyes: if yow knewe the right stone. Emrauldes: of the old and new rock, the greatest.'[33]

Thanks to globetrotting intermediaries such as Jacques de Coutre, it is no wonder so many Colombian emeralds ended up in India so quickly after their discovery. Still, as Benjamin Teensma has observed, there were profound things about India Coutre clearly did not understand:

[Gems] are subject to their own trade-ethic and gift-custom. Such codes were very different in Europe to what they were in Asia, and on various occasions de Coutre shows that he had an insufficient appreciation of the principles which prevailed in the Indian subcontinent in his day. He was unable to let go of the straightforward European principle that sale was sale and price was price, and this was very unwise for a purveyor to the court in Asia, as royal favour could only bring advantages in the long run. From the point of view of a ruler or a prince it was unthinkable that the subtle hint that he thought something beautiful or wished to possess it would not immediately be followed by the appropriate handing over of the gift. Such a person was unmannerly and should be corrected.[34]

In this world of lavish gifts and seemingly infantile princely urges, tactless European gem dealers like Jacques de Coutre were fortunate to get away with their heads.

As this and the previous chapter have shown, by the turn of the seventeenth century a small group of Sephardim and other Western European gem traders active in Asia had become key vectors in emeralds' steady eastern flow. Some of these merchants, notably the fearless Fleming Jacques de Coutre, penetrated deep into the kingdoms of South and southwestern Asia, hawking emeralds for diamonds and other locally produced luxuries. What men like Coutre learned was not just how to make a profit by exploiting price differences dictated by comparative advantage, political uncertainty or blips in supply and demand, but also how to span – or simply survive falling into – the vast cultural chasm that separated East from West, or at least 'gunpowder emperor' from 'Frankish merchant'.

1 Nadir Shah Bejeweled. This oil portrait of Nadir Shah, attributed to Muhammad Riza Hindi, is thought to date to just after the shah's 1739 sack of Delhi. Nadir Shah kneels piously on a Mughal carpet, a string of pearl prayer beads in his hand. His turban, arms, belt, weapons and flask are adorned with Mughal emeralds and other stones.

2 Topkapi Dagger. Pride of the Treasury of Istanbul's Topkapi Palace Museum, this 35 cm emerald-handled dagger was fashioned on orders of Ottoman Sultan Mahmud I in 1746-47 as a gift to placate Persia's Nadir Shah. In addition to the large emeralds set in the hilt, and the pendant on the scabbard, the dagger has a faceted emerald on top that conceals an English watch.

3 Emerald set in Gold Reptile. Excavated by University of Pennsylvania archaeologist
J. Alden Mason in 1940 from a gravesite at Sitio Conte, along the banks of Panama's Coclé
River near the Pacific coast, this jewel is a very rare example of a Colombian emerald set in
gold in pre-Columbian times. The gravesite is dated to *c.*700-900AD.

4 Llanos or Orinoco Plains from the Mines of Chivor-Somondoco. Looking east from the legendary Somondoco emerald mines of the conquest era is this spectacular view of the Orinoco Plains, described in several early colonial chronicles. Using the Franciscan chronicler Pedro de Aguado's description as a clue, Colombian mining engineer Francisco Restrepo rediscovered the deposits, now known by the name of Chivor, in the 1880s.

5 Habsburg Emerald Cluster. Long known mistakenly as the 'Montezuma Emerald,' this artificial cluster of Muzo and Chivor emeralds was a gift of Spain's Philip II to his Habsburg cousin in Tirol, Archduke Ferdinand II. A similar cluster was sent to Elector Augustus in Dresden by Rudolf II of Prague, later incorporated into a spectacular pearwood statue of a bejeweled black youth (Dresden Grünes Gewölbe VIII 303). Such exotic mineral samples crowded the Kunstkammers, or curiosity cabinets, of many European princes.

6 Modern Muzo and Coscuez Diggings. Thanks to geological quirks, these Colombian mines continue to produce the world's finest emeralds after nearly five centuries of digging. Emeralds occur in carbon-rich shales amid stringers of calcite, iron pyrite, quartz, and other minerals. Many miners rework tailings from underground shafts in the hopes of a lucky strike.

7 Francis Drake's 1586 Attack on Cartagena de Indias. Eyewitness and official cartographer Baptista Boazio rendered this and several other engravings of the 1585-86 Drake expedition to the Caribbean, which accompanied *A summarie and true discourse of Sir Francis Drake's West Indian Voyage*, published in London by Biggs and Croftes in 1588-89. Cartagena's elite women offered the great corsair hoards of emerald-and-gold jewellery to ransom the city.

8 Emeralds from the Wreck of the *Atocha*. Discovered off the Florida Keys by Mel Fisher and his team of salvage divers beginning in the 1980s, these Colombian emeralds were destined for Seville when the galleon *Our Lady of Atocha* sank in a hurricane in 1622. None was mentioned in a copy of the Atocha's manifest that survived aboard another vessel.

9 Inquisition Office and Torture Wrack, Cartagena de Indias. Established in 1610 in Cartagena, the Holy Office of the Inquisition spent its first fifty years or so persecuting alleged crypto-Jews, among them the city's wealthiest slave traders and dry goods merchants. It is among the confiscated goods – and correspondence – of several Portuguese Jews and New Christians that emeralds appear.

10 Cheapside Emerald Watch. Pièce de résistance of the famous Cheapside Hoard of Elizabethan and Jacobean jewellery discovered by London demolition workers in 1912, this emerald watch casing is among the few early modern western jewels to match the ostentation of the Mughals and Ottomans. The *c.*1600 watch mechanism is signed by Geneva master G. Ferlite. The watch's hexagonal shape is likely close to the original crystal form.

11 Emperor Jahangir Wearing a Tie-Dyed Patka, *c*.1620. Jahangir, arguably Mughal
India's most jewel-loving monarch, is painted here in full regalia, including emerald-pearl-
and-ruby prayer beads around the neck and turban. This masterfully rendered watercolour
miniature is by the court artist Balchand, who began his career under Akbar and continued
painting under Shah Jahan.

12 Emerald Prayer Bead Necklace and Floral Centrepiece. Comprised of 77 carved and polished emerald beads of highest quality, and weighing in all 518.8 carats, this rosary was probably worn by Jahangir or Shah Jahan. The deep-green, floral-patterned carved emerald centrepiece, weighing 161.2 carats and measuring 38 x 43 x 14 mm, is thought to date to the reign of Jahangir.

13 Inscribed Emerald Cup and Centrepiece. This small Mughal emerald cup, 41 mm high and weighing 252 carats, was inscribed with Persian verses by a court calligrapher using a diamond stylus. This beautifully coloured 85.6 carat rectangular centrepiece, measuring 29 x 34 mm, is inscribed with the Throne Verse from the Qur'an (2:255).

14 Lady with a Lotus Petal, *c.*1750-60. This delicate, late-Mughal portrait of an unknown lady shows how, over time, elite Indian women's jewellery began to incorporate more emeralds. The carved emerald bird turban ornament resembles surviving ones in the al-Sabah Collection, Kuwait.

15 Emerald Centrepiece Inscribed with Shii Prayer. Said to date to 1695, near the end of the reign of Mughal emperor Aurangzeb, this intricately carved 217.8 carat stone would have been sewn into a ritual garment as a protective amulet. The inscription is a Shii invocation in praise of the Twelve Imams.

16 Coscuez Miner Temístocles Reasgos with Gem Rough. Mining emeralds in Coscuez, Colombia, is still a hardscrabble business, but modest strikes are still had.

❖

CHAPTER 6

Emeralds of the Shahs

A s Jacques de Coutre's adventures suggest, Europeans were getting a taste not only of the wealth but also the tremendous power of Asia's gunpowder empires in their heyday. Coutre was not unique. Catholic missionaries, most of them Iberians and Italians, had long sought the ears of Asian sultans and shahs, particularly those of Mughal India and Safavid Persia. Embassies sent by the newly chartered trading companies of Protestant Europe followed closely on their heels. Indeed, in the years around 1600 the courts of the Mughal Akbar and Persia's Shah Abbas I were veritable hives of European activity, and the atmosphere of relative openness if not embrace continued for many decades after their deaths.

Ottoman sultans were sometimes less welcoming in these years to Iberian representatives, tied as most were to the enemy Habsburgs, but other foreigners, Christian, Jewish and otherwise, were not harassed. The French had allied with the Ottomans in 1535 against Charles V, and the legacy of this friendship endured. In general, merchants and diplomats, whether from France, the Netherlands, England, Russia or elsewhere, had little trouble finding safe passage through Ottoman lands. As noted in the last chapter, Venice's relationship with the Porte was often tense and occasionally explosive, but for the most part Venetian merchants were as mobile as Armenians and Moroccan

Sephardim. All members of these various trading diasporas exploited far-flung family and co-religionist networks.

Travel was nevertheless dangerous, all the more so when one trafficked in glimmering compact valuables. Pirates roved both the Mediterranean and Afrasian seas, and Bedouin and other bandit-nomads regularly attacked sojourners in the mountains and deserts of Syria. Some gem merchants were thus happy to join ambassadorial missions such as those sent by England's Levant and East India Companies around the turn of the seventeenth century. Globetrotting hangers-on frequently offered their services as interpreters, not just of languages, but also cultures. Men such as England's Robert Sherley and Thomas Roe soon discovered that before initiating trade concessions 'gunpowder emperors' demanded substantial gifts, including emeralds and other gems and jewels. How emeralds got sucked into the gift economies of South and southwestern Asia, and what this might have meant locally, are the subjects of this chapter.

Heirs of the Peacock Throne

On Thursday the twenty-second [2 December 1607], at Asaf Khan's request, I went to his house with the ladies of the harem and spent the night. The next day he presented his offerings for my approval. He had assembled ten *lacs* of rupees' worth of gems, jeweled utensils, textiles, elephants, and horses. Several rubies and emeralds, a couple of pearls, a few pieces of cloth, and several items of Central Asian and Chinese porcelain were accepted, but I gave the rest back to him.[1]—Jahangir Shah, Mughal Emperor of India

The Indian subcontinent has been the world's greatest gem producer, and gem consumer, since remote antiquity. Yet it was only in the early modern period, with the rise of the Mughals, that this jewelled opulence included substantial emeralds. Earlier Brahmanic and Islamic princes had employed low-quality Egyptian stones, and perhaps also green sapphires from Burma or Thailand, until the

Egyptian source was exhausted in late medieval times. Afghani and Pakistani emeralds also circulated on occasion, but were not actively mined as far as we know. With the rise of the Mughals, desire for emeralds grew, only to be satisfied by the arrival of Colombian stones in the later sixteenth century.

The beginnings of the Mughal Empire, which came to rule much of South Asia until the British inland invasions of the late eighteenth century, are usually traced to the rise of Babur (r. 1494–1530), an able warlord who commanded a large following of mounted fighters. Guns copied or imported from Europe aided and sped Babur's conquests, a fact that led Marshall Hodgson to regard the Mughals as the archetypal gunpowder empire.

Babur, a staunch Muslim and descendant of Timur, entered India from Afghanistan. His principal motive seems to have been booty rather than converts, since much of the Gangetic Plain region he eventually conquered was ruled by Muslim princes. The invaders' Turkic language survived in spoken form, but the official language of the Mughal court was Persian, tongue of poets and sages. Arabic was, of course, also required as it was the language of the Prophet and the sacred Qur'an.

It was not until the reign of Babur's grandson, later known as Akbar (literally 'the Great', r. 1556–1605) that the Mughal court came to be associated with opulent display of wealth. A contemporary of Ottoman Turkey's Suleiman the Magnificent, Habsburg Spain's Philip II and England's Elizabeth I, Akbar was as much a thinker as he was a conqueror. Surrounded by subjects and visitors of diverse religions and intellectual traditions, Akbar sought to minimize friction – and probably also make a name for himself – by creating his own hybrid faith.

Akbar's religion never took hold, but the sheer audacity of inventing one, plus the emperor's ruthlessly penetrating intelligence, stunned visitors. Akbar received numerous Europeans at his court, including Catholic priests and Protestant diplomats, but he remained aloof in the face of their attempts to impress him. Akbar was quite austere in his personal tastes, and always showed more interest in guns than jewels. Although illustrations show bejewelled female dancers and well-clad men, the *Akbarnama*, one of several contemporary chronicles, has little to say about gem consumption.[2]

The Mughal court took on a different character under Akbar's son by a Hindu princess, Jahangir (r. 1605–27). More hedonist than conqueror, Emperor Jahangir spent most of his roughly twenty-year reign hunting and relaxing with his harem. Despite his apparently sincere faith, he was an admittedly prodigious wine drinker and daily consumer of opium. Few of India's delights were unknown to him, and he frequently commented on the seductive charm of the subcontinent's female dancers. Despite his habits, Jahangir managed to be a capable administrator and reformer, and was generally loved and respected. He carried on his father Akbar's tradition of religious tolerance, but did not propagate the old man's proposed syncretic faith. Most of what we know about this often self-critical Muslim emperor's reign comes from his autobiographical memoir, the *Jahangirnama*.[3]

Like many Asiatic Muslim princes, Jahangir spent considerable time giving and receiving gifts – all of which he recorded in exquisite detail to demonstrate, or measure, his magnanimity. One of the most common gifts was the Islamic rosary, or string of prayer beads (*tasbih*). Many portraits of Jahangir show him sporting such strings, usually made from pearls, but often interspersed with emeralds and rubies (Plate 11). Some are entirely of emeralds. Similar strands adorn his turban, and also that of his favourite son, Prince Khurram, the future Shah Jahan. Some of these rosaries were part of gift assemblages presented on special occasions by subordinates.

In August 1608, for example, the emperor received pearl prayer beads from his former tutor, along with 'several rubies and emeralds' valued at 300,000 rupees (a rupee was worth about half a silver piece of eight).[4] Another visitor, about to take charge of a military campaign in August 1618, offered the emperor a string of prayer beads worth 2,000 rupees, apparently all made of emeralds.[5] In a portrait from about 1625 Jahangir wears just such a necklace, a similar example of which survives in the al-Sabah collection of the Kuwait National Museum (Plate 12).[6] Just as often, Jahangir notes giving pearl-and-emerald rosaries to others, and offering and receiving loose stones of many sizes and types.

Emeralds were incorprated into a wide variety of jewelled artefacts presented as gifts, and some exceptional stones were carved into free-standing items (Plate 13). Jahangir records numerous instances of giving jewel-studded swords, daggers, pen cases, inkpots, quivers, saddles and other such gifts to trusted commanders and bureaucrats. Many surviving examples from the period now scattered among museum collections contain numerous stones, mostly emeralds and spinel rubies. Just as important were 'robes of honour' and other textiles, and often fine riding horses. Substantial gifts of cash were also common, sometimes presented with great ceremony to men and women of rank and to others who were then expected to distribute them to the poor. Jahangir also gave and received emerald rings on more than one occasion.[7] An emerald signet ring engraved with the emperor's name is in the collection of the Victoria and Albert Museum in London, and another large stone inscribed with his name was incorporated into Iran's famous gem-studded globe.[8]

Jahangir enjoyed displaying his wealth. After arranging a ride for the emperor in a specially imported English carriage drawn by four horses, ambassador Sir Thomas Roe, hoping to advance the interests of the fledgling English East India Company, described Jahangir's 1616 departure from Ajmer (near Jaipur) as follows:

Then the King descended the stayres with such an acclamation of 'health to the King' [*Padshah salamat*] as would have out cryed cannons. At the stayres foote, wher I mett him, and shuffled to be next, one brought a mighty carp; another a dish of white stuff like starch, into which hee put his finger, and touched the fish and so rubd it on his forhead, a ceremony used presaging good fortune. Then a nother came and buckled on his sword and buckler, sett all over with great diamonds and rubyes, the belts of gould suteable. A nother hung on his quiver with 30 arrowes and his bow in a case, the same that was presented by the Persian ambassador. On his head he wore a rich turbant with a plume of herne tops, not many but long; on one side hung a ruby unsett, as big as a walnutt; on the other syde a diamond as great; in the middle an emralld like a heart, much bigger. His shash was wreathed about with a chayne of great pearle, rubyes, and diamonds drild. About his neck hee carried a chaine of most excellent pearle, three double (so great I never saw); at his elbowes, armletts sett with diamonds; and on his wrists three rows of several sorts. His hands bare, but almost on every finger a ring. . . .[9]

Jahangir prized emeralds, clearly, in this and other instances suggesting symbolic pride of place, but in truth he was no more interested in them than in diamonds, pearls or rubies.

In his official memoir, Jahangir remarks at some length on the quality of diamonds produced by mines under his control, and briefly describes unusual rubies and, to a lesser extent, pearls. William Hawkins, the English East India Company's first representative at Agra, offered an assessment of Jahangir's jewels around 1610 that seems to have been based on a royal account. He estimated the gross weight of the emperor's emerald holdings at 412½ English pounds. Diamonds above 2½ carats totalled some 124 pounds, rubies at least 164 pounds, and pearls some 990 pounds.[10] Although always fascinated by nature's oddities, including lemurs from Madagascar and the American turkey, Mughal rulers such as Jahangir did not generally share their European contemporaries' taste for baroque, or odd-shaped pearls; perfectly round ones were still best.

On the matter of emerald origins, Jahangir was familiar with the 'old mine/new mine' (or, as Roe put it, 'old rock/new rock') nomenclature that grew up around emeralds in India after the arrival of Europeans and their Colombian stones in the sixteenth century. On receiving a gift from a visiting prince in 1616, Jahangir counted among the treasures 'old emeralds fashioned in a peculiar shape', along with some 'European carnelians'.[11] These gems, brought to the court by a *sayyid*, or direct descendant of the Prophet, were appraised by the emperor's jewellers at 50,000 rupees. In October 1617 Jahangir received a substantial offering of gems from his son, the future Shah

Jahan, that included an emerald given him as tribute by the Adil Khan, ruler of Bijapur. Jahangir described this stone, which had likely arrived from Colombia via Goa, thus: 'Although it is from a new mine, it is of extremely good color and valuable. Until now nothing like it has been seen.'[12]

Even more Colombian emeralds were consumed in India under Jahangir's son, Shah Jahan (1592–1666, r. 1628–58). Most famous for commissioning the Taj Mahal, Shah Jahan was described by numerous foreign visitors as the richest monarch on earth. As the French gem trader Jean-Baptiste Tavernier noted after a visit to Agra in about 1648, he had tastes to match:

> On the side [of the temple at Agra] overlooking the river there is a projecting Divan or belvedere, where the Emperor comes to sit when he wishes to enjoy the pleasure of seeing his brigantines, and making his elephants fight. In front of this Divan there is a gallery which serves as a vestibule, and the design of Shah Jahan was to cover it throughout with a trellis of rubies and emeralds, which would represent, after nature, grapes green and commencing to become red; but this design, which made a great noise throughout the world, required more wealth than he had been able to furnish, and remains unfinished, having only two or three wreaths of gold with their leaves, as all the rest ought to be, and enamelled in their natural colours, emeralds, rubies, and garnets making the grapes.[13]

In the official chronicle of Shah Jahan's reign, the *Shah jahan ama*, emeralds are explicitly mentioned more than twenty times, nearly always in the context of royal gift giving. Many of the most opulent gifts were to Shah Jahan's favoured sons. In June 1633, fifteen-year-old Prince Muhammad Aurangzeb was weighed according to custom, and the gold he displaced distributed as charity. Shah Jahan then presented the prince with a number of gifts, including a dagger, a matching shield-and-spear set, an armlet, a turban ornament (*sarpech*) and 'a rosary of pearls embellished with rubies and emeralds'.[14]

For Prince Aurangzeb's wedding in 1636, Shah Jahan placed 'a tiara of pearls, strung with rubies and emeralds, on the brow of that noble youth'. On his promotion and first dispatch to the Deccan in 1637, Aurangzeb was given, among other things, 'a sarpech of priceless pearls and emeralds'. A similar send-off occurred in 1640, again with emeralds noted among the gifts, and another in 1647. At a promotion in 1652 Aurangzeb received from his father 'an armlet studded with rubies, pearls, and a single emerald'. While conquering Golconda in 1656 Aurangzeb was given a variety of gems by a subordinate, Mir Jumla, including 'a rough diamond, two rubies, nine emeralds, a sapphire, and sixty pearls'.[15]

Similar gifts were given to Shah Jahan's other most important son, Sultan Sulaiman Shikoh, but clearly it was the chosen heir Aurangzeb who got the most. The stones tended to add up. Of the emeralds incorporated into the fabled Peacock Throne at Aurangzeb's court in 1665, gem dealer Jean-Baptiste Tavernier offered this: 'As for the emeralds, there are plenty of good colour, but they have many flaws; the largest may weigh 60 carats, and the least 30 carats. I counted about 116; thus there are more emeralds than rubies.'[16]

As in the reign of Jahangir, these great, showy exchanges and bestowals of gems and jewel-studded items, usually along with fine horses and elephants, and sometimes textiles, were an almost daily event to judge from surviving chronicles. To celebrate the Shah Jahan's forty-fifth lunar birthday in 1635, a gift of 160 rubies, 250 emeralds, a female elephant, several gold items and fine fabrics were sent to Nazar Muhammad Khan, this in exchange for a similar range of items the emperor had received from the same subordinate. On Shah Jahan's sixty-second solar birthday, in 1654, he gave a subject prince a variety of jewelled items, plus 'a superb ruby and emerald'.[17]

Some gifts celebrated submission. In 1636, when the Adil Khan of Bijapur accepted Shah Jahan's authority, he too was given a sword and other items containing emeralds, pearls and rubies. Emeralds figured again among the emperor's gifts to the Adil Shah in 1649. Faithful civil servants, such as one Manji, *zamindar* of Chanda, who visited the emperor in 1653, were granted unset emeralds along with pearls, jewellery, fine robes and horses. A rare gift from 1654 consisted of a bezoar stone armlet surrounded by emeralds, rubies, sapphires and pearls. Like many Europeans of the time, Shah Jahan believed the bezoar stone to be a powerful aid against illness, in this case a sort of prophylaxis against a plague said to 'frequently prevail at Istanbul'.[18] The gift was sent to the Qaisar of the subordinate district of Rum.

The Meaning of Mughal Emeralds

The chronicles of the Mughal emperors challenge Western assumptions about power in several ways. First, they dwell less on war and celebration of victories – or even daily dispensation of justice – than on rites of passage. Second, they constantly record, in loving and precise detail, the incessant giving and receiving of exquisitely useless gifts. Emeralds, like pearls, rubies, diamonds and even elephants, were necessary only inasmuch as they served as symbols of power: exotic, colourful, outsized markers of magnanimity – and divinity.

That so many rare and precious things circulated so widely, and were given in such quantities, suggests not an economy of regal, despotic hoarding, as at least some European visitors – including keen observers such as Jacques de Coutre and Niccolao Manucci – tended to portray it, but of profligate philanthropy. A Mughal emerald was not only invested with the power of Allah, but also the extraordinary 'solar' charisma of the emperor, the undisputed 'King of the World'. Emerald gifts from the shah himself were like bits of life's verdant essence bestowed by the sun. They symbolized, perhaps better than any other material gift, the divine origins of kingship. (In this they almost echoed the seminal and solar meanings ascribed by the pre-Columbian Muiscas.)

As Harbans Mukhia has argued, the long tradition of royal gift giving was of central importance among the Mughal emperors for several reasons. First was the great man's need to prove himself a generous war captain, that is, to hand out booty to cement the loyalties of subordinates who aided him in martial exploits. As Dirk Kolff has shown, this was demanded of all descendants of Central Asian raiders.[19] Second was the urge (nearly mirroring baroque Catholic tendencies at this time) to give so as to visibly measure religious piety, to carry Islam's dictates of charity to unheard-of extremes that could be witnessed publicly and recorded. Thus, beginning with Akbar, a cult of royal selflessness combined with the redistributive urges of the mounted warrior arose to produce an almost potlatch-like atmosphere at court. As the chronicle of Shah Jahan suggests, this tradition of profligate giving did not diminish with time.

Yet as Shah Jahan's chronicle also shows, it was not always better to give than to receive. Indeed, there was another key aspect of royal prestations that emerges in the histories, what Mukhia calls 'the giving of gifts as an acknowledgement of status difference'.[20] As the late Annemarie Schimmel noted, each 'mogul' differed in his habits, yet from Akbar's time forward the receipt of jewelled gifts from subordinates was also mandated, either as they visited him or he visited them.[21] The gifts they gave were intended to demonstrate, and therefore clarify, their status, yet it was the emperor who finally decided what was appropriate. He reserved the right to refuse gifts. No one did this more artfully than Jahangir, who proved that royal generosity could also be expressed by denying extravagant gifts – because in giving them back he became the giver. Both civil servants and noble warriors knew their place as a result.

Tavernier relates numerous incidents of exchange with Mughal royalty that were carried out more in the manner of ritual prestation than sale. For example, in a 1666 visit to Emperor Aurangzeb's uncle, then the Nawab or governor of Bengal in Dacca, Tavernier states he 'went to salute the Nawab, and presented him with a mantle of gold brocade, with a grand golden lace of "point d'Espagne" round it, and a fine scarf of gold and silver of the same "point", and a jewel consisting of a very beautiful emerald'.[22]

There was no talk of price, and Tavernier received in return delicate foods and lodging, then sent more 'gifts', including a fine watch and a brace of silver-inlaid pistols, all things together valued by him at five thousand *livres*. Only later, and through an intermediary, did the nawab approve a letter of credit. Even this was not honoured, however, sparking a long discussion by Tavernier of the critical importance of bringing lavish gifts that would not in the end be compensated. Such were the 'start-up costs' of the South Asian jewel business for those wanting to stick around.

Of Aurangzeb himself (r. 1666–1707), Tavernier says that the austere and pious successor of Shah Jahan – and last great Mughal – much preferred gold and silver to gemstones. We know from other sources that he severely curtailed court patronage of architecture and the arts, but the Venetian amateur court physician Niccolao Manucci, who spent most of his long life in India, maintained that gems and jewels continued to be bestowed on the women of Aurangzeb's harem. Manucci offers a rare window on the meaning of gems among Mughal court women:

> The latter make it one of their diversions to examine and show to others their jewellery. But they have their reasons for this; for I have noticed several times myself when introduced into the rooms of these ladies, they having asserted that they had some reason for consulting me, that they often caused their ornaments and jewels to be brought, solely as an opening for a conversation. The things are brought on trays of gold. They would inquire from me their virtues and properties, and make other similar remarks. During this time I had sufficient leisure to examine them, and I may say I have seen every sort of stone, some of an extraordinary size, and strings of pearls very equal in size, which at the first start I often took for various kinds of fruit. . . . They wear these necklaces of jewels like scarves, on both shoulders. . . . In their ears are valuable stones, round the neck large pearls or strings of precious stones, and over these a valuable ornament having in its centre a big diamond, ruby, or emerald, or sapphire, and round it huge pearls. . . .[23]

Manucci suggests this female jewelled opulence was accepted as customary by Aurangzeb, despite his own personal austerity, but he also hints at its central function in the larger court drama: 'These queens and princesses . . . live in this way, with no cares or anxieties, occupying themselves with nothing beyond displaying great show and magnificence, an imposing and majestuous bearing, or making themselves attractive, getting talked about in the world, and pleasing the king.'[24] Display aside, jewels, as in the West, formed an integral part of Indian women's capital savings (Plate 14).

Aurangzeb, according to Manucci, wore almost no jewellery, '. . . nothing but a small plume or aigrette in the middle of his turban and a large precious stone in front; on his stomach another'. Surviving portraits bear this out. One at the British Library depicts the shah in old age with a large ruby ornamenting his turban and an emerald hanging from a necklace above his belly. Manucci continues: 'All the stones he wears have special names, almost always taken from some planet, such as the sun, the moon, or that of a star, or other similar names, such as he judges appropriate.' Emeralds were probably slotted into an astrological system of meanings, but Mughal emperors named everything they owned, including siege cannons. Many women of Aurangzeb's harem were given the names Diamond, Pearl, or Ruby, but not Emerald (*Samarad*). Only one eunuch was given this name.[25]

Among male merchants, princes and diplomats, the established custom of gift-giving kept gems and jewelled objects in circulation. According to Tavernier, just before any festival in his honour, Aurangzeb 'sends out of his treasury numerous diamonds, rubies, emeralds, and pearls, which the controller of the jewels entrusts to several merchants for sale to the nobles, who are bound to make presents to the emperor, and in this manner the emperor receives both the money and his jewels together'.[26] If Tavernier can be trusted, Aurangzeb had learnt to collapse the noble joys of giving and receiving into one simple transaction.

The situation was made worse still, according to Tavernier, by Aurangzeb's appointment of three court gem inspectors who 'do not neglect to extort all they can [from the merchant] in order to ruin him'. Pressures included bribes, gifts and forced adherence to deliberately low appraisal rates established by specialists in each type of stone. In a 1665 visit to Aurangzeb's court, Tavernier states he dispensed 23,187 *livres*' worth of gifts, including an emerald and ruby-encrusted Turkish saddle, 'a watch having a golden case covered with small emeralds' and 'a battle mace of rock crystal, all the sides of which were covered with rubies and emeralds inlaid in gold in the crystal'.[27] Several of these gifts were not for the emperor or his next of kin but for various court stewards and officials. For newcomers Tavernier offered this warning: 'So true it is that those who desire to do business at the courts of the Princes, in Turkey as well as in Persia and India, should not attempt to commence anything unless they have considerable presents ready prepared, and almost always an open purse for divers officers of trust of whose services they have need.'[28]

As Mukhia explains, an elaborate etiquette grew up around each of these diverse forms of gift giving, and with them the custom among the highest elites to ask for specific items. Some such luxuries, including elephants, dogs and fine gems, circulated among the Mughals, the Safavids and even the Ottomans. Shah Abbas I of Persia, for example, gave Jahangir an especially fine ruby, which he then passed on to his son, Shah Jahan.[29] As already noted at the beginning of this book, the legendary emerald-studded Topkapi Dagger, now on display in Istanbul, was another such item. It was dispatched by Ottoman Sultan Mahmud I to Iran's Nadir Shah in 1747, only to be brought back upon news of the latter's assassination. As previously discussed, Nadir Shah was so fond of Mughal emeralds he hoarded them like eggs following his 1739 sack of Delhi, although he did pass on a few to Tsarina Elizabeth of Russia in 1741.

Emeralds were of great importance to the Mughals from at least Jahangir's reign, but most significant of the emperor's gifts was the 'robe of honour', or *khila't*. This was in essence an extension of the emperor's skin, and 'wearing his coat' was to share in the resplendant glory of his divine charisma. Some such garments had emeralds sewn into them as protective amulets, often inscribed with the Throne Verse from the Qur'an (*Sura* 2: 255, Plate 13, or, in one case, a Shi'i prayer (plate 15).[30] Others were fastened with emerald-encrusted belts. Perhaps the most valuable emeralds, as far as the emperors were concerned, were those contained in the *sarpech* and *jiqa*-type turban ornaments, a number of which have survived in private collections.[31] Emperors wore the very finest ones, but they also gave them as gifts to nobles and high-ranking civil servants. They were only to be worn on Sundays.

Silks and Stones: the Safavids

Of Asia's three gunpowder empires, Iran under the Safavid dynasty remains the most enigmatic. Despite the extraordinary cachet of the Persian language – considered almost sacred by the more powerful Ottomans and Mughals – and the presence of court historians, poets and bards, the Safavid documentary record is somewhat thin by comparison with its neighbours. Outside observers were also fewer in Persia than in Turkey or India, and their surviving observations on the whole were less pithy. The dynasty's earlier and more sudden fall also hindered the survival of written records.

An exception to this rule is Eskandar Monshi's extraordinary history of the reign of Shah Abbas I (1587–1629), which compares well with the court chronicles of the Mughals.[32] Monshi unfortunately has little to say about exchanges – or pillage – of jewelled treasures. His great obsession is battles. An exception is Shah Abbas's receipt of a jewel-studded sword sent by the Mughal emperor Akbar with an ambassador during the shah's 1603 siege of Erevan. According to Monshi, 'The gift of a sword, coming at this particular time from a descendant of Timur, who had always triumphed over his Indian and Afghan enemies, was hailed as a happy augury of the Shah's ultimate victory in Azerbaijan and Sirvan.' During a break in the siege, Shah Abbas distributed other gifts sent by Akbar to his subordinates. It took three more years to win back Azerbaijan and Sirvan, which Shah Abbas celebrated by bequeathing his entire estate to the Prophet Mohammad, his daughter Fatima and the Twelve Imams. This gift included Chinese porcelain and substantial jewels.[33]

The Safavids' meteoric rise in the sixteenth century roughly coincided with gains and consolidations made by neighbours to the west and south. Like the Ottomans and Mughals, the Safavids had deep roots among the mounted warriors of Central Asia, but beginning with the reign of Shah Ismael in 1503 they set themselves apart by establishing Twelver Shi'ism as the state religion. Their embrace of this more or less indigenous branch of Islam was both profound and flexible. Certain tribal traditions and local customs (such as the consumption of Shiraz's famous wines) were allowed to persist in pragmatic fashion, despite the pressures of Shi'ite clerics. As for tolerance of unbelievers, non-Muslims for the most part lived peacefully in their quarters. In 1598, Shah Abbas I even set aside a large suburb of his new capital city of Isfahan, New Julfa, for Armenian Christians, many of whom were engaged in long-distance trade in gems and other compact valuables.

As Willem Floor and others have shown, Safavid Persia relied not on raiding and pillaging for subsistence and tax income but rather on peaceful overland trade and local artisan production.[34] Both were connected to Persia's ancient role as nexus of the Silk Road. Locally made products included fine textiles and carpets, high quality porcelain and metalwares, as well as agricultural produce such as wine, nuts and fruits. Pearls, as has been noted, came from the empire's satellite possessions in Bahrain. Given Iran's long-distance merchant connections (mostly through resident communities of Armenians, Jews, Banias and Russians) and the ruling dynasty's ceremonial gift exchanges with their prime allies and enemies, the Ottomans and Mughals, Colombian emeralds made their way to the capital of Isfahan by the turn of the seventeenth century. By 1660, a French Capuchin missionary stated that Persian traders sought 'emeralds from the West'.[35]

Such gem and jewel exchanges, official and private, carried on for many years. When the English and Dutch helped Shah Abbas I drive the Portuguese from Hurmuz in 1622, the volume of private gem trading expanded. Whether connected to the famous Cheapside Hoard or not, the story of Gerard Polman, the Dutchman whose treasure collected at Bandar Abbas (Gombroon to the Europeans) was scattered among London jewellers in the mid-1630s, offers just a hint of this thriving trade.

A signed and dated Persian dagger from 1621–22, now at the Hermitage Museum in St Petersburg, has a handle and scabbard encrusted with emeralds, the largest of them inscribed with a sacred verse.[36] The dagger is emblematic of a deeper matter. It was in Persia that Qur'anic exegesis emphasized the Prophet's journey to heaven accompanied by the archangel Gabriel. In heaven's seventh and highest level was found 'The Tree with Emerald Branches', marking the very centre of Paradise and source of the Nile and Euphrates, as well as the heavenly 'milk and honey' rivers, Selsebil and Kawthar. The sacred tree, as *axis mundi*, sprouted on the right-hand side of the Throne of Allah, celebrated in many emerald inscriptions and other artistic works. The scene parallels that of the Tree of Life and related rivers originating in Eden as described in Genesis II: 9–10.[37]

In an account of travels from Venice to Goa and back via the Levant, Iraq and Iran in the years 1671 to 1675, nobleman Ambrosio Bembo (from the family for whom the popular Bembo typeface is named) described several details of the overland gem trade in Safavid Persia and neighbouring territories. Bembo himself lacked the financial resources to engage much in it, but he noted how Persian gem traders hid their stones either in their clothes or inside a hen when searched by Ottoman customs agents near Baghdad in 1674.[38] Bembo also witnessed a thriving gem market in Isfahan, although to him the bazaar was most notable for the abundance of local stones, especially turquoise and lapis lazuli. Bembo encountered substantial communities of Armenian, Indian and other foreign traders in Isfahan, but he most admired the Persians themselves, whose honesty extended even to the jewel trade, in which, he said, 'one can easily be deceived'.[39]

Emeralds and Ottoman Splendour

The early eighteenth-century Topkapi Dagger mentioned at the start of this book is certainly the most famous emerald-encrusted Ottoman jewel, but Turkish interest in Colombian emeralds was at least as old as that of the Mughals and Safavids. Numerous emerald-studded turban ornaments, water flasks, pen cases, quivers and book covers now housed in the Topkapi Palace Museum date back to the sixteenth century, some to the reign of Suleiman the Magnificent, who was trained as a goldsmith. By the eighteenth century, Colombian emeralds were sent not only to placate aggressive neighbours such as Nadir Shah, but also as ex-votos to be displayed in the holy cities of Mecca and Medina.

What did such gifts and display items signify to the Ottomans, or can we know? Art historian Walter Denny has stressed the importance of outsize gems as essential props in an Ottoman theatre of power dating to the reign of Istanbul's conqueror Mehmed II (1451–81). According to Denny, there emerged a carefully choreographed alternation between secrecy and revelation, with the Topkapi palace complex coming to serve some of the functions of Beijing's Forbidden City. The sultan's treasury, like his harem, was intended to inspire awe rather than envy, though inevitably it did both. The sultan's occasional exits from the palace served as revelations, more than confirming the suspicions of his subjects. As Denny describes it:

> On the occasion of his weekly procession to Friday prayers at one of the capital's great Imperial mosques, he rode on horseback in the middle of a long procession of representatives of the military, the palace bureaucracy, and the judiciary – a procession that served as a sort of visual summary and personification of governmental power. The often very large scale of the designs on the sultan's costumes, the huge gems that adorned his mace, his turban ornament, and his ceremonial water flask, the brilliance of the gold and silver workmanship on his sword, and the huge size of his white silk turban, not to mention the opulent costumes, weapons, and trappings of his courtiers and servants, all served to project an image of royal power to the crowds who assembled to see him.[40]

As surviving miniatures and other artefacts suggest, this was court theatre of Alice-in-Wonderland proportions, and it demanded emeralds to match. Subsequent rulers commissioned numerous emerald-studded props. One of these is an extremely elaborate gold water flask from the era of Selim II (1566–74) or Murad III (1574–95), encrusted with more than one hundred emeralds, most of them of unmistakably bright, Muzo colour. An equally stunning mid-eighteenth-century jewel commissioned by Sultan Mustapha III (1757–74) to be sent to Mohammad's tomb at Medina but kept in Istanbul, consists of a huge Muzo emerald crystal set in a gold hanger with an attached seed-pearl tassel.[41] As previously discussed, in 1747 Sultan Mahmud I (1730–54) ordered the emerald-studded Topkapi Dagger made for his increasingly dangerous neighbour in Persia, Nadir Shah.[42] Luckily for theOttoman ruler, the gift rebounded.

As this chapter has shown, the great gunpowder empires of Islamic Asia, particularly Mughal India, but also Safavid Persia and Ottoman Turkey, absorbed considerable quantities of Colombian emeralds – along with many other gems – not so much because there was a 'pure market' for them but because there was a role for them to play in a wide range of gifting rituals and sacred royal dramas. At the least, South American emeralds were little more than expensive mosaic tiles, incorporated alongside rubies and pearls into royal accessories. The very best and biggest ones, however, were reserved for the shahs and sultans themselves as religious talismans, frequently carved with verses from the Qur'an and sewn into sacred garments and headdresses. Such centrepiece emeralds, combined with prayer beads and turban ornaments, constituted a kind of royal armour. If green was the colour of Paradise, then it must also be the colour of power.

❖

CHAPTER 7

Tax Dodgers and Smugglers

A s chance would have it, rising Asian demand for Colombian emeralds coincided with the decline of the Spanish Habsburgs, whose own gunpowder empire proved nearly as fragile as that of the Mughals. The rebellion of Portugal in 1640 and final capitulation in the Netherlands in 1648 signalled the end of a remarkable era of global maritime dominance. Dutch gains at the Iberians' expense began much earlier and reached as far as Manila, but they avalanched after the Twelve Year Truce expired in 1621. Portuguese trading forts from Elmina to Melaka fell to Dutch cannons, and by 1637 much of Brazil was governed not by the King of Spain or Portugal but by Prince John Maurice of Nassau.

Spanish America felt the Dutch lash, too, as the West India Company corsair Piet Heyn and his followers made off with millions in Mexican and Peruvian silver in 1628. Plunder, as in other contemporary gunpowder empires, was only the first step in Holland's larger imperial project. Primitive accumulation of this spectacular (and humiliating) kind was followed by the more mundane business of bulk trade. Protected by a steady stream of company-sponsored gunships, merchants set up shop on sun-baked Curaçao, spitting distance from the Spanish Main. In the River Plate district, Dutch contraband slavers drank up Potosí silver and sent it to Amsterdam, where it was repacked for Asia.

For a time it seemed the Iberians could not win. Yet it is crucial to remember that despite all this gunpowder-fuelled rearranging of global sea power, Dutch attacks and colonization schemes fell well short of eliminating the Iberians and their colonies. Indeed, as the costs of seaborne empire-making mounted, the never numerous Dutch settled into a kind of parasitical equilibrium with their old foes. Hispanic colonists from New Granada to Manila collaborated as frequently as they fought, preferring to devote their energies to contraband trade rather than defence.

Growing military and commercial attacks on Habsburg power had manifold repercussions in the Spanish American colonies. Creole elites gained a measure of autonomy as Crown authority weakened. Corruption flourished as state revenues were redirected to build family dynasties. Baroque anxieties fuelled religious donations, which in turn funded enormous church-building and frontier missionary projects. Meanwhile, many indigenous populations bottomed out, only to begin a slow recovery. Some just disappeared. In the hot lowlands of New Granada, the void left by extinct peoples such as the Muzos was increasingly filled by Africans and mixed people of colour.

As described at the end of Chapter 3, the emerald mines of Muzo were in crisis by the time of the Portuguese Revolt of 1640. The great 1646 earthquake seemed almost to seal their fate. Yet as this chapter will show, long-ignored Colombian and Spanish documents hint at a slow but steady seventeenth-century revival in Muzo. As early as the 1650s, new finds sparked growth, reviving the old impulses to commit fraud and engage in contraband trade. Word of these practices in turn drew government attention.

Fraud investigations beginning around 1660 reveal how merchants had wormed their way into the mines from both Bogotá and Cartagena, buying up emeralds in exchange for slaves and luxury goods. Mine owners hid their yields from Crown officials, or sought to buy their silence. Gem cutters and mineworkers, too, some of them slaves, established new underground trading networks. What many of these enterprising individuals and clans failed to realize was that Habsburg Spain was a weakened, even humiliated, beast, but hardly a dead one. The imperial bureaucracy still had teeth, usually in the form of careerist martinets, but sometimes also activist courts with Crown support. When they felt the urge, these magistrates and judges could in an instant shred a vibrant and far-reaching trading web established over decades.

New Granada's ties to global trade were nevertheless forever changed after Dutch refugees from Brazil settled in Curaçao in 1654 and the English seized Jamaica in 1655. Once Muzo emeralds reached the Caribbean coast, they entered a zone of near-free trade, picked up by foreign slavers and contrabandists. Many of those who bought and resold Muzo stones on Curaçao or Jamaica were from the same Sephardic families driven from the Luso-Hispanic world by the Inquisition. Some Ashkenazim also joined the mix, and a few Jewish families found refuge in French St Domingue, Martinique and Cayenne. Many of the stones we can trace were sent to factors in Amsterdam, as discussed in previous chapters, but increasingly they went to London, where they hitched rides on East India Company vessels carrying Spanish silver and Mediterranean coral to Madras to trade for diamonds. Though still easily smuggled, Colombian emeralds show up frequently in ships' manifests as registered cargo by the early eighteenth century.

Muzo's Baroque Revival

Local tax records suggest that even before the 1646 earthquake, Muzo's wealthier families had shifted their assets to cattle-raising and small-scale sugar production. Instead of mines and shops being sold on a more or less regular basis, sale documents show it was *estancias*, or farming plots and pastures, and *trapiches*, or crude, ox-driven sugar-cane mills. A few sales of enslaved Africans were also noted, but without specific mention of mining as their chief occupation. The cloth industry of the late sixteenth and early seventeenth centuries was abandoned for lack of hands. Yet even as the once-feared indigenous

Muzo population dwindled to extinction, the regional economy was becoming diversified, shifting away from dependence on emerald mining.

Healthy as this product diversification may have been from the perspective of those with something to invest, emeralds were still being produced. According to tax records, these included some rather large and fine ones. A mine purchase was recorded in 1659 after a long hiatus, but it sold for only 30 silver pesos when a modest plot of land sold for 50 pesos, a wheat farm for 80, and a small house in town for 65. A reminder of the value of labourers was the sale of an enslaved African in the same year for 425 silver pesos. That in subsequent years several elite women sold enslaved African women suggests most of the latter were engaged in domestic service rather than mining. As discussed below, however, this was not always true.[1]

On 1 July 1663, Muzo joined many New Granadan mining towns in celebrating the birth of Habsburg Crown Prince Charles Joseph.[2] The misshapen, dim-witted and ultimately sterile prince would rule as Carlos II until his death and Bourbon takeover in 1700, but this unhappy coda to nearly two centuries of Habsburg pre-eminence was not yet evident. Because the good news nearly coincided with the feast of Corpus Christi, a special mass was held to honour the Holy Sacrament, followed by a procession in La Trinidad's main plaza. Three terraces were built, along with four temporary outdoor altars. Music was supplied by bagpipers, an organist and a choir, plus a small army of drummers, fifers and miscellaneous noisemakers.

The local militia head, Field Marshal-General Francisco de Tovar Alvarado, used the occasion to muster followers for his campaign to 'punish the Indians who have withdrawn to the ends of this province'. It is unclear to which Indian 'guerrillas' he was referring, but they were most likely the nomadic Carares of the Middle Magdalena basin, not surviving Muzos. After this proclamation came four days of equestrian games, including jousting with canes and bull-baiting. According to testimony, all of Muzo's elites, including two Inquisition field officers, participated fully, engaging in 'very lucid horsemanship with four squadrons in their costly and varied livery'. Each night ended in a memorable fireworks display, a reminder that gunpowder could also be used for peaceful purposes.

The gaiety of these events was soon to be severely mitigated. It so happened that the whole New Kingdom of Granada was undergoing a general Crown audit between 1657 and 1663, and in charge of the Muzo district was a contraband snoop named Francisco de Useche y Cárdenas. Whereas earlier *visitas* had emphasized (if not corrected) mistreatment of indigenous labourers, this audit obsessively pursued allegations of sales of untaxed emeralds to merchants in Cartagena. The ailing Spanish treasury was, as always, desperate to tap revenue streams, and Muzo's small trickles appeared to have been sneakily diverted.

In his opening comments to Spain's Indies Council, Useche y Cárdenas's boss, Visitor-General Juan de Cornejo, spoke of a strange 'emerald calamity' afflicting the empire. He cited treasury officials in Seville who were perplexed to record the arrival of 'very lucid shipments of this commodity, which is to say emeralds of great value' amid the many chests of private treasure, when the king's share seemed to be only 'a tiny and very limited amount'. On orders from his superior, Useche y Cárdenas wasted no time in trying to get to the bottom of this supply-side 'calamity'.

In Muzo, the auditor took testimonies from many householders, including mine administrators and lapidaries. He apparently assumed these to be the sort of vulnerable people who might tell the truth about their sponsors and clients, imagining it would save their skins. Interestingly, Useche y Cárdenas did not question any women, Amerindians, African or mulatto slaves, or indeed any people of colour. He seemed especially intent to collect testimonies from bona fide *vecinos*, or ranking householders, presumably since these held up best in the status-obsessed Baroque courtroom. The testimonies quickly showed up all the town's main players, which ones were striking it rich, and who resented them for it.

At the pinnacle was Muzo's Field Marshal-General Francisco de Tovar Alvarado, a major emerald producer since the 1640s. Most of his holdings were concentrated in the mines of Cañaveral, part of the old Traza Grande diggings from the first days of discovery. Just below Tovar was Sergeant Major Juan de Poveda, said to own and work mines on the equally venerable Cerro de Miguel Ruiz, in company with the town's parish priest, Bachelor Nicolás Flores. Another powerful mine owner was Alonso Ximénez, said to be the sole boss of the Cerro de Yacopí, famous for emeralds of a distinctly beautiful lustre.

All these men were notable for working their mines with squadrons of enslaved Africans and mulattos. Another old-timer, who had begun as an overseer of African slaves and was now a major mine owner, was Francisco Ovalle. He had claims scattered all over the Muzo district, but his enslaved workers had been most lucky of late in the fabled Peñol de Busto, one of the oldest strikes. It is difficult to account for the sudden upturn in emerald production beginning in the 1650s, but one factor that must be considered, though it would never have been described as such in elite-generated documents, was the rising skill level of both enslaved and free workers in the mines. It was they, individual Africans, Amerindians and their offspring, who are mentioned by name in later fraud documents as having discovered (and often hidden or sold) the biggest and best stones.

Some Muzo mine owners saw their stars rise dramatically thanks to the efforts of their workers. Indeed, a few self-described 'lords of slaves and mines' were literally transformed from rags to riches as a consequence of a lucky strike. One was Francisco de Poveda, a relative of sergeant major Juan and scion of an original Muzo mining family who, with his assistant Juan Beltrán, found his fortune in the mines formerly set aside for the king. He paid a third rather than a fifth of his produce in taxes as a result of this fact, yet still managed to prosper.

Similar was Francisco Pacheco, who after striking it rich entrusted his 'largest and most lucid' stones to Muzo's chief lapidary, Francisco Ruiz. Yet another winner was Diego de Aldana. He and other newly rich mine owners sent their emeralds, raw, cut and set, with roving merchant factors to Cartagena. A smaller number of stones was sent to Bogotá. Merchant factors named in the 1663 inquest included Josef Díaz, Francisco Camero, Josef Salgado and Juan de Arce Penagos. Several, including Arce Penagos, were descendants of the mines' original claimants, some of them conquistadors.

Crown officials wanted to be sure *quintos*, or severance taxes, were being collected, yet they were also interested in other sources of revenue, such as the payment of tribute by indigenous men and free people of whole or part African descent, both male and female. Non-enslaved individuals described as 'mulatto', 'zambo', and 'negro' by colonial officials were assessed an annual tribute throughout New Granada, beginning just before the turn of the seventeenth century. The tax, collected in silver, was initially described as their 'gracious donation' to Spain's chronic war effort, but like many taxes it proved hard to live without once its collection became routine. Taxing free people of colour in cash-starved Muzo unintentionally encouraged 'high-grading' and clandestine emerald sales to procure the needed silver coins.

Of special interest here are two women described in the audit documents as *mulatas* living 'in the mines'. In other testimonies from the 1663 *visita* there were said to be several slave barracks, or *rancherías*, located alongside the Itoco Hill and other diggings. They were described as wattle-and-daub structures with thatched roofs. It is unclear whether the women living in the *rancherías* engaged in mine work directly or only in support tasks such as food preparation, clothes washing or even ore sorting, but there is ample evidence of women of African descent working in all types of mine labour in New Granada in this period.[3]

Úrsula *mulata* lived in the mines with her enslaved black husband, Mateo, and there raised five children: Ana María, Pascuala, Francisca, Dominga and Pedro. Caring for the family was probably more than enough work without taking into account mining. A more likely candidate for female mine labour was Gregoria *mulata*, listed as unmarried and childless. Enslaved African women, not listed here as they were not subject to tribute, were even more likely than free women of colour to be engaged in mine work, and even those who were not assigned to it apparently searched for emeralds following landslides and other chance occurrences. One great slide at the Cañaveral diggings in 1657 was described by local *caudillo* Francisco de Tovar Alvarado:

> The hill had fallen on a Saturday around ten at night according to my majordomo in charge of those mines, but he did not advise me of this until about nine in the morning the following day, Sunday, after which I dispatched him and one of my sons to see what was happening with the slide. There they drove away more than 100 people, including black men, black women, mulattos, mestizos, and Indians, all of whom had been there since five in the morning searching and sifting through what had fallen. I was later advised that these people had made off with great quantities of emerald stones according to popular rumour. I could do nothing to stop this since I was in town, and although Your Majesty suffered a loss of one-fifth, I lost four-fifths.[4]

King's and master's losses were workers' and plebeians' gains thanks to this 'act of God', and Muzo's growing number of free people of colour, male and female, young and old, appear to have known precisely what they were looking for.

Other Muzo elites testified that as in earlier times an underground emerald market thrived among this mixed-race, plebeian class, mostly in 'stolen' or high-graded stones. The first clear use of the term *moralleros*, in this case meaning small-scale raw stone buyers rather than miners, is from a 1655 case when two big strikes occurred in the mines of Cerro Miguel Ruiz. According to testimony, some of these peddlers were free men of colour.

The 1655 strikes occurred during Holy Week, when a group of hired peons working for one Antonio Suárez cleared a terrace, or *banco*, and uncovered a rich vein. It was quickly covered back up, according to law, and an enslaved black man named Francisco was set to guard it until Suárez returned from town with a magistrate to witness the extraction of gem crystals and take a fifth for the king. While in town Suárez heard from a just-arrived 'black *zambo*' who served as mine overseer for a parish priest in the same Cerro Miguel Ruiz that there, too, a rich vein had been struck.

Such a large quantity of 'fat crystals', as one witness called them, was in fact coming out of the second strike that the *moralleros* who had rushed there to trade for stones had quickly run out of money and were hurrying back to La Trinidad to get more. Among those named was one 'mulatto Luis'. He and other informal buyers had abandoned the bull-baiting and other holiday festivities in town to get a piece of the action in the mines.

Those allegedly selling the stones to the *moralleros* included two of the priest's servants at Cerro Miguel Ruiz: 'don Juan Indio, whom they call Tartamudo (The Stutterer)', and 'Francisco Suárez, *mulato*, whom they call Pachango (Chubby)'.[5] Don Juan was later listed as a cacique among 'fugitive Indians' in a 1663 tribute roll and 'Chubby' Francisco Suárez was named son of a free *mulata*, Francisca Suárez of La Trinidad. Given these webs of knowledge and apparent purchasing power among what Crown officals derisively called *la plebe*, it appears the self-styled white elite of Muzo was forced to negotiate with a wide range of social subordinates to hang on to some part of the emerald business.

The Last Bonanza

Tax records through the late 1660s note sales of local products, including raw cotton, maize, beef and sugar syrup (used to make kill-devil rum, or *aguardiente*), and imports from the highlands and neighbouring lowlands, such as salt, cheese, tobacco, jerked beef and ham. Other items were brought to Muzo by travelling merchants with ties to Spain, and included wine, soap, spices and dry goods. Special taxes on sugar syrup and cotton, used to fund Spain's Caribbean anti-pirate navy, the so-called Windward and Gulf of Mexico Fleet, suggest especially heavy emphasis on these agricultural products, perhaps as a more reliable source of income than emeralds. That individual farm owners were registering sales of 20 to 30 *arrobas* (about 275 to 410 kg) of cotton annually suggests something less than plantation agriculture, but clearly more than enough for homespun.

Evidence of a new mining bonanza shows up in Muzo's tax records from 1667, when Captain Diego de Guzmán y Saavedra purchased rights to half of an emerald mine and an enslaved black man. This might not otherwise signal anything, except that Guzmán would soon emerge as a major figure in the brief emerald boom of the 1670s. There would be others. Also in 1667, Antonio Suárez de Alvarado purchased no less than seven emerald mines. It was still a buyer's market, however, as all these (likely moribund) mines were valued together at only 90 silver pesos – not much money when in the same year an 'estancia-and-a-half', plus a cane field and *trapiche* sold for 850 pesos. Land planted with cash crops was still clearly more of a sure thing than a luck-of-the-draw emerald mine.

But in Muzo only mines could make you rich. Further evidence of the return of emeralds shows up in tax records for 1668, when merchant Francisco Pérez's estate was confiscated by royal officials. Pérez, who died intestate, left behind a number of emeralds that appeared not to have been taxed. The stones, that Muzo's mine magistrate affirmed he had never seen or registered, included seven ounces (about one thousand carats) of raw crystals classed as *segunda suerte*, or decent gem-quality material, along with some four-and-a-half pounds 'good' third-class, 'of the type called *morallón*'. More interesting were 165 worked stones, 'among them six small drops, clear to deeply coloured'. Although Muzo's officials did not call it such, they were reporting on contraband trade in polished emeralds very close to the point of production.[6]

By 1670 new finds were shaking up the local labour and real estate markets. In this year Guzmán and his wife Margarita de Riaño sold their cane farm and *trapiche* and purchased five slaves, four men and one woman. The woman, Eugenia, described as *mulata*, was likely going to work either in the mines as a sifter or as a cook in the slaves' quarters nearby. The following year Guzmán and his wife's investment paid off, when they registered a four-and-a-half ounce (about 647-carat) grade-one emerald, which was sold at auction for two thousand silver pesos. This was the highest price registered for a single emerald since the 1570s, suggesting that the stone was truly exceptional. Unlike in early eighteenth-century Brazil, where vigilant diamond sifters could be freed for finding large stones, no credit was given to the enslaved African who found this prized emerald.

Guzmán used this great stone, and more importantly the credit it gave him, to go on a buying spree. He purchased two emerald mines from Muzo's parish priest, then another from a layman, then half a share in a mine of another. The mines cost a total of 540 pesos, suggesting a general climb in the value of pay dirt, but this was still well short of the 1,580-peso cost of the four enslaved men who worked them. Guzmán also used his personal 'emerald futures' to purchase another enslaved African man, unnamed in the sales tax record but no doubt destined to work in the mines. Guzmán and his wife also purchased more arable land, which was always a safer bet than mines or slaves in the long run.[7]

Antonio Suárez de Alvarado, the purchaser of seven mines in 1667, saw his luck improve in 1672, when he registered a grade-one stone that auctioned for 250 pesos. This was well short of Guzmán's great rock, but not a bad return on the 90-peso cost of the mines. Mine sales suddenly became common for the first time in fifty years, and real estate sales in general picked up and rose in value. A half-block lot in La Trinidad with a number of tamped-earth and woven bamboo storefronts sold for 1,440 pesos in 1672. In the same year Crown officials collected tributes from two indigenous men working in the region and one Afro-indigenous man, Francisco Cevillas. It is possible, perhaps even likely, that all three had been brought or drawn to the mines to serve as paid day labourers.

By 1673, Guzmán's son, alderman and captain Enrique de Guzmán, was purchasing grade-one stones produced by others. In 1674, he and his father together purchased a mine for one hundred pesos from Doña Petronila de Figueroa. This would be Don Diego's last investment, as he died later that year. In part as a result of this male tendency to die early, elite women, especially widows, were as prominent in Muzo as in other Spanish colonial towns. Such women were often highly active in the elite market sphere. Brothers Juan and Francisco Vallejo, the former a royal accountant in Muzo, purchased a mine from Doña Juana Flores de Guzmán. In 1677, Doña Juana García sold a mine, and Margarita Flores purchased one. Other women would soon be implicated in fraud investigations.

Suggestion of a lower tier of producers appears in the 1674 record, with a number of mine sales among men without the honourific Don before their names. One frequent seller at this level was Juan Delgado Matajudíos, whose blunt second surname ('Jew-killer') linked him to Muzo's first European settlers. Matajudíos appears to have cashed in on his family's long-moribund holdings on the Cerro de Itoco, where he sold eight mines in quick succession. Most of these second-tier sales were for less than fifty pesos. Another tier of producers was less visible, the *moralleros* or freelance prospector-dealers, although they do appear again in a 1680 inquest. Most indigenous and mixed-race labourers (unlike enslaved Africans) were by 1674 referred to explicitly as *concertados*, or debt-peons, almost certainly forced or tricked into mine work.

The rush tipped off by Captain Diego de Guzmán y Saavedra continued to yield notable emeralds, among them a grade-one stone auctioned for 340 pesos in 1677 and another for 300 in 1679. The former had come from the mines of Captain Juan Ramírez de Poveda, head of a prominent Muzo family, and the latter from the similarly well-situated Doña Ana María Alvarez de Noriega, who had also paid taxes on 140 pesos' worth of high-grade stones in 1678. Also in 1678, tributes were paid by mine owners for *concertados*. Local slave sales for most years are not mentioned in the royal account summaries, although they are mentioned frequently in a series of fraud investigations begun in 1678.

By 1679 a major Crown inquest was well under way, and in 1680 ordinary taxes on emerald production ceased to be recorded. Instead, local elites were charged with more than one thousand pesos in what the new auditor Don Francisco de Vergara Azcarate called 'compositions of emerald quintos'. These were essentially fines on stones that had allegedly gone untaxed and otherwise unregistered since the lucky strike of 1668. Fines continued to mount, and if surviving records are indicative, the Crown's inquest, whatever its intentions, had the effect of strangling a just-resuscitated Muzo.

A New Scandal

Beyond the mines, of course, lay the equally fraught and tangled world of transoceanic trade. What the Crown's 1678–80 fraud investigation reveals here is how things had changed since the expulsion of most of Cartagena's gem-trading New Christian and crypto-Jewish communities by *c.*1650. Some New Christians were no doubt still active in the Spanish colonies, but it appears that a new group of Seville-based merchants had moved into the emerald trade by the late 1660s, if not earlier. A few of these merchants managed to penetrate the Muzo mining zone as well as Bogotá's lapidary-jeweller networks hoping to corner the market by the late 1670s. Of their connections back in Spain I have yet to find details, but documentation of their activities in New Granada is rich. Among other things, it suggests *quinto* records for this period are but a dim reflection of production, especially of best-quality stones.

The case began when charges of tax fraud surfaced in late 1677. Bogotá merchants cut out of too many emerald deals grumbled to royal treasury officials that outsiders were buying up stones and sending them off to Spain untaxed, with 'much concealment'. The value of these emerald packets was said to range from two thousand to twelve thousand silver pesos, significant sums in a place where two thousand pesos bought a fine town house in the capital or a small crew of enslaved Africans. Total sales were said to be in the hundreds of thousands of pesos a year, and it was 'a shame' how the Crown did not benefit. Virtually all of Muzo's mine-owning families, about thirteen of them, were implicated, but investigators also went after 'blacks and other poor folks' said to 'prospect in deserted mines'. They were the ones said to sell stones 'under the cord, hidden'.[8] Priests were also suspects.

Merchants, both creole and peninsular, were examined rigorously, and their sworn testimonies and confiscated papers are revealing. According to merchant correspondence, emerald prices dropped in

Cartagena in the early 1670s, perhaps as a result of the big finds of the late 1660s. Roving and stationary factors wrote to each other complaining of sudden shifts in price, the periodic lack of decent stones and the unreliablity of Spain's transatlantic fleet system. One merchant even wrote that Muzo's mine owners had developed a ruse of their own: they would send news of new discoveries to the coast to attract creditors, then come up empty-handed after accepting money and merchandise. The goods going to Muzo's upper class in exchange for promised emeralds mostly consisted of luxury items such as taffeta, linen and other fine fabrics, but the second most-listed commodity type was East Indian spices: pepper, cinnamon, cloves and cumin.[9] Here at last was evidence of global reciprocity!

As in the past, emerald dealers participated in that more lamentable business associated with Cartagena: the transatlantic slave trade. Several merchants said that it was common practice to exchange slaves for emeralds in Muzo, and one mentioned in a September 1677 letter to a colleague the possibility of directly investing emerald profits in the Spanish slave trade monopoly.[10]

The biggest of the new dealers was one Gerónimo de Estrada of Seville, and he complained in his August 1679 testimony of having advanced a number of slaves (along with an assortment of fine fabrics) to Muzo mine owner Doña Ana María Alvarez de Noriega, and not having received the promised 'top colour' stones in return. Alvarez de Noriega was said to have already supplied Estrada with six thousand pesos' worth of emeralds from mines of Noriega's administered by Jesuits.

We know nothing about these Jesuits, but the possibilities and problems of expanding the ranks of enslaved Africans in Muzo were seemingly on everyone's mind. Merchants spoke of trying to sell young black girls (*negritas*) in the mines, while several owners testified that enslaved African men routinely discovered, and occasionally sold against their masters' wishes, some of the finest and largest stones unearthed in the 1670s.[11]

Other Bogotá-based merchants called to testify included Gerónimo de Estrada's godson, thirty-nine-year-old Juan Márquez

Poyete, along with Josef de Ricaurte, Cristóbal Pantoja, Juan Calvo, Josef Machado, Francisco and Andrés de Grandas (father and son) and Luis Jorge. With the exception of Márquez Poyete, most of these roving factors were not apparently linked to Estrada or other peninsular buyers, who included Antonio de Quesada, Felipe de Velasco and Domingo de Barasorda.

The Bogotá merchants mostly made runs back and forth to Muzo, although a few also mentioned travelling to Cartagena. Márquez Poyete described numerous payments of silver coin to Muzo miners in exchange for stones, as did Pantoja and Ricaurte. Ricaurte's testimony is the only one to give some specifics on price: he stated he had purchased two marks (about 2,300 carats) of grade-one emerald at 350 silver pesos of eight reales per mark (i.e., about $1\frac{1}{2}$ pesos/gram or $2\frac{1}{2}$ reales/carat). His testimony seems to refer to cut stones, as he says he bought 'rough at 180 pesos per mark', but the context is not clear. Whatever the case, most of what Ricaurte gathered he sold to Estrada.[12] If these prices for *primera suerte* emerald are even close to accurate, gains for exporters like Estrada must have been stratospheric.

An Emerald Underworld Revealed

As it was centred in Bogotá, the Crown's investigation also focused on the capital city's small gem-cutting and goldsmithing community. Several lapidaries noted how their work served a number of constituencies, including local elites, religious institutions and overseas markets. Gem cutter and jeweller Lorenzo Herrero testified that some of his pieces had been sold profitably in Madrid by merchant Cristóbal Pantoja.[13] Much finished work from Bogotá, he said, was sent to Cartagena, but because of the big 1677 run on all available raw and finished emeralds in the entire district nothing had been fashioned since. Everything had been scooped up by Gerónimo de Estrada.

One of Estrada's factors was Josef de Ricaurte, owner of the enslaved African lapidary Juan de Argüelles. Forty-nine-year-old Argüelles testified that he had been cutting stones for thirty years following a rigorous apprenticeship and 'perfection' (*perfección*) with his former master, an eighty-eight-year-old goldsmith and stonecutter who shared his name. They had worked together mostly in Bogotá, but lived for a time in Cartagena 'repairing broken stones' for Governor Pedro Zapata. The elder Argüelles had recently retired, but said he had required his enslaved namesake to cut more than one thousand emeralds to learn the trade. The two had occasionally gone to Muzo to buy rough, and also worked together on a large jewelled retable for the Dominican Order's Chapel of the Rosary.[14]

Jewellers Josef Ramos and Felipe López de Torres said they had cut stones or fashioned jewellery on order for Gerónimo de Estrada and other Cartagena merchants. Free mulatto lapidary Josef López de Arias would not name names, but said he had been commissioned to cut both Mariquita amethyst and Muzo emeralds, some in the drop, or 'avocado' form. Several lapidaries said they made trips to Muzo to buy stones occasionally, but more often received them from travelling merchants. Mysterious characters appeared at the edges of this trade. Thirty-three-year-old master jeweller Juan Navarro said he had been commissioned to make a number of emerald-encrusted chokers for a man he knew only as 'The Captive'. He added that he and another jeweller, Fernando Valenzuela, had set some very large stones for a sergeant-major who bought them in Muzo from a now-dead man called 'Big Head' (*Cabezón*). Another Muzo miner was known as *Ojo de Patacón*, or 'Silver-dollar Eye'.[15]

When Gerónimo de Estrada's estate was embargoed in Cartagena in February 1679 he was waiting with his wife and children for the annual fleet to arrive so he could make his way home to Spain. Some six thousand pesos in silver coin were confiscated, 214 marks of worked silver, some gold and emerald jewellery said to belong to his wife, twelve finely worked saddles, and twenty oil paintings. Suspiciously, no loose emeralds were found, cut or rough. Angry that he was suspected of defrauding the Crown, Estrada called on witnesses to testify how he had personally mustered, paid and armed a militia in the Magdalena River port of Mompóx in 1678 to fight

French pirates threatening Cartagena. He then produced receipts for emeralds purchased from the widow Ana María de Noriega and copies of Muzo's own *quinto* records. Despite this, Estrada was ordered to put up a forty thousand-peso bond; a Bogotá merchant, Andrés de Liaño, signed for the sum.[16]

Crown investigators then turned on Muzo's mine owners, forcing them to come up with a seemingly more reasonable 6,000-peso bond. In the event they produced only 4,600 pesos, and complained of 'losing our slave rents'. The biggest miners in the region, Francisco de Tovar Justiniano and Juan Ramírez de Poveda, could offer nothing; their estates had been embargoed since the beginning of the investigation.[17]

Aftermath

In 1681, Crown investigator Francisco de Vergara Azcarate wrote to his superiors of how he hoped to prosecute Muzo's small-scale scavengers and rough dealers, the *moralleros* and *rescatadores*. They practised all sorts of subterfuge, he had discovered, including tossing stones into gullies to be retrieved after the mines closed for the day.[18] It appears he had run out of more serious and potentially lucrative targets, and indeed the documents suggest Estrada and the other 'big fish' gem dealers were wriggling out of his grasp, calling in favours in both Spain and Bogotá.

The Crown auditor's attempt to go after Muzo's local mining elite had also collapsed, and he argued in favour of either dropping the case against them or settling out of court. They were now broke on account of legal fees, or so they said. One mine owner said his slaves had run away when he was called to Bogotá to testify, and another, a Jesuit named Ximénez, claimed ecclesiastical exemption from prosecution in civil courts. Even Vergara Azcarate's attempt to auction a number of emeralds collected as *quintos* failed to attract bidders, suggesting all contact with green stones had been cursed.[19]

A long hiatus in the documentary record would suggest the Crown audit of 1678–80 was another death knell for Muzo like the 1646 earthquake, but a case from 1688 argues for at least a small revival, and a near repetition of history. Crown officials again seeking *quintos* found a few of Muzo's mines back in operation and charges of subterfuge again began to fly. The new fraud investigation centred on mines in the Cerro Miguel Ruiz diggings belonging to the Ruisinque family. Their major-domo, Toribio Alvarez de Noriega, and mine magistrate Clemente Gómez de Cancelada, were the prime suspects. Trouble arose in the form of temptation when four enslaved African men discovered a promising stringer one Saturday and followed it into a kind of 'glory hole', or *buraco*.[20] They immediately notified their overseer and the magistrate, both of whom arrived at once to supervise removal of any emeralds.

A thirty-year-old slave, Manuel Bran, testified that, while working in the diggings one Saturday, one of his companions, Sebastián Mandinga, using his iron crowbar, 'struck verdigris' and out came two talon-like pieces of host rock 'with emeralds in the middle'. Mandinga also found a huge crystal, 'three by two fingers' in size, and immediately gave it to the magistrate, Gómez de Cancelada. Gómez ordered work stopped and the hole covered. Within a few days, according to various witnesses, the site was picked clean. Henrique Ruisinque blamed peons working for Gómez de Cancelada, while Gómez and Alvarez de Noriega blamed the slaves. It was difficult to say who, exactly, had 'cleaned up', although Manuel Bran said he had tried but had arrived too late.

A woman in Gómez's household, Josefa de Aguilar, testified that Sebastián Mandinga and another enslaved miner had brought her some stones, which she then sold to Muzo lapidary Vittorino Sandé. Sandé downplayed their value, calling them 'breadcrumbs' (*migasitas*). Valuable or not, the stones travelled through a local contraband network linking enslaved Africans to female householders and gem cutters.

Many larger stones quickly passed to the hands of bigger players, perhaps in part because they could be quite dangerous to move, or even hold. Crown officials were indeed far more interested in the large stone the slaves said they had given to Clemente Gómez de Cancelada. It was described as being 'the colour of heaven' (*laya del cielo*) and locally worth at least one thousand silver pesos. Gómez and the major-domo were jailed, but no resolution appears in surviving records. Gómez stated he had never seen the big stone.

The emerald diggings truly seem to have fallen moribund after this inauspicious find, and by late 1702, just as the War of the Spanish Succession was shaping up, visiting officials reported that most of Muzo's mines had been closed for more than twenty years. The officials also wrote that, as in the aftermath of the 1646 earthquake, a major fire had destroyed much of the town of La Trinidad in 1688.[21] It would be many years before the mines returned to anything like full production, and they never again produced as many top-grade stones as they did in the seventeenth century.

Smugglers' Beachheads

After 1655, the English occupation of Jamaica gave rise to a new and, to some, infamous Caribbean trading post. The unlikely city of Port Royal, the most populous in English America in its heyday, sat on a thin sand spit jutting out along Jamaica's south coast to encompass Kingston Harbour. According to several pious commentators, both English and Spanish, the sins of its residents were duly punished when half the city slid into the sea in a 1692 earthquake. Until then, Port Royal boasted a thriving and diverse merchant community. A portion of the old town and its adjoining fort remained, but most survivors moved across the bay to malaria-prone Kingston, and inland to the healthier site of Santiago de la Vega, or Spanish Town.

A number of Jewish traders, mostly Portuguese Sephardim, set up shop in Port Royal by 1660, but they were hardly as numerous as on Dutch Curaçao. Dyewood cut by English rovers in Mexico and Belize was an early Jamaican export, along with ginger, sugar, tobacco and cocoa, but as the Portuguese and Dutch had discovered long before, the real money to be made was in the illicit slave trade to Spanish America – that and piracy. This was precisely the era of news-grabbing buccaneers such as Henry Morgan, Alexander Exquemelin and William Dampier. Given England's political instability and perennial hostility towards Spain, little was done to interfere with either buccaneering or contraband trade. Both were seen as forms of war in that nebulous world 'beyond the line'.[22]

Historian Nuala Zahedieh has studied late seventeenth-century contraband trading in Port Royal in great detail, and she cites occasional mention of precious stones in governors' reports and other correspondence. In a 1672 letter, Governor Thomas Lynch complained that trading with the Spanish was nearly impossible given that they were 'the most senseless, ungrateful people in the world', and could not be made to purchase 'as much as an emerald'.[23] Clearly the governor had his commodities reversed, as no self-respecting Spanish subject would have bought an emerald from an Englishman.

Despite the governor's complaints, English vessels had already been trading vigorously all along the Spanish Main from Venezuela to Panama. As with the Curaçao trade at Willemstad described in previous chapters, cruising the Colombian coast was carried out under cover of darkness, with foreign visitors fading in and out of view and sending boats ashore on deserted beaches. The Spanish globetrotter Gregorio de Robles, who reported on illicit commerce in emeralds and other valuables at Cartagena and nearby Barú Island in the early 1690s, backs this up and adds colourful details.[24]

In such furtive circumstances only compact valuables were accepted in return for textiles, wine and enslaved Africans. Gold, silver, emeralds and pearls were perfectly suited for the task, and they changed hands routinely from Tolú, southwest of Cartagena, to Margarita Island, off the coast of Venezuela. It was also true that despite Spain's obvious inability to curb it, contraband trading, like mining tax evasion, could still get you killed if you were careless or poorly informed of the latest shift in political winds.

Typical of the uncertainty of Baroque times, interspersed with the standard shrill decrees, were long stretches of legality. Operating from Port Royal, the English Royal African Company held the Spanish *asiento*, or slave trade monopoly, in 1665, then again from 1677 to 1690, when it was transferred to a Portuguese firm. In the interim it was briefly held by Genoese merchants based on Curaçao. Gregorio de Robles, who visited Port Royal in 1690, lamented that the *asiento* allowed the 'English, Dutch, and Jews' to enjoy the 'gold, silver, pearls, emeralds, and other fruits of Your Majesty's dominions through this illicit medium'.[25]

Port Royal's Jewish merchants were not the only traders likely to be dealing in emeralds, but as discussed in previous chapters their close association with the slave trade and moneylending, along with established links to gem merchants in London, Amsterdam and various Indian factories, renders them the most likely contributors.[26] Nuala Zahedieh cites a 1664 incident directly linking two Jewish Port Royal merchants to Amsterdam-based investors, and many years ago Meyer Kayserling noted the connections between the Sephardim of Jamaica, Curaçao and Barbados after 1655.[27] Why Jamaica instead of Curaçao might be preferred by these merchants was partly because of geography. Curaçao was closer to Spanish shores, indeed perfect for tapping the high quality cocoa and tobacco of Venezuela, but it was difficult to reach from Cartagena or Santa Marta because of the Caribbean's prevailing easterly winds.

Other Port Royal regulars likely to have been handling emeralds in this period included several hundred rum-soaked, polyglot buccaneers, but their activities were by nature unsustainable. Pirates and gem merchants did rub elbows. Robert Ritchie tells the story of the Jewish gem merchant Benjamin Franks, who hitched a ride to India with the pirate-hunter turned pirate William Kidd in 1696.[28] Franks, from an Ashkenazi family with ties to Hamburg, had apparently lost his fortune in the 1692 Port Royal earthquake. There is no mention of emeralds in Franks's deposition, according to Ritchie, but anyone in his business working in Jamaica – especially if he had ties to India – was likely to have traded for them at some point.

On the Franks family's later fortunes in England and North America, Ritchie defers to the painstaking work of economic historian Gedalia Yogev. Yogev's landmark 1978 book, *Diamonds and Coral*, traces links between Jewish merchants, mostly Sephardim, with experience in both Iberian and Dutch overseas colonies but also Ashkenazis like Franks from Hamburg and other northern cities, and the English East India Company.[29]

In keeping with the bullion-hoarding mercantilist policy of the time, England's East India Company encouraged Jewish merchants to send Mediterranean coral to India instead of silver or gold to trade for diamonds. Although they did so, as shown in some detail below, most merchants continued shipping significant quantities of Spanish American silver pesos, along with pearls, emeralds and Baltic amber.[30] How exactly these merchants obtained Colombian emeralds Yogev does not say, but as already mentioned, most probably travelled through Jamaica or Curaçao by the time of Franks and Kidd. Other stones arrived through family contacts in Lisbon, Seville or Cádiz before being repackaged for export from London.

Whatever their path to London, Jewish merchants routinely asked East India Company officials for licences to ship Colombian emeralds to India at reduced rates. As early as 1703, emeralds, pearls and coral beads were charged only 2 per cent of appraised value, and raw coral 4 per cent.[31] Yogev cites a 1709 resolution, periodically renewed throughout the eighteenth century:

> That licence be granted for exporting to Surrat, Fort St. George [Madras] and Borneo all sorts of Corall, corall beads, amber beads, pearl, emeralds or any sort of precious stones, the exporters giving security, if required, that the produce be brought home in diamonds, diamond boart, musk, ambergreece or bezoar, and in no other goods whatsoever.[32]

There are no surprises here regarding India, but what about Borneo? It so happens that in the first decades of the eighteenth century the English East India Company was trying to break into the Dutch trade in south Borneo, the world's only other significant source of diamonds besides India at the time. These efforts failed, and I have found no record of Colombian emeralds making their way to Borneo. Meanwhile, the Jewish-dominated private trade in coral, amber and emeralds to India began a new cycle.

Stowaway Commodities Go (Barely) Legal

The substantial European coral trade to India, as described by Gedalia Yogev in 1978, and more recently by Francesca Trivellato, may illuminate our understanding of the parallel but smaller and more secretive trade in emeralds.[33] Coral of a deep red colour was found only in the western Mediterranean, retrieved by divers and trawlers from the waters adjacent to Marseilles, Genoa, Livorno, Sardinia and Naples. Like pearls, coral was a renewable but fragile resource, easily overharvested and destroyed and also highly variable in quality. Among Catholics it was most often used to make rosary beads and votive objects.

Though found in western European and Middle Eastern ornament and jewellery – and like other minerals thought to be invested with a variety of occult curative powers – coral was never in such high demand in the West to make it truly precious. In India, by contrast, particularly western India, demand for fine red coral ran deep and wide. Unlike the essentially regal desire for high-priced gems discussed previously in the Mughal and similar cases, coral was a more common form of adornment. As European travellers noted, people of several castes and religions donned heavy coral necklaces and bracelets as everyday expressions of wealth and status.

The Indian coral market was more elastic than the transparent gem market for several reasons. First, in a world without banks, hoarding coral beads as a form of money made economic sense. They were valuable but not so much so as to incite thieves to rip them from one's person in broad daylight. Second, for religious reasons some people burnt substantial amounts of raw coral, what Jewish merchants sometimes listed on their manifests as 'coral branches', on highly esteemed persons' funeral pyres.[34] As long as esteemed people kept dying, coral was actually being 'consumed', not just hoarded. Thus, coral consumption in early modern India seems to have been driven by a mix of cultural and economic impulses more profound than inconstant fashion trends in jewellery. Jewish merchants soon discovered that even the coral market had limits, however, and learned to withhold stock as needed.

There were other factors, in part because of the constantly shifting politics of Europe, at play. As Trivellato has shown, a complex coral-diamond trading network developed in the late seventeenth century, tying the Sephardic merchants of Amsterdam to Lisbon-based Italian Catholics, mostly from Livorno, back to Brahmin merchants from the Saraswat caste in Goa. The interdependence of these quite different trading communities intensified in the eighteenth century, even as the main diamond market shifted south to Madras. European demand for diamonds, meanwhile, remained strong, if not bottomless, throughout most of the eighteenth century.

The diamond business was prone to shocks, too, however, as happened following massive new discoveries in Brazil beginning around 1725. Suddenly, European demand for more expensive Indian stones was dampened. As Yogev demonstrates, patient Jewish gem traders rode out the storm in two ways. First, they moved quickly into the trade in Brazilian rough to restrict its flow. Second, they temporarily reduced, but did not eliminate, purchases of diamonds in India. When it became clear around 1750 that the Brazilian source was not inexaustible, demand for Indian stones again picked up. Thanks to all this careful manoeuvring, the same merchant families who had always been involved in the trade were still there to take up the slack.[35]

Rapid capital accumulation and general demographic growth in eighteenth-century Europe seemed to help drive up demand there as well, and it was only in the 1780s that the diamond business in India suffered a major crisis. Business cycles could be long or short for gem dealers as in other trades, but with exclusive luxury items crashes tended to be more drastic and unforeseeable. Maintaining the 'secret' and exclusive cachet of the world's rarest gemstones while also expanding their consumption was a delicate business, yet in this instance it was production that proved to be the greater problem. Coincidentally, as discussed in the next chapter, Colombia's emerald mines fell into ruin about the same time that diamonds crashed in India, Brazil and Europe.

In the midst of the supply-side confusion in the diamond trading world caused by the Brazilian discovery, an interesting claim emerged, probably planted and propagated by East India gem traders of several castes and affiliations: Brazilian diamonds were not 'oriental' enough; they were American, and therefore second-rate. While some diamond connoisseurs still maintain today that the world's most brilliant diamonds come only from India's venerable Golconda fields, this charge was more clearly motivated by fear and spite. Again, it was as if the New World could not possibly be old enough to have produced 'sufficiently cooked' gemstones.

Counting Rocks

In reviewing English East India Company records in London, I found I could only add minor details to Yogev's work that might highlight what was happening with emeralds. Following the 1709 freight-charge decree quoted above, the company created a standard entry space in its accounts for 'bullion' or 'foreign silver' (mostly Mexican pesos) along with coral, emeralds, pearls, amber and assorted jewels, all sent by private traders to India expressly 'to trade for diamonds'.

In exchange for what was possibly the safest and fastest global delivery service available at the time (quite unlike the old Portuguese *carreira*), London gem merchants, nearly all of them Sephardic Jews, paid minimal freight charges plus the 2 to 4 per cent duty on their stones' appraised sale value. They paid the same low rates on diamonds coming back. Gem merchants minimized risk further by splitting their shipments among the half-dozen or so East India Company vessels that made the trip each year.

According to the documents, most merchants sending emeralds to Madras, or more rarely, Bombay or Bengal, did so on behalf of consigners who were also Sephardim. These individuals were usually listed in records by their mark or brand rather than by name, so it is difficult to say who, if anyone, specialized in green stones. Most emeralds were sent rough, although a few went out polished and even fewer were set in finished jewels. Pearls were sent in about the same quantity as emeralds in the records I was able to examine, and it is likely some originated in the Caribbean. Surprisingly, even a few diamonds, presumably Brazilian, were sent to the Indian market after 1730. As Table 2 amply demonstrates, however, the vast bulk of this business, or

Table 2 Registered Private Treasure Sent to India to Buy Diamonds*

Year	'Foreign Silver'	Coral	Amber/Pearls	Emeralds
1730		£49,796 (appr.)		£75 (2pkts.)
1731		13,079		
1732		12,231		
1733	2,500 oz	16,043		1 pkt. (no val.)
1734		34,772		1 box (no val.)
1735		48,159		
1736		43,878		£450 (1 box + 1 pkt.)
1737		47,320		£25 (1 pkt.)
1738		32,979		£937 (2 boxes rough, 1 box jewels)
1739		15,416		£500 (1 box)
1740	1,350	25,900		£110 (1 box)
1741		37,430		
1742	57,715	43,829	£300 pearls, £25 amber beads	£150 (1 box)
1743	106,700	55,273		
1744	66,550	19,922	'Liso' pearls	
1745	112,850	37,094	c. £200 pearls	c. £1,200 + jewels, rings
1746	91,501	71,922	c. £1,000 pearls + some amber beads	c. £2,200 (some boxed w/pearls)
1747	152,500	68,286	c. £2,500 pearls + amber beads, diamonds	c. 2,500 lb (most boxed w/pearls)
1748	345,616	45,994	c. £2,000 + some jewels	c. £1,000
1749	652,350	74,520	c. £3,000 pearls + £700 amber beads	None named, but some precious stones
1750	131,828	44,373	c. £400 amber, precious stones	£285 (2 boxes)

1751	172,869	59,943	c. £4,000 pearls + diamonds, precious stones	c. £2,000
1752	25,706	39,262	Some amber	£50
1753 (partial)		14,185	£220 amber	c. £200

* East India Company Letterbooks, British Library, OIAC E/3/105–11.

at least the registered part, was in Mediterranean coral and Spanish-American silver. As K.N. Chaudhuri noted in his massive 1978 study of the company's silver-for-textile trade, authorities included in their correspondence updated exchange rates for pesos and rupees, listing precise silver content in various Mexican mint issues.[36]

There were at least forty or fifty men active in the English East India Company-sponsored diamond trade in the first half of the eighteenth century, notable among them Jacob and Isaac Salvador, Phineas Serra, Haim Supino, Assur Isaac Levy, Lewis Mendes, Jacob Fernandes Nunes, David de Castro, Alexander Ramires da Costa, Joseph and Samuel Moses, Henry Isaac, Moses Henriques, Abraham da Fonseca, Isaac Lindo, Nathan Salomons, Isaac Ciprut de Gabay, Jacob de Natal Levy, Aron Goldsmid, Abraham Elias, Barent Gompertz, Samuel Cohen and Naphtaly and Moses Franks.

Ashkenazim, evident in the last several names, were slow to enter the London-centred India diamond trade, and likewise the emerald business. In terms of both volume and value, the Sephardic merchants Abraham and Jacob Franco dominated the business until the mid-century. Non-Jews were few, but they included well-travelled men such as Thomas Godfrey, James Porten and George Arnold, along with a few Italians and at least one Armenian.

As Yogev also notes, the flow of silver grew despite company officials' efforts to flood the Indian market with coral instead. Hundreds of thousands of ounces of silver went out annually alongside boxes of coral fragments and beads valued at tens of thousands of pounds sterling. By comparison, emeralds, like pearls, played only a minuscule role in this registered trade, not making up even a fraction of a per cent of the total in any given year. Although some surely went below decks, emeralds were now a kind of tag-along commodity rather than a super-secret stowaway.

Although I did not find itemized lists of emerald exports before 1730 or after 1753, the records for the years in between suggest an established pattern of movement. One might expect emerald numbers to pale against silver and coral given the deeper demand or wider market for these money-commodities, but my guess is that emerald's poor showing in these records is indicative of two additional aspects: first, trade in green stones to India through older Portuguese or contraband channels was probably still going on, and second (and probably far more important), there was a general crisis in the Muzo mines. As discussed in the following and final chapter, it so happened that emeralds were at this time in shorter supply than ever.

What this chapter has shown is how the Muzo mines revived in the second half of the seventeenth century and sent emeralds furtively abroad through shifting and frequently contraband trade networks. Tax evasion was rife from Muzo to Cartagena, but the wobbly Spanish Habsburg state still proved its ability to interfere with colonial business affairs from time to time. Thanks to a series of fraud investigations, by 1680 the Crown appears to have all but crushed New Granada's emerald mining industry. Yet emeralds still flowed from Colombia to India, sometimes in significant quantities. In the Atlantic context, emeralds remained stowaways in a shifting trade built mostly around specie and enslaved Africans. Spain's Atlantic treasure fleets still carried significant amounts of emeralds, as a number of shipwrecks such as that of the *Maravillas* in 1656 attest, but they were increasingly sent east by other means. More and more, Colombian emeralds travelled through Curaçao and Jamaica to Amsterdam and London. The way to Asia had also shifted by the end of the seventeenth century. Displacing Lisbon and the Portuguese *carreira da Índia* to Goa, emeralds regularly – and officially – left Europe for Surat, Madras and other factories in East India Company vessels.

❖

CHAPTER 8

Twilight of Imperial Emeralds

IN the midst of the 1702–13 War of the Spanish Succession, an English squadron attacked the Tierra Firme treasure fleet just as it was reaching Cartagena de Indias from Portobello, on the coast of Panama. The attack, which took place on the afternoon and evening of 8 June 1708, led to the sinking of the 1,200-ton flagship *San José*, killing all but a dozen of her six hundred-odd crew-members and sending several million pesos' worth of treasure – mostly Peruvian silver – to the bottom. It has yet to be recovered. The *San José* may have carried emeralds, too, as historian Carla Rahn Phillips surmises, but because the galleon was heading back to Cartagena to pick up more treasure before sailing for Spain, this was unlikely.

The *San José*'s surviving sister ship, the *San Joaquín*, did however, sail for Spain from Cartagena after a long delay with at least some emeralds on board. Carla Rahn Phillips found in the *San Joaquín*'s manifest several parcels of second- and third-grade emeralds, about 3,200 pesos' worth according to Crown appraisers, stowed in 1711.[1] These emeralds may have been derived from taxes collected at the Muzo mines, but the record for these years is silent. Were there likely many more emeralds on board that had not been registered?

Sources closer to the diggings suggest Muzo remained in crisis in the first years of Bourbon rule. A few old seventeenth-century mining clans remained active, and smuggling charges continued to fly. Contraband trade became such a generalized scandal all over New Granada following the War of the Spanish Succession that Philip V (1700–46) elevated the colony to a viceroyalty, with Bogotá as capital, in 1739. The plan had been proposed in the 1710s. Creation of the viceroyalty did not end smuggling, however, and in fact it only worsened with the expansion of Colombia's massive Pacific Coast goldfields – staffed by enslaved Africans supplied by mostly English purveyors.[2]

Another type of Bourbon royal intervention failed to revive Muzo. By 1760, when Charles III's (1759–88) enlightened ministers attempted to resuscitate the diggings through a Crown takeover and the application of scientific excavation methods, only a few prospectors were still grubbing. Even with Crown attention, investment and scientific study, however, Muzo proved unprofitable. By 1792, royal overseers abandoned the state enterprise in disgust, and the mines produced virtually nothing – at least officially – until Bolívar secured Colombian independence in the early 1820s.

The eighteenth century witnessed a range of profound global reorientations. In the Atlantic, many such shifts grew out of Anglo-French rivalry. For Spain and its colonies, most major changes, including new monopolies and 'sin' taxes, only came to a head after the mid-century. Portugal followed suit, monopolizing the diamond fields of newly rich Brazil and shifting the colonial capital from Salvador to Rio. The rights to tax and channel trade were, as before, the main stakes, but increased firepower, shipping capacity and civilian participation in warfare ratcheted up the scale of violence. Fortresses protecting port cities grew enormous. In southwestern Asia, meanwhile, French and English observers watched transfixed as Nadir Shah came out of nowhere to trounce his neighbours, then bring about his own murder and subsequent Persian decline. East India Company officials took careful note of Mughal weakness.

Such telluric shifts and reversals of fortune seemed the order of the day. By the 1750s, Qing generals took horses and light cannons to conquer distant Tibet. A newly belligerent Russia raced in the opposite direction to Pacific shores. Austria-Hungary and Egypt successfully carved out new spaces and challenged Ottoman resolve. A weakened Spain relied on France against Britain, and a beleaguered Portugal on Britain against Spain and France. Key ports (Manila and Havana), then whole colonies (New France and Florida) were traded like gaming chips. The resilient Dutch consolidated holdings in Indonesia, only to see their storied East India Company dissolve in bankruptcy. The true costs of coffee and tea were finally coming up for a reckoning, and not only in the metropole. Talk of anti-imperial 'people's' revolutions began to brew.

In the midst of all these swings and upheavals, and the increasingly long and deadly wars they spawned, gem merchants found themselves profoundly challenged. Disruptions in trade were not the only problem: tastes were changing. Opulence had by no means gone out of fashion, and was in fact likely to become more democratized in thriving European cities with fast-breeding bourgeoisies. Yet throughout Eurasia stable markets for a particular kind of 'Baroque' or 'marvellous' gemstone appear to have been dying. Asia's old gunpowder empires were fading fast, and what was coming to replace them was not yet clear. Undoubtedly, it would be different, but would it still crave emeralds?

Muzo Decadent

I have spent these days looking for emeralds and all I found were three or four folded papers' worth, of such low colour and so small that all of them together were not worth 2,000 pesos.[3]—a Spanish visitor to Bogotá in 1741

After the 1713 Treaty of Utrecht, Spain was forced to open the Caribbean port of Cartagena to English slavers. The agreement, which also allowed for limited trade in cloth and other merchandise, formalized the old contraband trade to Port Royal, Jamaica, but also fostered more widespread smuggling. Historian Lance Grahn has studied Spanish documents detailing the seizure of contraband vessels along Colombia's coast in the early eighteenth century, but since these are almost entirely records of incoming vessels' cargoes, emeralds figure only in vague lists of desiderata.[4] Meanwhile, the official English supplier of slaves to New Granada, the state-backed South Sea Company (whose famous 1720 bubble only briefly interrupted business), became intertwined with the more venerable East India Company.

The rapid ascendancy of the English East India Company in the first half of the eighteenth century, and with it the community of mostly Jewish gem traders discussed in the previous chapter, was not matched by a rise in emerald production in Muzo, although slavery seems to have expanded somewhat in the diggings. What few emeralds became available through factors in Cartagena or Jamaica were sent off to Fort St George and other Indian ports as East India Company letterbooks attest, but at least in part because of a prolonged mining crisis emeralds remained a barely noted shadow commodity.

Records from eighteenth-century Muzo are few and lean before the 1760s, when the Crown stepped in to attempt a revival, but as early as 1702 a dispute arose between two mine owners who also happened to be local officials. The project, at the ancient Cascarón mine, was apparently a large one, employing numerous enslaved Africans and costing some 1,500 silver pesos.[5] One investor was Doña María de Tovar Justiniano, daughter and granddaughter of the region's biggest mine owners of the previous century.[6] As for the miners themselves, a Muzo lawsuit from 1704 reveals that enslaved African descendants and 'concerted' indigenous workers were still excavating emeralds together in the Itoco basin, often drinking together and getting into fights.[7]

Other archival fragments hint at the general dearth of emerald rough. In 1712 mine owners feuded over a find in the Cañaveral diggings, but the documents offer few details beyond the fact that one was a priest and the other the treasurer of Bogotá's mint.[8] Having received no news for some time, royal officials left Bogotá in 1720 to inspect Muzo's treasury. They found the royal chest empty, save for a gem scale and a few papers, including records of taxes collected on the slopes of the Cerro de Itoco itself in the first quarter of 1719.[9]

Few emeralds had been registered, but they included some large and apparently fine ones. In a curious sidenote, one-fourth of the April registry was pledged to one 'señor San Josef of Mompox'.[10] Mompóx was a key river port located about three-quarters of the way down the Magdalena River towards Cartagena, famous for its contraband trade via Riohacha and Lake Maracaibo. It's a clue, but nothing more. In 1726, Muzo's royal mine magistrate wrote to superiors in Bogotá begging to be recalled. He was, he said, 'trembling from the contagions so common in this land, of plague and evacuations of blood that have killed so many'.[11] The prognosis for Muzo's mines was just as grim, but Bourbon scientists would soon intervene to attempt resuscitation.

Freemasons and Scientists

The two provinces of Santa Fe and Popayán have no other way of supplying themselves with [manufactured goods] than from Cartagena. Their traders bring gold and silver in specie, ingots, and dust, and also emeralds; as, besides the silver mines worked at Santa Fe [Mariquita], and which daily increase by fresh discoveries, there are others which yield the finest emeralds. But the value of these gems being now fallen in Europe, and particularly in Spain, the trade of them, formerly so considerable, is now greatly lessened, and consequently the reward for finding them.[12]—Jorge Juan and Antonio Ulloa, *A Voyage to South America*, 1748

Despite what Spanish savants Juan and Ulloa stated after their visit to Cartagena in the 1730s, European demand for emeralds may have grown in the eighteenth century, although prices suggest they remained well behind diamonds. The gemologist John Sinkankas cited a 1747 mineralogical treatise published in Stockholm by Johann Gottschalk Wallerius as giving some sense of then-current emerald prices in northern Europe. Decent emeralds of any size were extremely rare, and those of good quality ranged from thirty to eighty *riksdalers* per carat. One-carat diamonds were said to sell in Hamburg for at least sixty-four *riksdalers*, and for seventy in Amsterdam. Sinkankas concludes by saying that on average good diamonds appear to have outpriced good emeralds by roughly two to one in northern Europe.[13]

To the south, meanwhile, Lisbon returned to its former status as a gem trade hub. The discovery of diamonds in Brazil in the 1720s had breathed new life into the Bragança court, and with newfound wealth and opulence came a new wave of immigrant lapidaries to Lisbon. The Inquisition was still making life miserable for Jews, although its investigators and theologians were surprised to discover a brand new heresy among the city's stone-cutting and jewel-setting community in the age of enlightenment.

The secret sect à la mode was *pedraria livre*, or Freemasonry, and it appears to have been especially popular among foreign merchants and artisans. A case from the early 1740s centred on the Frenchman Jacques Mouton, a Parisian lapidary who specialized in diamonds. He and several other Frenchmen, plus an Englishman and an Armenian, all stonecutters, jewellers or apothecaries, were accused of participating in Masonic rituals.

The foreign lapidaries' leader, said to be the only grand master in Portugal, was a Swiss diamond cutter named Cousteau (or Coustos) who had joined the order in England, 'where the books are kept'. The investigation revealed a second group of Freemasons whose members were Irish, German, Belgian and English, and included clockmakers and locksmiths as well as jewellers. Their leader was a Mr Gordon.

Witnesses said a total of about fifty artisans were known as practising Freemasons in Portugal *c.*1743, all with the aim of mutual economic aid, and presumably also social interests. When asked the meaning of their ceremonies, deponents protested that they had always been, and continued to be, good Catholics, and that *pedraria livre* had risen from the ashes of the crusading orders and was no heresy. Theirs was simply a secret brotherhood based on an old-fashioned, knightly honour code; its rituals were not religious. Inquisitors disagreed, and after an auto-da-fé the leader of the first group, Cousteau, was sentenced to four years penal exile and threatened with excommunication in case of relapse. He published an account of his tortures and trials in London in 1746.[14]

Throughout Europe, artisans such as Lisbon's persecuted lapidaries increasingly saw themselves as agents of a new, enlightened worldview. Some no doubt proudly claimed membership in an increasingly open and sceptical transnational scientific community that took tinkering and innovation seriously. The shadowy rituals of Freemasonry were, as the stonecutters insisted, essentially secular stand-ins for those familiar from religious confraternities. But why risk tangling with the Inquisition? Perhaps because secret rites of passage were truly needed to cement social and therefore economic bonds between craftsmen of such varied backgrounds. Trust in an era of inquisitions was always at a premium; to be in on the gem-trading game one had to join the *pedraria* club.

Elsewhere in Europe, by the 1750s, interest in emeralds was thoroughly scientific and experiments to determine fusibility, refraction, hardness, crystal geometry and other inherent characteristics were carried out by mineralogists and chemists. In 1757, U.F.B. Brückmann, famous for his taxonomic *System of Mineralogy*, commented on emerald's physical properties at some length. He also mentioned price: decent emeralds were once again very hard to find, but good ones fetched only one-fourth of what one could expect to get for a similarly sized diamond.[15]

Before long, Spain's King Ferdinand VI (1746–59) caught the scientific bug. In November 1752 he issued an order requiring subjects to collect all order of minerals to form the Royal Cabinet of Natural History relating 'to the mines found in His Majesty's dominions in the two Americas'. Most important were 'metals and precious stones'.[16]

Ore samples poured in from established silver districts throughout Mexico and Peru, along with newer and lesser-known ones in the Philippines, Chile, Paraguay and Cuba. Where minerals could not be had, exotic birds, plants and animals were packed – or caged – and sent. The Enlightenment also inspired a new way of looking at human diversity and the unknown past, and for the first time since the sixteenth century ethnographic and archaeological information was collected throughout the Spanish Empire with purely scientific rather than transformative religious aims.

But it took shiny rocks rather than pretty birds or fantastic origin stories to make money, and thus Spain's more practical Enlightenment thinkers turned to a revival and expansion of mining, hoping this industry would pay off like it once had. The line between curiosity and profitability was thin. It was already known by 1750 that the most prized and possibly unique mineral products of the Spanish Indies were New Granada's platinum and emeralds, and prime samples of both were specifically requested. Hundreds of pounds of platinum were hastily recovered from waste heaps where they had been accumulating for decades and shipped to a new royal workshop.[17] Emeralds, by contrast, were not found lying around, and in fact Muzo's mines were in such decline when the order for samples arrived it was not filled for over twenty years.

By 1775, when a large chunk of host mineral studded with fine crystals was at last sent to the king, the vigorous reformer Charles III, Muzo's mines had been run by a Crown-appointed administrator for more than a decade. Two years later, following a lucky strike in the Cañaveral diggings, more than four-and-a-half pounds of grade-one emeralds were sent, along with ten pounds of second- and third-class stones and several more slabs of scientifically interesting host rock.

Muzo Resuscitated

By the mid-1760s the Spanish Crown's interest in reviving its numerous mines was at an all-time high. The Seven Years War, though entered late, proved as expensive as it was humiliating, and Spain's many losses persuaded Charles III of the need to raise revenue by whatever means. Promoting precious metals production seemed a logical first, but any natural resource likely to turn a profit or find a use in some new manufacture, medicine or dye was pursued.

When it came to fixing Spanish America's broken or 'backward' mines, it was believed northern Europeans knew best. For chronically self-flagellating Iberians, cold-country Protestants, in particular, were models of the new rationality and discipline that decadent Spain and its underexploited colonies desperately lacked. As for Spanish-American science, or even homegrown practical knowledge, colonists were all but universally assumed to be ignorant and unteachable.

Saxon Germans were preferred, but, when unavailable, Spaniards trained in northern European universities were given a try. By the 1770s, under the direction of Spain's new Minister of the Indies, José de Gálvez, special mining missions were organized and sent to New Spain, Peru and New Granada. The head of the New Granada mission, Basque metallurgist Juan José D'Elhuyar, eventually reached Muzo and wrote a brief but detailed report of his findings (partially quoted in Chapter 1).

Well before the creation of the D'Elhuyar mission, however, the Crown had stepped in to improve Muzo's emerald output. On 28 February 1764, Charles III decreed an immediate royal takeover of the Muzo mines. A little over a year later, Bogotá officials dispatched Feliciano Casal to establish the Crown monopoly and oversee operations. Casal remained the king's man in charge for nearly two decades.

The feisty Casal, whose official title was 'Interventor de las Minerales de Esmeraldas de la Ciudad de Muzo', received an annual subsidy of four thousand pesos from the royal treasury in Bogotá to cover his salary and that of two overseers, plus day wages for up to forty hired peons. The subsidy, which rose slightly in some years and fell into arrears in others, was also used to cover the cost of tools, transport, building supplies and incidentals.

As required in this era of enlightened accounting, every last *real* of income and expenditure was entered in neat ledger books. Of those that survive, the fattest cover the years of lowest emerald output. Most years seemed to end in loss, but because the stones produced by the royal mines were accounted for only by weight and grade rather than potential market value, it is virtually impossible to determine profitability. Casal attempted such calculations at the end of his tenure based on what he had heard were going prices in Madrid, but his estimates were fiercely challenged by Royal Treasury superiors.

Casal would have a few good years, yet despite the celebrated arrival of modern science in the colonies, the work of mining emeralds remained virtually unchanged. Workers' lives may even have worsened under the new regime. Immediately on Crown takeover in 1764, the overseer Don Martín Morales put eight hired peons to work in the Traza Grande diggings. They were to receive wages of one-and-a-half *reales* per day, and three if they worked through the night. Night work was increasingly common, and mostly involved maintenance of floodgates and canals.

In Muzo, trusted peons known as *tambreros* were charged with directing the flow of water over the day's debris. Accumulated water from afternoon rains was released at night after pick-and-bar men had done their work clearing away surface material in search of paying veins. Wage receipts suggest other peons were also frequently called on to work at night, either to handle emergencies or help channel sudden rains into the hushing dams. There is also frequent mention of the need to use torches for illumination, and they show up in Casal's ledger books.

Such enlightened administrators as Casal tended not to value local knowledge. Within months of his arrival in Muzo, Casal complained in letters that his efforts to have a new hushing dam up and running had been frustrated by 'the many crests of these uneven hills'. He and his subordinates had searched for the 'blessed water' of natural springs, but had found none. The lack of reliable water sources left him, he said, 'completely sunk'.[18] Had Casal bothered to ask local miners their opinion, they might have told him to wait a few months. Indeed, by October, the first rains of 'winter' arrived and the administrator was heartened to see how readily the reservoirs filled. He ordered a new one built. Water was periodically short, Casal wrote highland officials, but the real problem was the lack of 'adaptable peons'.

Casal had only begun when he wrote to his superiors in Bogotá complaining bitterly of his 'godless', intractable labourers. Local peons were worthless, he said, because of 'the deep-rooted idleness with which they live'. Most of them went from mine to mine begging for money and making false promises to work. Or so it seemed to him. Some would work for two weeks at a stretch, collect their pay and disappear. There was no way to compel them to stay on site, and nothing but the vague threat of lost wages made them work at all. Stealing emeralds discovered with the least possible exertion seemed to be their central aim in life. Casal asked for convicts, but none were sent.

Under Bourbon administration, the work-week ran from Monday to Saturday, sunrise to 5:00 p.m. (about an hour before sunset at this latitude), with an hour's break for lunch. Night work began whenever the rains let up after dinner. Despite numerous plans for mineside barracks and 'prisons', for almost the entire period of Crown administration, Muzo's emerald mineworkers did not live on-site, but rather in the nearby villages, or house clusters, of Itoco, Quípama and Avipí. Only in 1786 was a mineworker bunkhouse built next to the Itoco diggings. With it came a new system of daily time cards. Rainy mornings went unpaid, and labourers' wages were calculated with greater precision according to 'strength, age, and ability'. The trend, in short, was towards a more rationalized work regimen, and with it, increased surveillance.[19]

In a 1776 report, Casal said his first three years of work in Muzo (1764–7) had been 'lost', with only thirty-six marks [about eighteen lbs] of junk stone to show after ten thousand pesos' investment. The next three years had been better, after some significant finds were made when black-powder blasting was introduced in 1771. New mines had been opened and had yielded some choice gems. Still, labour problems continued to plague the enterprise. Casal all but begged his superiors for fifty 'African blacks', with 'their captains'. After observing an enslaved work gang belonging to a private mine operator, he said, he had determined that enslaved miners did as much work in four years as a comparable number of peons did in six.

African slaves not only had the proper 'robustness' for mine work, but also 'worked steadily'. Casal appears unaware he was echoing, almost verbatim, elite requests from the sixteenth and seventeenth centuries.

As in those earlier centuries, Crown officials refused to purchase enslaved Africans for the Muzo emerald mines. In this case, the mines had yet to promise sufficient returns to justify the outlay. Under a new administrator, the Crown mines finally closed on 26 October 1792. In a final report, the administrator wrote that he had sent the king's treasurers more than fifty pounds of emeralds from the mines of San Josef, San Antonio, El Aguardiente and Cascarón, and gave account of their quality and likely market value. One big stone of 'happy green colour' he guessed would fetch four thousand pesos.[20] Crown officials ordered the mines cordoned off and put up for auction, but no buyers came forward. The viceregal government was still seeking takers in 1797, but without luck.[21]

Workers' Farewell

As with most commodity fetishism stories, it was the usually nameless, faceless workers who offered an alternative ending. In 1792, just as the Crown gave up on its enlightened monopoly project, fraud charges surfaced. Several peons who had worked in the royal mines of Cascarón and El Aguardiente were charged with selling stones under the table to a variety of merchants and jewellers in Muzo, Bogotá and other highland towns. The miners had allegedly entered the diggings after dark and on weekends to grub for high-grade stones, later trading choice rough for food and liquor.

The workers' cleverness may seem amusing, but perhaps the most revealing detail to emerge from this fraud case is the absolutely wretched poverty suffered by Muzo's mine labourers. Most unfortunate was one Roque Martínez, who was beaten to death for trying to escape what amounted to police custody. Apparently without dissimulation, Martínez confessed to have smuggled emeralds the size of fingers in hollowed candles to trade in La Trinidad for a hunk of beef, a few loaves of bread or a shot of rum. Clearly the miners' two-*real* per day wage was insufficient to live on in a hard-luck mining town.[22]

The 1792 fraud investigation also offers a much-appreciated window on the 'real' emerald industry. Officially, the mines were moribund, yet unofficially there was a thriving traffic in raw and cut stones linking highlands to lowlands, rich to poor, creoles to peninsulars. An otherwise invisible trade network linked low-ranking miners to low-ranking lapidaries, who then traded upward to make a living. There was an international dimension to this business as well, but we have only the scarcest clues as to its shape. Back in 1782 the Crown lapidary Pedro Puig had reported to Spain's Indies Minister, José de Gálvez, that when he had visited the Muzo mines in 1766 the best stones always seemed to disappear, leaving the Crown with only fractured bits of second-class rough and many marks of useless *moralla*. Puig wrote:

> Moved by curiosity, I began to cautiously investigate what commerce there was in all the stones taken from those mines, and I discovered that all those of first quality were purchased by various subjects commissioned by some Dutch merchants, citizens of the island of Curaçao. And I was assured that one of them invested every year 20,000 pesos in this, trading [emeralds] for goods kept hidden in various sites along the seacoast.[23]

If Puig was correct, and it appears he was as he offered to provide still more detailed testimony, Curaçao had returned to (or never really lost) its early seventeenth-century role as a contraband nexus for Colombian emeralds. Buyers were most likely to be the now quite numerous Sephardim of Willemstad, who had maintained their long-established connections to gem cutters and wholesalers in Amsterdam and London. Even direct Crown administration could not prevent the secret trade in these exclusive stones, which Puig admitted were 'unique in the world'.

According to surviving accounts, the Crown's operation of Muzo's mines proved a terrible money loser throughout its approximately thirty-year duration. Costs always exceeded the value of emeralds produced, and the situation only worsened with time. In the final two years, 6,500 pesos' investment had yielded only 1,400 *reales'*-worth of emeralds. Administrators explored previously abandoned diggings in later years, but known deposits played out and no genuinely new ones were discovered. The basic Enlightenment argument was that earlier miners had been fools – even klutzes in handling stones – and had missed all sorts of good ore that science and rationality would reveal. Modern labour management and bookkeeping were expected to sort things out. The introduction of explosives boosted production some-what in the early 1770s, but otherwise the promise of enlightened emerald mining never delivered.

Denouement of Gunpowder Empires

The eighteenth century witnessed the extinction of the Safavid Dynasty in Persia, the fall of the Mughal Empire in India and the steady erosion of Ottoman power from Eastern Europe to North Africa. Gunpowder and Timurid charisma, it seemed, were no longer sufficient to hold together vast, heterogeneous states. All of this presumably affected the global emerald trade, although exactly how remains unclear. Nadir Shah obtained his emeralds through plunder, and his successors wore them with pride until the fall of the House of Pahlavi in 1979. Mughal successors of Muhammad Shah similarly continued to sport considerable emerald jewellery until the end of the colonial period in 1947. As for the Ottomans, many showpiece emer-alds date to the late eighteenth and even early nineteenth centuries, long after the heyday of the Muzo mines. Emerald-encrusted scab-bards and other ritual paraphernalia were produced right up to the creation of modern Turkey in 1922.

As these examples imply, later phases and other aspects of global emerald trading remain to be examined. Scholars will surely explore the significance of the many emeralds worn by prominent Sikhs and Hindus in the eighteenth and nineteenth centuries, as documented in numerous paintings and photographs. Others may explain emeralds' prominence in certain Sikh and Brahmanic temple jewels. In these cases, as in certain Christian and Buddhist contexts, emeralds must have meant something different to what they signified in the Islamic world (assuming they were ascribed any meaning at all). In some cases it seems likely emeralds were used simply to copy Mughal fashions in an orientalist, romantic way, as in the 1790s when the East India Company Governor-General John Shore had an emerald signet ring inscribed with his name and an Arabic verse.

The company's most famous employee, Sir Robert Clive, had already received, along with his admiral, Charles Watson, a set of emerald-encrusted turban ornaments in the Mughal style from the Nawab of Bengal, Mir Jafar. Now housed in the Victoria and Albert Museum in London, one ornament has a deep green emerald at its core, surrounded by tiny diamonds, flanked by rubies and hung with a pearl. The other, more feather-like, ornament has emerald inlay and a dramatic green drop on top, but at the centre is a large and brilliant blue sapphire. For the nawabs of Bengal, it seems, paradise could have other colours besides green. This extraordinary gift was presented following the 1757 Battle of Plassey, in which Mir Jafar's former boss, Nawab Siraj ad-Daula, was defeated, in part by a newer brand of gunpowder warfare imported by globe-trotting Europeans. The nawab's emeralds were a far cry from Atahuallpa's – or Chief Bogotá's – but nevertheless they signified that British rule in India had begun.

❖

Conclusion

THE discovery and dissemination of Colombian emeralds, beginning around 1540 and ending in the 1790s, was not globally transformative. Emerald mining and trading were minuscule and irregular enterprises next to the constant, high-volume traffic in spices, textiles and precious metals. Even within Colombia, emeralds were a minor story next to gold. As this book has sought to demonstrate, however, the mining, transoceanic circulation and often ritualized consumption and 'gifting' of emeralds in early modern times still amounts to more than a curious, three-part tale of production, circulation and consumption. The emerald story may illustrate better than almost any other commodity how a prized and exclusive mineral of no obvious utility shifted in value and meaning as it changed hands and crossed oceans over the course of two-and-a-half centuries. By absorbing projected attributes in so many global contexts, emerald was a chameleon that never had to change colour.

Emerald's genuine rarity, ascribed and shifting cultural meanings and ultimate uselessness gave rise, I would argue, to a special type of commodity chain, perhaps the essential one. Because emeralds were found in only a few isolated locales and traded in such small quantities, factors as diverse as the precise geographical location of Colombia's richest mines and the aggressive – or as Freud and

Veblen would have it, aggressively generous – whims of individual Central Asian despots like Nadir Shah made this singular emblem of 'conspicuous waste' all the more special. That emeralds' production entailed great suffering in distant and unimaginable lands, and were often traded at great personal risk (and therefore in secrecy), may have only added to their lustrous mystique.

On a more mundane level, the history of emeralds in the age of sail and gunpowder was marked by unpredictable cycles of production and consumption, as well as eddies and disruptions in the flow of global trade. If there was irony it was that a gemstone so many believed could come only from the 'ancient' Orient had in fact to be sent there from the 'immature' Occident. In an older understanding of the Indies, East and West were not supposed to complement, or even mirror, each other, but rather simply supply Europeans with the luxuries their newfound power and wealth demanded. That emeralds flowed mostly to the Islamic gunpowder empires of Asia rather than to the scattered courts and cities of Christian Europe (along with a large share of Spanish America's silver) supports recent claims of a different centre of power in early modern times, at least in commercial and demo-graphic terms. The Muslim-dominated world of South and south-western Asia may have lacked the economic gravity of China, as studies of the silver-for-textile trade suggest, but not by much.

If Mughal India was a non-traditional centre, colonial Colombia was a perfectly traditional periphery: a thinly populated producer of raw commodities reliant on forced labour and working for the benefit of a distant metropolis. Yet even here there were other stories to tell, among them contraband subplots and counternarratives of resistance, collaboration and betrayal. Chronic landslides, hurricanes and other environmental factors added to the mix of terror, tenacity and luck. Even the conquistadors could not resist telling and embel-lishing tales of doomed sorties and clever guerrillas, of snakebites, mantraps and the dreaded 'twenty-four hour herb'. Colombia, it seems, had its own Jungle Book. Still, in the end the fabled Muzos, who fought so hard to keep Spanish invaders at bay, have been forgotten in modern times. In another irony Marx might have savoured, their once feared name is now the globally accepted standard for perfect emerald colour.

Of the enslaved African miners who followed the Muzos and Muiscas into the coal-black pits and streams of Itoco, Coscuez and Somondoco we know almost as little, and not much more about their mixed offspring. Occasionally an individual offers a brief testimony from beyond the grave on how he and his companions followed a promising stringer to a glittering bonanza. Elsewhere a fragmentary testimony mentions an enslaved African woman working in the mines, or a mother grieving for her malnourished child. Other documents mention runaway communities, free black and mulatto contraband traders, and hired and enslaved high graders. Theirs was a complex and sometimes contradictory world that, as Michael Taussig has argued for Colombia's many thousands of African-descended gold miners up to present times, has been more effectively erased than that of their native American predecessors.[1] If this book has tried to recover and amplify a silenced past, it is that of 'black' and 'subaltern' Muzo.

Of the mine owners a great deal more is known, or at least recorded, and little they did seems worthy of praise today. Still, Muzo was no easy destination even for whites, and only a few individuals managed to escape to healthier climes. What generations of Spanish, Portuguese and other European conquistadors, militiamen, freelance prospectors and their wives and widows managed to do, for better or worse, was to keep Muzo productive, despite what they described as positively biblical challenges (only locusts and boils escape mention). Mine owners' persistent hopes and desperate fears were arguably the motors that kept emeralds in the world marketplace for centuries.

Local elites continued to sink money into emerald mines with no help from Crown, church or local authorities, often assuming risks few modern corporations would consider. Over time, owners worked out deals with their subordinates that at least partially mitigated the worst abuses – but were aimed at spreading risk and minimizing capital outlay. Pragmatism, not Christian charity, dictated these compromises. Perfect surveillance was as impossible for the rich as keeping a valuable emerald perfectly secret for the poor. If Crown investigators' reports are any indication, newcomers had a hard time fathoming the bounds and rules of the resulting shell game, and this only fuelled rumours of rampant tax fraud and contraband trading.

Of the merchants who registered and smuggled Colombian emeralds across oceans at great personal risk, we also know little, but there are a few good stories. What emerges from the fragments is an odd cast of individual entrepreneurs and semi-clandestine merchant communities moving in and out of such far-flung cities as Cartagena, Lisbon, London and Goa. We know most about the several dozen Sephardic clans at the centre of the global gem and jewel trade, because it was their bad luck to live caught up in a world of religious paranoia. In their case, like that of certain Armenians, Banias and Gujaratis, clan ties made the gem business just profitable enough in the absence of consistent state protection to be worth the considerable risks to life and limb. Rare individuals like the Fleming Jacques de Coutre provide still more details of the gem trade's specific risks and payoffs in their personal narratives. Archival clues in the form of criminal investigations tend to enhance and complicate rather than solve the mysteries of early modern gem dealing, although occasionally a great shipwreck find like that of the *Atocha* confirms our wildest suspicions.

Of emerald consumers, European, American and Asian, we know a bit more, at least in terms of taste and function. Emeralds in the early modern West were essentially a feminine accessory, although not simply a 'wasteful' one, as Veblen might have claimed. A Spanish woman's dowry, on the Peninsula or in the colonies, was hardly complete without them, and dowries were more than symbolic capital. Considerable emeralds also went to the saints of the Catholic tradition in the form of votive offerings to intercessors and protectors, often 'housed' in local or hometown shrines. In Colombia the protector was (and remains) Our Lady of Chiquinquirá, quite close to the mines of Muzo. Profligate piety was certainly a form of conspicuous consumption, but seen another way, it was the saints or local cults who were competing to accumulate the precious assemblages required by their divinity. From this perspective emeralds, like gold or diamonds, were a variety of divine residue that all but pleaded to be mined, polished and heaped back on the divine.

In much of Muslim Asia, by contrast, emeralds found a distinctly masculine niche, and were worn as amulets or displayed prominently in turban ornaments. Others covered sacred water flasks, scabbards and quivers, usually pertaining to the shah, sultan or crown prince. At their largest and very best, Colombian emeralds served as reflections of the divine seminal energies of godhead. For the Safavids, Ottomans and especially Mughals, they encapsulated as no other earthly material could the visions and journeys of the Prophet in the form of the green pastures and palms of Paradise. Inscribed with a verse of thanks to the all-powerful or strung in a necklace of prayer beads, what better tangible symbol of protection, what better gift, could a ruler hope to receive or bestow – or, in Nadir Shah's case, steal from a rival?

From the perspective of Western science as it developed in the eighteenth century, emerald was no longer associated with solar divinity, snakebite curing or soothsaying. It had even lost its claim on the guardianship of female chastity. If emerald was special it was because it possessed a unique chemical composition, a singular crystalline geometry, a scaled hardness, a specific gravity, a refractive index. Emerald was but one of nature's many mineral combinations, 'mysterious' only inasmuch as it was a mathematical puzzle to be solved. With perseverance and the right instruments it could be properly classified, and perhaps one day synthesized, in the laboratory. For merchants and Crown administrators, emerald was at last reduced to a commodity in the modern, neoclassical sense (and therefore a 'pure' fetish in the Marxian one): emerald's value was a simple function of market price, determined by supply and demand.

The shift towards appraising emeralds in terms of scientific and 'raw' economic values brought with it a new narrative, a version of history in which those who had dug and died for them were individually irrelevant. Labour was but a troublesome factor of production – or fact of production, like excessive rainfall or landslides. It was presumed to be unskilled, ignorant and nameless. It had only to be 'managed', and thus only managers (plus a phalanx of geologists and engineers) could direct the struggle against nature that unearthing gemstones in a rational, efficient (read: profit-making) way required. When romantics revived the mythic prospector, they saw him as a grizzled white man, not an Indian or ex-slave.

Indeed, Aztecs and Incas might be added here and there in a shareholder report or auction catalogue for spice, along with a conquistador or two, but gone were the Muzos and slaves, along with emerald's own occult qualities. Gone were the adventurous Jewish traders of Iberia's globe-encompassing heyday, periodically robbed of their estates, tortured and sometimes killed by predatory imperialists in sacred guise. Gone, too, were the magnificent Asian shahs and sultans, great hoarders and bestowers of the green stones of paradise. Their gunpowder-propped empires were now but a distant memory, their weak descendants sad reminders of the fickle, unseen hand of history. By the early nineteenth century there was only folklore, chemistry and the grail-like quest to manipulate, if not control, international prices. Only at the outer limits of the modern world-system, where snakes still bit and female chastity remained insecure, could one find hints of that more magical and dangerous time when emeralds were something more than mere shiny green rocks.

❖

Postscript
From British Adventurers to Today's Esmeralderos

THE story of Colombian emeralds did not end with the decline and fall of gunpowder empires. The Muzo mines reopened soon after independence in the 1820s thanks to British interest and local initiative, although they still struggled. Various Colombian and European partnerships formed and dissolved through the turn of the twentieth century, with most emeralds going to European and U.S. markets via Amsterdam, Antwerp, London and New York. Some stones went to Calcutta for cutting and polishing. An attempted government takeover of Muzo around 1910 failed, and the mines returned to private hands. By this time, U.S. investors and engineers began displacing British, French and German ones.

The conquest-era Somondoco mines were rediscovered around 1890 near the village of Chivor, prompting new foreign investment and some extraordinary finds, mostly in the 1920s and 1930s. In a new wave of nationalization following the Great Depression and World War II, the Muzo diggings were taken over by Colombia's national bank. (Chivor remained private.) Bulldozers and dynamite boosted Muzo's emerald output in the 1950s, but the state's new, closed system bred corruption and an increasingly violent contraband scene. By the time the state shuttered operations in 1973, emerald bosses, or *esmeralderos*, had become virtual feudal lords, complete with warring private armies. Although their image is now of well-heeled businessmen rather than pistol-wielding prospectors, *esmeralderos* with names like 'Big-eared Pedro' are still in control of Muzo as of writing this.

Mining Emeralds in a Capitalist Age

Emerald mining in Muzo likely continued on a small scale after the 1792 royal monopoly failure, but it was not until after Colombian independence in 1824 that a friend of Simón Bolívar, José Ignacio 'Pepe' Paris y Ricaurte (1780–1849), along with Charles Stuart Cochrane, brother of Scottish admiral and Latin American independence guarantor Sir Thomas Cochrane, sought to reopen the Muzo works on a large scale.[1] Paris and Cochrane were joined by Peruvian naturalist Mariano Rivero, who also assisted a French team in establishing a School of Mines and a national mineralogical cabinet in Bogotá. The three entrepreneurs signed a contract with Gran Colombia's fledgling government, which granted them a ten-year monopoly on emerald extraction in exchange for a tenth of sales revenues.

Despite great hopes, the company failed. The mines were apparently not to blame, but rather the disinterest of the principals. Cochrane and Rivero quickly moved on to other pursuits, leaving Paris alone in Colombia. In 1828 he had the contract revised. After working with little capital and no significant finds, Paris renegotiated terms with the national government yet again in 1830, reducing his obligation to the state to 5 per cent of sales and extending his exclusive rights to Muzo's original mine works to twenty years.[2]

The mines still failed to produce, and 'Pepe' Paris found himself hounded by Bogotá treasury officials scrambling for any revenue they could find. Gran Colombia was dissolving: Venezuela and Ecuador had declared themselves sovereign republics by 1830, and Bolívar the Liberator was dead. Finally, one of Paris's brothers invited an English mining engineer, George Cheyne, to examine operations. Contrary to expectations, Cheyne recommended a return to opencast works, essentially reverting to pre-Columbian methods.[3] A government census from 1835 counted only 7,800 residents in the entire jurisdiction of Muzo, making it, for its area, one of the least populated regions in Colombia.[4]

Once the floodgates opened, as in former days, Muzo's fabled deposits began to yield gems. Paris left Colombia for Europe in 1839, where he sold a number of emeralds and also exhibited other unusual crystals he had found in Muzo. A strange, amber-coloured mineral, too soft for a gem but of interest to scientists and collectors, was named Parisite in his honour. Some of Paris's emerald earnings were spent contracting with the Italian sculptor Pietro Tenerani for a bronze statue of Bolívar, the one now standing in the centre of Bogotá's main plaza. Cast in Munich and shipped with great difficulty up the Magdalena River and over the mountains, it arrived in the capital amid great ceremony in 1845. Paris returned to Colombia to run the Muzo mines until both he and his contract expired in 1848.[5]

Colombia's emerald deposits were officially declared national patrimony on 9 June 1847 by General Tomás Cipriano de Mosquera, and placed under the direction of a salaried Irish mining engineer, Thomas Fallon. Fallon's efforts yielded 60,181 carats of emeralds within a year, but for reasons of cost the government quickly chose to revert to the contract system. The emerald contract then went to Juan de Francisco Martín and his English associate, Patrick Wilson. The two agreed to the 5 per cent tax on sales for eight years, plus an annual rent of 142,000 silver *reales*. Though seemingly quite expensive, the agreement paid off for investors. At least 120 men were said to have laboured under the direction of engineer Fallon, who was kept on, by 1850.[6] Manuel Ancízar, who visited Muzo in 1850, described the diggings as follows:

> In order to discover the vein of emeralds the workers descend with admirable dexterity down a near-vertical wall, chopping out tiny footholds with iron bars until they reach the designated spot to

carve a bench, or perpendicular cut in the wall in the manner of a great staircase. The spectator witnessing this work for the first time fearfully expects to see the peons fall from the rocks at any moment, to be crushed at the base of the excavation. Indeed, there have been cases in which, as a result of poor footing or the fall of a rock from above hitting the legs, they have fallen all the way to the patio below, torn to pieces. It is certain that only force of habit and emulation could inspire the miners to be so audacious and indifferent, stepping from one crumbling foothold to another as if they were ants on a vertical wall. Arranged in a line at the designated spot for the bench they begin to chop and shovel, producing a large mass of earth that slides unpushed all the way down to a pile. . . . When the pile gets large enough the overseer rings a bell and the *tambrero*, already on watch, opens the floodgate of the *tambre*, sending an impetuous torrent of water from the highest part of the hill all the way down to the patio, and being well directed it carries away all the accumulated rock and earth from the dump pile, then exits the patio through a drainage tunnel. This process, repeated many times, leads eventually to the discovery of many horizontal or diagonal calcite and quartz veins in whose bosom are found the desired emeralds. Their presence is announced by a greenish quartz crystal, some small crystals called green earth, plus stringers of iron pyrite in brilliant yellow and rainbow-hued clusters, until finally there appear the *gangas*, or crystaline masses, in whose centre there shine the precious stones.[7]

Ancízar was far less impressed with the nearly three-hundred-year-old colonial 'city' of La Trinidad, 'today the sad and miserable town of Muzo'. Like a romantic on tour, Ancízar lovingly described brick and stone ruins that locals knew to be the remains of five colonial churches and at least two monasteries (there had been three). Now all these structures were abandoned, overgrown with trees and vines, 'guarding in harmony the desolation of the ancient villa'.[8] Finding even the parish church in a state of total abandon, its priest absent and most of its two hundred citizens (nine hundred in the larger parish) sickly, poor and uneducated, Ancízar concluded that Muzo was the victim of its own greed. Syphilis raged, he said, and 60 per cent of births were illegitimate. He could have been describing most nineteenth-century mining towns.

Sick or not, Muzo and its mines carried on well after Ancízar's departure. According to Otero Muñoz, during three months in 1858 workers uncovered nineteen pounds of quality emerald. De Francisco and Wilson managed to extend their contract to 1861. The mines failed to attract new investors during one of Colombia's perennial civil wars, but they continued to operate on behalf of the state, run by the Irishman Fallon until his death in 1863.

The next emerald contractor was the Frenchman Gustave Lehmann, who promised a rent of 14,700 pesos in 1864 in exchange for ten years' monopoly. Labourers were encouraged to sign on with state exemptions from military service. Lehmann enjoyed at least three lucky days in early February 1865, when some 66,940 carats of emeralds were discovered and registered, yet by 1870 the national government annulled the agreement and opened numerous Muzo and Coscuez-area mines to public claimants.

Bids on individual mines came in from European and Colombian firms, including Koppel & Schrader, Pittar Leverson & Co., Juan Sordo, Gustave Lehmann himself and the Government of Boyacá. After some shrill fraud denunciations in Bogotá, the Colombian government created the post of 'Inspector of the Mines of Muzo'.[9] The man named to the position, Felipe Fermín Paúl, was one of the first officials since early colonial times to call for better working conditions. Paúl had been a state employee in Muzo off and on since the Fallon administration.

Between 1875 and 1885 the state-claimed mines, including virtually all the Muzo diggings known since colonial times, were run by a group of Colombian investors, most with illustrious surnames (Samper, Uribe, Restrepo). The main contractor was Juan Sordo, who promised to pay 20,606 pesos per year. Workers were also granted the now-standard military service exemption, but it is difficult to say if this was of greater benefit to them or to the company.[10] In the midst of the Sordo contract a fight broke out between the departments (then called 'sovereign states') of Cundinamarca and Boyacá over jurisdiction. The solution was to share the emerald annuities.

The nation reclaimed sole legal control of the mines and their revenues in 1886, by which time a new contractor, the English subject Lorenzo Merino, was in place. In 1894 the mines passed to the Frenchman Alexandre Mancini. By this time the state was charging 30,000 pesos a year in rents, plus a good-faith payment of 400,000 pesos. The high cost of entry was a result of public bidding, and Mancini's ace in the hole was a firm he represented, The English Mining Syndicate, Ltd.[11]

Mining operations were handed over to the syndicate's man on the ground, Christopher Dixon, in 1896. Despite assertions by Conservative Party journalists beginning in 1899 that the syndicate was making millions at the nation's expense, Mancini offered to end the contract and return the diggings to the government for 500,000 pesos. The offer was ignored, and in the midst of the ensuing War of the Thousand Days the syndicate faced even greater problems. The engineer Enrique González was charged with recruiting mineworkers for his rebel batallion, suggesting a return to conquest-era paramilitarism. Even after the contract passed to a Colombian, Lorenzo Cuéllar, in 1901, trouble with roving paramilitaries stymied mining operations. Engineer Dixon, who had stayed on, was treated as a suspect and hauled off to the highlands for interrogation.[12]

The Colombian Emerald Company Ltd.

When the War of the Thousand Days ended in 1902, Colombia's government began renegotiating and consolidating its debt. One strategy was to use emerald rents to help back the new *peso de oro*, or gold peso currency. Despite troubles, some 268,211 carats of emeralds were registered between November 1902 and May 1903, when the mines were run by salaried overseers. Even with foreign specialists on the ground and significant capital investment, little about emerald mining appears to have changed since colonial times, except perhaps expanded use of explosives. Transport was similarly timeless, as suggested by a 4 December 1903 dispatch to Bogotá from the Muzo mines:

> Ministry of the Treasury. – Today at 7 a.m. left here in direction of that city carrying emerald remittance with escort of twenty soldiers and companion Sr. Leovigildo Nieto. On crossing the Minero River, which was running very high, a mule drowned; farther on after crossing the river another mule carrying said remittance doubled back by another trail and in trying to intercept her she fell in the river according to the peon who was driving her. Until now it has not been possible to find her. I will continue doing all I can to find the load. On coming back from the outskirts of Muzo in search of the load I received notice that mine administrator Maldonado had just fractured his leg in a fall. As a result I resolved to return to the mines. I have just sent a peon to Ubaté to fetch physician Dr. Zenon Solano. – Your servant, Estanislao Franco.[13]

In addition, there were security problems, as the military escort suggests, and both Franco and Maldonado sent a number of 'suspect persons' to Bogotá whom they had discovered near the diggings. The lost mule's skeleton was later found, but no trace of the emeralds.

The mines were run from 1904 to 1909 by a private Colombian company, the Banco de Exportadores or 'Sindicato de Muzo', which paid the government its share of revenues and did reasonably well. Between 29 March 1904 and 11 June 1909 the company registered 737,047 carats of 'first class' (*primera clase*) emeralds, 704,812 carats of second, 1,268,017 of third and 1,738,559 of fourth. The stones were sold for 2,177,008 pesos against costs totalling 606,866 pesos. Although it is difficult to know the exact meaning of the grading terms in use by this time, this was as good as Muzo's mines ever produced in the colonial era. One great emerald found in May 1907 weighed 2,462 carats and was dubbed 'El Gran Felibre'.[14]

In early 1909 the contract went to an Anglo-Colombian syndicate registered in London as The Colombian Emerald Company Ltd., and an international dispute immediately broke out. In one version of the story, the company, which had ties to South African diamond interests in the Transvaal and which sent emerald rough to be cut in Amsterdam, New York and Calcutta, was to pay £100,000 sterling to seal the deal, arranged primarily by one of the previous syndicate leaders from the 1904 to 1909 period, Laureano García Ortiz. Another claim was that the payment was £250,000 plus another £71,073 in indemnities to the former syndicate. The contract was nullified amid fierce denunciations by the Colombian government in May 1910.[15]

The nullification of the Colombian Emerald Company's contract was hotly debated for several years, often in quite specific terms. The Conservative politician Laureano Gómez cut his teeth arguing the case in print as a young journalist.[16] In his 1915 tract, *Renta de esmeraldas*, the government lawyer Francisco Montaña stated that Colombia was being short-changed in part by poor cutting practices in Europe. The company's dealings with diamond polishers in Antwerp were a financial disaster, according to Montaña, as 'these specialists in diamonds know absolutely nothing of the cutting and marketing of emeralds'. Why were the stones not being cut in Colombia, he asked, where there had never been a shortage of trained lapidaries?[17] Whatever the truth, the debates of the 1910s did not drive away foreign investors, prospectors and engineers. Some simply abandoned Muzo for Coscuez or Chivor.

The mines of Chivor, or Somondoco, were rediscovered in 1889 by Francisco Restrepo. It was not until 1912, however, when Restrepo's partner, German gemologist Fritz Klein, managed to start operations. The project was soon aborted with the beginning of the Second World War, and Klein did not return to Colombia until 1919. By this time his concession had been sold to The Colombian Emerald Development Corporation of New York. The company hired Klein as manager, and he made a number of significant finds, including the 632-carat Patricia Emerald, now displayed by the American Museum of Natural History in New York City.

Klein left Colombia in 1933, just as political violence engulfed the region and prompted the closure of the mines. He published an illustrated memoir in 1941.[18] In a similar vein, the British engineer Peter Rainier published a self-aggrandizing account of his work at Chivor in 1942, under the title *Green Fire*.[19] Not until after the Second World War were the mines reopened, run by the Delaware-based Chivor Emerald Mines. It was in these years that a young farm boy from the nearby village of Guateque named Víctor Carranza Niño first learned to appreciate emeralds.

The Colombian government ran the Muzo mines again from 1920 to 1927, allegedly without success. Yet success must be understood in relative terms, as García Manjarrés and Vargas Ayala claim 265,000 carats of emerald were extracted – or registered – between 1924 and 1927, when the mines were closed. Perhaps the stones were mostly of poor quality. In 1931, Oscar Heyman Brothers of New York signed a monopoly contract with the Colombian government to cut and sell Muzo's emeralds worldwide, but this deal was as sharply criticized as the Colombian Emerald Syndicate's previous contract of twenty-odd years. The Heyman Brothers deal also struggled to make money, which was perhaps unsurprising amidst the Great Depression. There was also a great burst of violence from 1930 to 1932, led by Boyacá's Conservatives that halted production and terrorized Liberal miners.

An attempted revival of the mines beginning in 1933 also failed to yield profits, with total production from 1933 to 1938 totalling only 93,287 carats, 25,645 carats of it *moralla*, or junk stone, and none of it *primera clase*. Finally, in 1945, partly as a result of Depression-era legislation, the Muzo emerald mines were handed over to the Bank of the Republic. In line with a pan-Latin American trend towards economic nationalism, the Colombian government created a ministry of mines and petroleum in 1940, and set about taking over the nation's numerous mineral deposits. The state also intervened to develop the gem-cutting sector, almost entirely concentrated in Bogotá.

Monopoly and Murder

The federal bank's mining operations in Muzo were not opened until 1947, and as in colonial times in the interim a number of clandestine miners were said to have invaded the old diggings. *Guaquería*, or freelance grubbing, was, as always, a primary means of survival on the rough-and-tumble frontier. Vigilance improved somewhat when the mines opened, and between 1947 and 1968, registered output totalled 463,750 carats of gem-quality emerald and 2,250,495 carats of *moralla*. Yet amidst reorganization came more waves of partisan violence and the emergence of politicized bandits such as José María Sosa, alias 'Cucacho'. The end of the 1960s marked the rise of locally recruited Conservative policemen and assassins known as *chulavitas*. Their handiwork soon spread far beyond the emerald districts surrounding Muzo.[20]

The Bank of the Republic's production numbers may sound significant, but as in the days of royal administration, Muzo's yields never came close to offsetting costs. The best efforts of mining engineer and bank-appointed director Dr Miguel Alvarez Uribe proved as insufficient as those of his colonial predecessors. Alvarez Uribe had publicly laughed off statements in the press that Muzo was an 'accursed treasure', yet it was just as operations began that Colombia collapsed amid the great *Violencia* that followed the 9 April 1948 assasination of the Liberal firebrand Jorge Eliécer Gaitán.[21] Violence in Muzo grew so severe that the mines were closed between September 1949 and January 1951. The situation remained tense, but one extraordinary find was made shortly after the reopening on 9 May 1951. Two crystals, one weighing 1,796 carats and the other 1,483 carats, were unearthed; they remain the pride of the Banco de la República's collection.

The bank and federal government tried various schemes to make the mines viable in the 1950s and 1960s, and in June 1968 legislators tried to form a state emerald company structurally similar to the state airline, Avianca. The plan was ditched later the same year, however, and the mines were put under the larger administration of the Empresa Colombiana de Minas (ECOMINAS). The state company's registered sales of emeralds for 1969 totalled nearly US$4.4m, but trouble was again brewing.[22] Even before this, in 1960, new, clandestine finds at Peñas Blancas, near Coscuez, had led to a series of vendetta killings.

Before his death in 1965, the instigator of what the press labelled the 'War of the Emeralds', Efraín González, had all but sewn up the illicit trade in green stones with help from two brothers who worked in the state-owned diggings. After more murderous score settling, a new emerald boss arose in the person of Humberto Ariza, a.k.a. 'The Swan'. Waiting in the wings, however, was a much subtler figure, the now mature Víctor Carranza Niño, aided by investors and a long-time legal partner from Cartagena, Juan Beetar. These men came from Chivor and would soon dominate Muzo. They established a firm called TecMinas, and Carranza began buying up loose rough from anyone who would sell it.[23]

The anthropologist Martha Rojas, who had direct access to ECOMINAS officials and data, plus information gathered by *El Tiempo* newspaper reporter Abel Rodríguez, offers the best descriptions of Muzo in the tumultuous period from 1969 to 1973, when the mines were closed for a mix of social and economic reasons. Muzo was apparently deemed too dangerous for Rojas to visit personally at the time, and access was officially limited to miners and other locals by police roadblocks.

ECOMINAS leased non-emerald bearing lands to local farmers to raise livestock and food crops to help supply legally employed miners, yet the arrival of thousands of *guaqueros*, or rootless prospectors, made even the farmers' lives miserable. The *guaqueros* allegedly stole crops and animals at night, and grubbed for emeralds at will, often within fenced-off company diggings. Enemies of the farmers, the invaders still found friends. Hundreds of company officials, guards and policemen were quickly discovered to be complicit in allowing the *guaqueros* to mine for emeralds on the sly in exchange for a cut of the findings.

For their part, some thirty thousand *guaqueros* were by the early 1970s trying to support families living in tarpaper shacks built in flood-prone ravines. A roll of bread cost four times what it did in Bogotá. Even when lucky enough to find an emerald amid the waste sent downstream by the company, or in illegal tunnels, the *guaqueros* faced double-crossing mates, common thieves and what Rojas calls the 'mafia verde', or Green Mafia. Although ECOMINAS technically reserved the right to buy and even cut stones found in and around Muzo, an underground network of buyers and lapidaries quickly emerged when the mines restarted in 1969, echoing the era of Crown monopoly two centuries previously.

As for law in this lawless land, *guaqueros* were accustomed to receiving notes advising them to move on within six hours. Failure to follow the warning was rewarded with murder. The best protection, according to Rojas, was to organize into units of six or eight *socios*, or 'associates', often kinsmen who then found sponsors at the buying level to advance them tools, food and other supplies. Policemen were also considered essential protectors as long as they received their cut. Most of the *guaqueros* by this time were said to gather in the Quebrada de las Ánimas ('All Souls Creek') to wash material mined illegally at night. Buyers lined up by 7:00 a.m. to greet them. As is true today, many *guaqueros* worked underground by carbide lamp or flashlight, mostly with picks and short-handled sledgehammers. Those who could afford it used dynamite and power tools.

Behind its fences, ECOMINAS exploited its extensive holdings at Muzo, Coscuez and Peñas Blancas. Although bulldozers were now standard equipment, the old techniques of mining were still in place. Bulldozers shaved the tops off steep hills to form gently inclined planes where possible, enabling expansion or opening of old-style *bancos*. These were worked from top to bottom by men with crowbars as in colonial times, flushed periodically with water gathered higher up in reservoirs, still called *tambres*. Bulldozers then removed mounds of detritus that subsequently accumulated at the base of the diggings. Pneumatic drills were used to break up especially hard material, but once the rock began to 'paint', the work of gem extraction was done by hand. On receiving reports of growing violence among *esmeralderos*, or Green Mafia families, plus news that the mines were running a huge deficit despite a thriving secret trade in stones, the Colombian government decided to shutter the mines and expel the *guaqueros* in July 1973.

Emerald-related struggles only intensified in the decades following the 1973 closure of the Muzo diggings. Money made in emeralds was invested in the emerging narcotics trade, and vice-versa, pulling in new players and raising the stakes. At the margins lurked the eleventh and twenty-second fronts of the Fuerzas Armadas Revolucionarias de Colombia, or FARC, whose fundraising methods included extortion, kidnapping and other forms of criminal parasitism. Paramilitary gangs fought the guerrillas and also common criminals, who flowed in from the highlands. The tide of violence crested with a series of massacres in the 1980s, but by this time far more attention was being paid to bombings and assassinations associated with the M-19 guerrilla group and with drug kingpin Pablo Escobar of Medellín.

When the dust settled, one *esmeraldero* held sway: Víctor Carranza Niño. Carranza, who had started as a child *guaquero* in the northern Boyacá highlands and was now middle-aged, became the boss of bosses in the so-called Green Mafia. As evidence of his power, he helped broker a peace deal in the emerald zone aided by the Bishop of Chiquinquirá in 1990. Even after the peace, Carranza's sponsorship of paramilitaries and freelance assassins, both in the emerald district and in the eastern Llanos where he owned cattle ranches, has been amply documented.

Despite the legacy of murderous violence and drug trafficking, plus time spent in federal custody in the early 2000s, Carranza has many admirers in the business world as at this time of writing. A recent biography by Jeanette Erazo Heufelder, while acknowledging his ruthless rise to power, treats the 'Emerald King', as she calls him, as a kind of Colombian peasant version of Horatio Alger's Ragged Dick. A would-be Cecil Rhodes, too, Carranza is seen by many international gem traders as the necessary kingpin capable of containing the world flow of Colombian emeralds needed to keep prices high.[24] Do ordinary people share this view? In my several visits to Muzo, Coscuez and Chivor, I have been afraid to ask too many questions for fear of further endangering people whose lives are already at considerable risk, but when Heufelder interviewed the men and, especially, women of Muzo, she found little love for Carranza. In bringing peace, they said, he had helped only himself and the big Bogotá and foreign shareholders; he had done nothing to ease the poverty of mineworkers and their families.

Colombian emeralds have meanwhile enjoyed new popularity in India, where the rise of a vast bourgeoisie has helped spur a revival of Mughal jewellery fashions.

❖

Note on Weights and Measures

L IKE most gemstones, emeralds are measured in carats, now standardized at one-fifth of a gram. The original karat, or *qirat*, referred to a carob seed of near uniform weight. In early modern times, carats (*quilates* in Spanish and Portuguese) were used by most European and Mediterranean gem merchants. Several different but analogous systems of gem-weighing were employed in South Asia and the Middle East in the period covered by this book. Perhaps because of ignorance of any of these systems, in New Granada and other parts of the Spanish Indies emeralds were usually weighed using the same measures applied to gold dust. The *peso de oro de minas*, or *castellano*, is generally believed to have weighed 4.6 grams (100 castellanos went into a Castilian pound, which is known to have weighed 460 g). *Castellanos*, or *pesos de oro*, were divided into eight *tomines*, and sometimes 24 carats (rendering them close to the modern measure at 0.192 g). Things become less clear at the level of grains, or *granos*, which varied depending on which grain – literally – was being used. Whole or partial wheat, rice and maize grains have since colonial times been used for these fractions among Colombian miners, merchants and lapidaries. In most districts in the period covered here, a *tomín* officially consisted of twelve grains. The *adarme*, or dram, an apothecary's measure amounting to one-sixteenth of an ounce, shows up in emerald production records from the eighteenth century.

Mine claims were measured in terms of the Spanish yard, or *vara*, of roughly 0.835 m, or 35 inches. In Muzo, most mine claims were rectangular surface lots measuring 30 by 20 *varas* (about 25 × 17 m).

quintal = 4 arrobas/100 lbs/46 kg
arroba = 25 lbs/50 marcos (marks)/11.5 kg
libra = 2 marcos/460 g
marco = 8 onzas/230 g
onza = 8 ochavas/16 adarmes/28.75 g

peso = 8 tomines/24 quilates (carats, old style)/4.6 g
ochava = 2 adarmes/6 tomines/3.6 g
adarme = 3 tomines/9 quilates/1.8 g
tomín = 3 quilates/12 granos/0.60 g
quilate = 4 granos/0.20 g
grano = 0.05 g

ducado = 375 maravedís (account money based on Venetian gold ducat)
escudo de oro = 340 maravedís (22.5k gold coin weighing about 3.3 g)
patacón, peso duro or peso de a ocho = about 28 g silver coin worth 272 maravedís
peso de oro de minas = 450 maravedís (used as weight measure and account money)
real = 34 maravedís (coin and money of account equal to 1/8 of a peso de a ocho)

legua = 5.57 km
braza = 1.67 m
vara = 0.835 m

$$\diamond$$

Appendices

Production, Appraisal and Brazil's Fabled Emerald Range

UNLIKE gold or silver, emeralds cannot be reduced to simple units of standard purity. As a result, tallying production using tax ledgers and other records is difficult. There is also the problem of untaxed stones, for which only occasional, anecdotal records survive. Despite these deficiencies, Spanish treasury officials tried hard to tax emerald production, and left substantial evidence of their efforts. The following is an attempt to summarize surviving production data from 1539 to 1792, and also to explain the evaluation criteria used by colonial and Spanish Crown appraisers over this long period. Last is a brief examination of Brazil's fabled 'emerald mountains', not discovered until the 1960s.

1. Production Records

1a. Somondoco/Chivor

The earliest surviving post-conquest tax records, now housed in the Archive of the Indies in Seville, show a dwindling number of emeralds making their way into the Bogotá treasury following the Muisca conquest in 1538, which was said to have yielded about 1,800 plundered emeralds.[1] Later stones arrived as tribute payments offered by conquered Muisca chieftains, suggesting they had not been mined but rather collected from graves or sanctuaries. The term *plasma* refers to cloudy stones of less than gem quality, some of which were probably in the form of beads. None were specifically described as having come from the Somondoco diggings. The *quinto real*, or 'royal fifth', amounted to the following:

Years	'Fine' emeralds	'Plasmas'
1539–43	536	47
1543–7	84	29
1562	49 (left in *caja real* from earlier years)	
1563	9	

Source: AGI Contaduría 1293.

Emeralds were also taxed by treasury officials in the far southern jurisdiction of Popayán, more closely tied to Quito than Bogotá, in the 1550s. In 1553 116 'small emeralds of all grades' were listed, then between January 1554 and June 1555, 160 'small and medium emerald stones of average colour plus some plasmas'.[2] Although Popayán's ledgers offer no explanation, these stones were likely collected as taxes on either locally excavated grave goods or emeralds hoarded by soldiers who had been involved in the recent conquest of the Muiscas. Quito's mining tax ledgers do not list emeralds.

1b. Muzo

Below is a first attempt at graphing production using Muzo's emerald *quinto* (twenty per cent royal severance tax) records. The most complete series is housed in the Archive of the Indies, but many years of accounts are also preserved in Colombia's National Archive in Bogotá. Records consulted include Bogotá's and Muzo's treasury records, copies of which were periodically sent to Spain, along with some receipts of emeralds belonging to the royal treasury as recorded in Seville. In several cases numbers can be verified or adjusted by comparing these different ledgers. Unfortunately, most of the top-grade stones in the left-hand column were not listed by weight, although big ones were afforded precise, paragraph-long descriptions. These were most likely the centrepiece and dagger-handle emeralds of the shahs, as they were of best colour and greatest size.

Registered Emerald *Quintos* in Muzo, 1564–1634* (in 'gold' pesos of 4.6 g each)

Year	Primera Suerte	Segunda Suerte	Tercera Suerte	Cash Quintos
1564	782 stones			80 (pesos Au)
1567	792 stones			'_'
1569	5 stones	17		764
1570	49 stones	223		183
1571	111 stones	675		106
1572	16 stones	467		'_'
1573	7 stones	288		64
1574	19 stones	344	452	35
1575	61 stones	183		35
1576	113 stones	680	852	72
1577		153	230	70
1578		46	500	38
1579	1 stone	135	187	65
1580		164	360	27
1581	1 stone	711	1782	111
1582	3 stones	1351	1785	93
1583	2 stones	911	488	79
1584		516	403	10
1585		632	737	54
1586		645	1475	50
1587	1 stone	784	675	133
1588		956	939	194
1589		333	452	56
1590		597	1720	109
1591		193	1327	156
1592	11 stones	1068	2567	438
1593		791	1999	4
1594	1 stone	296	1610	80.3

1595		255	635	11
1596	6 stones	701	4400	66
1597		526	1353	29
1598		782	2435	82
1599		660	2401	28
1600		939	2277	44
1601		1764	2202	63
1602		751	1527	33
1603		516	1249	33
1604		172	418	12
1605		198	1474	6
1606–7	1 stone	650	3086	39
1608	1 stone	2486	2431	29
1609		71	661	30
1610		180	182	4
1611		309	902	12
1612	84 stone (guaca)[†]	504	1627	57
1613		87	520	29
1614	1 stone	92	790	8
1615		194	434	30
1616–17	1 stone	98	957	33
1618		134	625	15
1619		167	933	8
1620		270	831	29
1621		212	647	8
1622		650	1262	'–'
1623		427	983	20
1624		548	1377	19
1625–6		224	1159	22
1627		170	613	11
1628		35	155	5.5
1629		226	468	2.5
1630–3		351	1048	'–'
1634		42	255	13
TOTALS	2,069 stones	28,550 pesos	62,857 pesos	3,937.3 pesos

* Source AGI Contaduría 1587, 1295.

† Recovered from an indigenous gravesite, or guaca.

These numbers seem unimpressive, and certainly they do not represent total production, but when one converts *quinto* amounts from pesos to grams, then to carats (0.2 g), and finally multiplies by five for total output, the significance of registered production grows. Below I have excluded the loose and first-grade stones and cash *quintos* listed above since these are impossible to render into carats. It should be kept in mind that a few large, grade-one stones could exceed the value of all second- and third-grade stones in terms of overseas market value (the numbers below are charted on p. 81).

Registered Emerald Production in Muzo, 1569–1634 (in carats)

Year	Segunda Suerte	Tercera Suerte
1569	1,955	
1570	25,645	
1571	77,625	
1572	53,705	
1573	33,120	
1574	39,560	51,980
1575	21,045	
1576	78,200	97,980
1577	17,595	26,450
1578	5,290	57,500
1579	15,525	21,505
1580	18,860	41,400
1581	81,765	204,930
1582	155,365	205,275
1583	104,765	56,120
1584	59,340	46,345
1585	72,680	84,755
1586	74,175	169,625
1587	90,160	77,625
1588	109,940	107,985
1589	38,295	51,980
1590	68,655	197,800
1591	22,195	152,605
1592	122,820	295,205
1593	90,965	229,885

1594	34,040	185,150
1595	29,325	73,025
1596	80,615	506,000
1597	60,490	155,595
1598	89,930	280,025
1599	75,900	276,115
1600	107,985	261,855
1601	202,860	253,230
1602	86,365	175,605
1603	59,340	143,635
1604	19,780	48,070
1605	22,770	169,510
1606–7	74,750	354,890
1608	285,890	279,565
1609	8,165	76,015
1610	20,700	20,930
1611	35,535	103,730
1612	57,960	187,105
1613	10,005	59,800
1614	10,580	90,850
1615	22,310	49,910
1616–17	11,270	110,055
1618	15,410	71,875
1619	19,205	107,295
1620	31,050	95,565
1621	24,380	74,405
1622	74,750	145,130
1623	49,105	113,045
1624	63,020	158,355
1625–6	25,760	133,285
1627	19,550	70,495
1628	4,025	17,825
1629	25,990	53,820
1630–3	40,365	120,520
1634	4,830	29,325
TOTALS	3,283,250	7,228,585

Source: AGI Contaduría 1587, 1295.

Solid as these numbers look, the *quinto* records on which they are based are shaky. Aside from the problem of subjective assessment, emerald miners, dealers and occasionally gem cutters dealt with the inflexible 20 per cent Crown duty by giving the king their worst stones. Further complicating matters, treasury officials ordered large and exceptionally fine stones auctioned to avoid being falsely appraised (or cut to pieces) to pay the fifth. Willingly or not, the seller paid the tax from the resulting cash settlement.

Royal officials established this tradition of auctioning large stones after a 1568 visit to Muzo. As the mines were so new at the time and emeralds still very rare, officials offered to buy the best specimens in town in the name of the king. They promised to pay between 16,000 and 18,000 ducats for one huge crystal weighing 102 pesos (2,346 carats), 3,000 ducats for one weighing 40 pesos (920 carats) and 3,000 for a third, finer one weighing 15 pesos (345 carats).[3] Unsure of these values, the three miners in possession of the stones balked and asked that they be paid after the stones were appraised in Spain.

Because sending any stones across the Atlantic untaxed would diminish Bogotá treasury income, colonial officials decided to require cash payment of taxes based on a local auction price. Portuguese lapidary and goldsmith then resident in Muzo, Diego Hernández, said that miners were already avoiding *quinto* payment because of the still uncertain nature of emerald appraisals. Hernández noted that the king of Portugal wisely employed a special appraiser to handle diamond shipments coming from India, but stopped short of recommending Philip II to do the same for emeralds.

Apparently out of fear that Muzo locals would engage in fraud, emerald taxes were collected in Bogotá, the regional capital, until the mid-1590s. The fifth was usually paid by travelling merchants, and in some cases servants and even soldiers who had participated in the conquest. Only when it appeared that the amounts rendered bore little relation to ups and downs in the mines did Crown officials deem it wiser to collect taxes nearer the Muzo diggings, going right to the slopes of the Cerro de Itoco.[4] It was even ordered that a magistrate be called and work stopped as soon as stones of any value were unearthed – in part so that multiple witnesses would be on hand to testify as to the value of any strike. Officials hoped taxing at the source would keep emeralds from 'leaking' downstream, where they would quickly disappear into competing trade vortices.

Charges of contraband trade and *quinto* fraud were rife immediately after the great discoveries of 1564. In 1574, the mine-discoverer Alonso Ramírez Gasco charged Bogotá's *audiencia* president, Dr Venero de Leiva, along with his wife, with taking prized emeralds worth some 1,500 gold pesos.[5] The misdeed dated to 1565, but Ramírez was forced to wait for the new incoming president to begin his investigation, or *residencia*, of Venero de Leiva. In his petition, Ramírez said he had been ordered by Dr Venero to display all stones in his possession to pay the *quinto*. This was done in the president's house, and after Venero selected the three finest stones 'for the king and Council of the Indies', the doctor's wife, Doña María de Ondegardo, took her pick of the rest, a total of some fifty emeralds. Venero maintained that the stones were in fact 'clear', and of little value, but witnesses recalled otherwise. Here was a disincentive to reporting.

After 1595, monthly *quinto* records were kept in the town council building of La Trinidad de los Muzos, and copies of these records, along with the gem-rough *quintos* themselves, were sent annually to the capital and then to royal treasury officials in Spain. Although Muzo's local records have been lost, enough copies of the yearly registers survive in Bogotá and Seville to tentatively estimate production.

With the exception of prime emeralds, called *piedras de cuenta*, or 'stones of account', which were always extremely rare, miners preferred to pay the fifth in kind, not cash. The Crown in fact demanded as much for reasons that were never clearly stated but seem to have referred to Islamic and Reconquest traditions of pillage and rightful shares. Crown officials quickly caught on to the ruse of the 'worthless fifth', and ordered miners to put all their emeralds in a bag, from which a fifth would be selected at random. Variations on this practice, including the chance selection of two fifths, of which the miner was allowed to take the better (as an incentive to be honest and still bring in all stones), seem not to have improved the quality of taxed stones.

As unhappy Crown officials noted across the entire colonial period, the king's emeralds seemed strangely unrepresentative of what was circulating among merchants.

Stones given the designation of third class, or *tercera suerte*, prevailed, followed by those of second class, or *segunda suerte*. Respectable gems could be cut from both second- and third-class emeralds, but *segunda* was far above *tercera*. 'Second grade' usually meant stones with some inclusions or flaws but of prime, deep-green colour, precisely what set Colombian emeralds apart from those of Egypt or Austria. Third-class stones included those with less colour, more fractures, or more inclusions. *Plasmas*, as seen above, were cloudy stones, but worst of all were *morallas* or *morallón*, fractured bits or hunks of crystal with little gem potential. Miners loved to pay taxes in these.

Registered Emerald *Quintos* and Totals in Muzo, 1657–79* (in gold pesos/carats)

Year	Segunda Suerte	Tercera Suerte	Segunda Total	Tercera Total
1657	n/a	n/a	2,465	5,348
1659	85	292	1,955	6,716
1662	89	420	2,047	9,660
1664	5	3	115	69
1665		15		345
1666	12	20	276	460
1667	116	273	2,668	6,279
1668	149	499	3,427	11,477
1669		11		253
1670	125	348	2,875	8,004
1671	173	584	3,979	13,432
1672	50	107	1,150	2,461
1673	84	298	1,932	6,854
1674	13	150	299	3,450
1675	102	696	2,346	16,008
1676	186	590	4,278	13,570
1677	58	279	1,334	6,417

1678	39	910	897	20,930
1679†	15	308	585	18,430
TOTALS	1,301	5,803	32,628	150,163

* Source: AGI Contaduria 1587, 1588 (from *quintos* rounded to nearest whole peso).
† Monthly quinto records for this year are fragmentary, but annual totals survive, as recorded in the two right-hand columns.

Registered Emerald *Quintos* and Totals in Muzo, 1686–1760* (in gold pesos/carats)

Year	Segunda Suerte	Tercera Suerte	Segunda Total	Tercera Total
1686	77	467	1,771	10,741
1687	81	601	1,863	13,823
1688	22	237	506	5,451
1689	68	936	1,564	21,528
1690	15	271	345	6,233
1696	88	521	2,024	11,983
1699†	30	117	1,725	10,410
1700	77	174	467	4,002
1701	36	92	828	2,116
1702	97	265	2,231	6,095
1703	96	357	2,208	8,211
1704	55	120	1,265	2,760
1705	76	246	1,748	5,658
1706	130	529	2,990	12,167
1711	200	2,005	4,600	46,115
1719	41	116	943	2,668
1720	56	31	1,288	713
1721		2,338		53,774
1749	24 ozs.	6,342	3,450	145,866
1750	199	213	4,577	4,899
1751–60‡				
TOTALS	1,594	15,978	36,393	375,213

* Source: AGI Contaduría 1587, 1588; AGNC Real Hacienda.
† Monthly quinto records for this year are fragmentary, but annual totals survive, as recorded in the two right-hand columns.
‡ For this decade the crown required Muzo miners to pay a collective tax of 75 pesos in cash per year. Emerald production was thus not recorded.

Total Registered Emerald Production in Muzo, 1766–84* (in marks – ounces – adarmes)

Year	Primera Suerte	Segunda Suerte	Tercera Suerte	Cash Quintos
1766	-0-	2.3.0	9.7.8	4 pesos Ag
1767	-0-	1.3.8	5.0.6	4 pesos Ag
1768	2.0.5	3.4.2	11.5.11	
1769	8.1.2	8.6.4	36.3.9	
1770	9.3.9	5.2.8	17.7.0	
1771	3.2.7	1.5.13	3.5.16	5 pesos Ag
1772	1.1.2	3.1.1	3.5.10	
1773	0.4.4	0.9.15	13.4.0	22 pesos Ag+
1774	0.7.2	1.2.14	4.1.7	
1775	16.0.6	18.1.15	30.0.5	
1776	18.6.2	9.7.12	20.7.10	
1777	8.0.8	6.4.16	8.2.0	
1778	7.3.15	4.6.0	15.4.4	
1779	*none registered*	('por ser . . .	. . . mina nueva')	
1780	0.7.1	0.5.2	10.2.12	
1781	9.1.10	3.1.3	23.7.2	
1782	10.4.8	14.1.0	51.2.12	
1783	1.1.9	1.6.8	15.6.0	
1784	0.1.2	0.4.12	3.7.10	

* Source AGI Santa Fé 877; AGNC Minas de Boyacá 2.

Total Registered Emerald Production in Muzo, 1766–84* (in carats)

Year	Primera Suerte	Segunda Suerte	Tercera Suerte
1766	-0-	2,731	11,428
1767	-0-	1,653	5,840
1768	2,345	4,043	13,468
1769	9,362	10,099	41,912
1770	10,862	6,110	20,556
1771	3,801	1,986	4,313
1772	1,312	3,603	4,259
1773	611	1,429	15,525
1774	1,024	1,564	4,807
1775	18,454	20,979	34,545

1776	21,581	11,464	24,096
1777	9,272	7,619	9,488
1778	8,616	5,463	17,861
1779	*none registered*	('por ser ...	... mina nueva')
1780	1,015	737	11,896
1781	10,584	3,675	27,474
1782	12,147	16,244	59,046
1783	1,375	2,085	18,113
1784	162	683	4,546
TOTALS	112,523	102,167	329,173

* Source AGI Santa Fé; AGNC Minas de Boyacá 2.

2. *Lapidaries and Appraisers*

Appraising and cutting emeralds was as much an art as mining them. The purpose of this section is to highlight the presence of gem cutters in colonial Colombia from the discovery of the mines to late colonial times, then to look briefly at how these stones were appraised, cut and set in the colonies versus Spain or Portugal.

2a. Colonial Lapidaries

Within a few years of discovery of the Muzo mines there emerged a class of gem cutters, or *lapidarios*, from among New Granada's small goldsmithing community. They appear not to have formed a guild separate from the broader profession of goldsmiths, but lapidaries were recognized as specialized craftsmen in documents spanning more than two centuries. As early as 1569 gem cutters were expressly forbidden by order of the royal *audiencia* from practising their trade in Muzo, and some were charged with visiting the mines to barter with Amerindian serfs and enslaved Africans for stones.

Ordinances reiterated and expanded in 1614 forbade lapidaries from handling rough without proof of taxation, and added that only certified craftsmen could cut gems of any kind. A 1643 *visita* led to further tightening, calling for periodic examination of 'lapidary workshops' (*obrajes de lapidaria*) and harsh punishments for anyone convicted of working untaxed emeralds. As 'traitor to the Royal Treasury' such scofflaws could expect two hundred lashes and permanent exile twenty leagues from home.[6] Crown officials rightly feared untaxed stones would be cut and set in jewellery soon after their discovery, then 'lost' in the local or export markets.

Although some colonial lapidaries gravitated back to Muzo when authorities lost interest and turned to other matters, most settled down in the capital. Bogotá, as a result, developed a minor polished gem market by about the turn of the seventeenth century, if not before.[7] A few other gem cutters set up shop in the towns of Villa de Leiva and Tunja, which were somewhat closer to the mines and boasted wealthy patrons. Others surely worked in Cartagena and Santa Marta, and in the southwestern cities of Cali and Popayán.

A few early master gem cutters in New Granada undoubtedly came from Portugal, Italy and the Low Countries, but the records offer few giveaway names. Only one sixteenth-century lapidary was explicitly described as Portuguese. Two lapidaries who appraised stones for the Crown in Muzo in the 1610s were Micael de Vega, whose origins are not listed, and Hernando Ortiz, a Basque from Bilbao.[8] By the time we get more information on individuals, as when Crown officials raided the shops of several Bogotá jewellers and lapidaries suspected of contraband trade in 1677, they turn out to be poor Creoles or free men of colour.

One Muzo-based lapidary questioned in the course of this multiyear fraud investigation, Felipe Lópes de Torres, said he had been apprenticed in Bogotá with the late 'Mateo Vicenzio, chapetón', almost certainly a 'peninsular' craftsman of Italian origin, cutting more than 2,500 stones before leaving to set up his own shop. Another likely Italian Muzo lapidary from the late seventeenth century was Vittorino Sandé. Lópes de Torres and most of his fellow tradesmen shrugged off the order not to work in Muzo and charges of cutting untaxed stones, citing a prevailing 'don't ask, don't tell' custom.[9]

Some emerald cutters mentioned in seventeenth- and eighteenth-century documents were enslaved Africans, such as Juan de Argüelles of Bogotá, who had undergone lengthy apprenticeships. A free mulatto lapidary named José López de Arias testified in 1677 that he had visited Argüelles in his master's house, 'where he has his workbench'. Argüelles had been trained by his master, also a lapidary. That men of colour would be active and even independent gem cutters in seventeenth-century Colombia is not surprising. Throughout colonial Spanish and Portuguese America all manual trades were disparaged from the first generations after conquest, giving rise to a large class of artisans of indigenous, African and mixed heritage.

Cutting and Setting Styles

To judge from surviving personal jewels and religious artefacts from the sixteenth and early seventeenth centuries, emeralds in the Habsburg era were rather crudely faceted – or polished in rounded cabochon form – then set deeply in soft, high-karat gold. This was not as developed as the celebrated *kundan* technique of the Mughals described by Manuel Keene, but it could have a similar visual effect.[10]

Most stones were cut square or rectangular, and usually quite shallow. Contemporary descriptions offer few details, not even on the cutting wheels, or *ruedas*, sometimes mentioned in inventories. In 1629 royal officials confiscated 215 cut stones from two merchants leaving Muzo. The emeralds were described as mostly 'small, worked stones of good colour' plus 'two eight-sided stones worked in point', 'three small, clear, table-cut stones' and 'one pendant'. Also counted were 62 *ojuelos*, or 'little eyes', presumably referring to cabochons.[11] Although setting styles and cutting techniques changed dramatically in the late seventeenth century thanks to Italian innovations, early modern gemstones of any kind were almost never propped up in the high, clawlike settings popular today.

Gem presentation or arrangement patterns were also distinct in early modern times, and they changed considerably between the sixteenth and eighteenth centuries. Still, with few exceptions, in both Iberia and the colonies Muzo emeralds were rarely showcased in an individual way except in small rings and as curiosities. Instead, they were most often cut into squares and used to fill and colour as much space as possible, often in combination with enamelwork and interspersed with other gemstones and hung pearls.

The verb used most was *engastar*, 'to encrust', and many stones were classified at the mines themselves as *engastes*, roughly: 'encrustables'. Despite this tendency to use emeralds like Byzantine mosaic tiles, there are also numerous surviving examples of cabochons, lozenges and dangling 'teardrop' beads. These last were usually called *aguacates*, or 'avocados', in Spanish colonial documents. In the sixteenth and early seventeenth centuries, exceptional stones, like baroque pearls, were sometimes set in the breasts of gold animals or mythical creatures. One of the only sixteenth-century illustrations of western stone-cutting specific to gem types is in Juan de Arfe y Villafañe's 1572 treatise, *Quilatador de la plata, oro, y piedras* (roughly 'Appraiser's manual for silver, gold, and gemstones', discussed further below).[12]

2b. Appraising Colombian Emeralds in Europe

They tell a tale of a Spaniard in Italy who, soon after these gems were found in the Indies, showed an emerald to a lapidary and asked the price of it. The other, seeing that it was of excellent size and quality, told him a hundred *escudos*; the Spaniard showed him another, larger one, and he said three hundred. Delighted with his trade, the Spaniard took the lapidary to his house and showed him a large box full of emeralds; when he saw so many, the Italian said, 'Sir, these are worth but one *escudo*.' This is what has happened both in the Indies and Spain, for such an abundance of these gems has been found that their value has declined. . . . In the fleet in which I came from the Indies in 1587 two boxes of emeralds were brought, each weighing at least a hundred pounds, which shows how abundant they are.[13]

Such was the story of Colombian emeralds according to the Spanish Jesuit José de Acosta, whose 1590 *Natural and Moral History of the Indies* was widely translated and cited for centuries. Acosta was no gem dealer, however, and the story of the Spaniard and the Italian led him to exaggerate both the abundance of New World emeralds and their decline in value. He clearly had no idea they were finding new markets in Asia. Who was appraising Colombian emeralds in Europe, then, and how much did prices change? Fortunately, an authoritative late sixteenth-century source survives, that of court jeweller to Philip II, Juan de Arfe y Villafañe.[14]

In 1572, Arfe, son of a Spanish woman and a German court goldsmith employed by Charles V, laid out a series of tables to help jewellers and merchants appraise all manner of precious stones and metals. Just as importantly, he updated price information for a 1598 edition, which shows a substantial decline in emerald prices consonant with the intermediate flood of stones from Muzo described by Acosta. As Earl Hamilton showed many years ago, prices in general were thrown out of equilibrium in Spain because of the massive influx of silver in the second half of the sixteenth century. For things like food, which became relatively scarce, prices went way up.[15]

Arfe y Villafañe discusses emeralds in some detail, and unlike diamonds, rubies and even pearls, he splits them into two broad categories: Eastern and Western. The wording is almost identical in both editions of his book. First, the Eastern, or Oriental emerald:

The emerald occupies third place among stones, and after the diamond and the ruby it is the most valuable, and this is because it is green and so radiant that no other creation so delights the eye. In another time they were more esteemed than diamonds, size for size, until in the Western Indies they found another species of them, and some large pieces, which for having arrived in such quantity they have come to be less valuable than they once were.

So far this echoes Acosta (and Pliny), but then it becomes more interesting:

Despite all this, oriental stones from the Province of Egypt, known as 'old emeralds', are highly esteemed, because there are but few. They are said to counteract gout and aid in augmenting wealth, and are of a calming temperament. They are faceted on top like diamonds, but their edges and corners are rounded, because this better conserves their colour as well as their size and shape, according to the colour of each, thinning as necessary to help bring this out. Their colour should be as if lit afire, with great force and radiance, and the green must tend a little toward yellow, and not black, and if they are perfect they shall be appraised according to the scale used for diamonds.[16]

Arfe then provides a table, or scale, advising appraisers to discount for flaws, colour variations, fractions of carats and so on. Prices are in Spanish ducats, each equivalent to a little more than an ounce of fine silver, and weights in old-style carats (about 0.192g).

Although its buying power declined considerably because of price inflation, the Spanish ducat was worth ten silver *reales* in both 1572 and 1598. Thus, a prime one-carat emerald of the 'old' or 'oriental' type would have traded for about 50 'pieces of eight' (the more common 8-*real* peso coin) among wholesalers in 1572, but only 7½ silver pesos in 1598. Gains in size, being three-dimensional, followed the double multiplier six, but by 1598, even with the

Table for Old Emeralds (1572 edition *v.* 1598 edition)

Quilates (1572)	Ducats (1572)	Quilates (1598)	Ducats (1598)
1	40	1	6
2	160	2	24
3	360	3	54
4	640	4	96
5	1,000	5	150
6	1,440	6	216
7	1,960	7	294
8	2,560	8	384
9	3,240	9	486
10	4,000	10	600
11	4,840*	11	726

* Not listed in original, but consistent with multipliers used.

mystique of Egypt on one's side, by Arfe's measure a stone had to reach a whopping twelve carats (about 2.4 g) to break the 1,000 silver-peso barrier. The same stone would have been worth 7,200 pesos in 1572, roughly the cost of a huge mansion in Seville, or a fine ocean-going vessel. In 1598, 1,000 silver pesos was a decent bureaucratic salary – hardly small change, but no great fortune.

Here is what Arfe had to say about 'western', or 'new' stones:

> For the other emeralds of Peru and the New Kingdom [of Granada] they use another, lower price, and it is half that of the old ones. This is such that if an emerald of the kind they call new is as large as a diamond of one carat, they give it the value of three or four ducats, and with these four they multiply the rest, as with the old ones.

Given what we now know, both about world emerald sources in the sixteenth century and the peculiar yellow-green colour of Muzo stones, it appears that what educated European connoisseurs like Arfe were calling 'Egyptian' or 'oriental' or 'old' emeralds were

Table for New Emeralds 1572 ed. *v.* 1598 ed.

Quilates (1572)	Ducats (1572)	Quilates (1598)	Ducats (1598)
1	20	1	4
2	80	2	16
3	180	3	36
4	320	4	64
5	500	5	100
6	720	6	144
7	980	7	196
8	1,280	8	256
9	1,620	9	324
10	2,000	10	400
11	2,420*	11	484
12	2,880*	12	576

* Not listed in original, but consistent with multipliers used.

simply the choicest ones coming from colonial Muzo, Colombia. As with so many things American in Europe at this time (except perhaps gold and silver), there was a built-in prejudice against New World gems.

As Padre Acosta and others suggested, usually with disdain, not only the native inhabitants but even the land itself was not quite mature. Instead of tigers it had *tigrillos*, and in lieu of bona fide camels, only llamas and alpacas. Unknown to the Ancients, America, North, South and in between, was not allowed to compete with the neoscholastics' favourite exotic locales – even its emeralds were a kind of natural fake. Who were the emerald-mining Muiscas, after all, when compared with the Egyptians? True riches, as Marco Polo had reminded everyone, came only from the East.

3. The Fabled Emerald Range of Brazil

Fernão Dias Pais was one of Brazil's most famous seventeenth-century *bandeirantes*, epitome of the tropical backwoodsman. Like the conquistadors of Spanish America, the *bandeirantes* of Brazil were fortune-seeking fighters of Amerindians who relied on a mix of guerrilla tactics and modern firearms to achieve their aims. They sought Crown aid only for monopoly licences after the fact of 'discovery' or conquest. Self-styled American *fidalgos*, or knights, men such as Dias hoped to find native kingdoms and mineral wealth to rival Cortés and Pizarro. Most simply became slave hunters, scourge of the great *sertão*, or rugged backlands. A native of São Paulo, Dias spent nearly all his considerable inheritance searching not for indigenous slaves or gold mines, but rather the 'lost' Serra das Esmeraldas, or Emerald Range, said to have been discovered in the second half of the sixteenth century in the coastal mountains south of the colonial capital of Salvador.

As early as 1550, claims of 'emerald mountains' located somewhere between the districts, or captaincies, of Porto Seguro and Santo Espiritu surfaced in a letter to King João III. In florid language more typical of medieval travellers, one Filipe Guilhem described how he had encountered a settlement of 'blacks' living along an unnamed river near where the Portuguese had first touched Brazilian shores fifty years before. They showed him stones of varying colours, mostly yellow, and known locally as 'sun of the earth'. He had been assured, he said, that in the shimmering mountains on the horizon there lay fabulous mines of emeralds. He only needed a royal licence and a specialist capable of mapping the region to make good on the promise of gems. Guilhem maintained only his advanced age had prevented him from exploring further.[17] Expeditions under Captains Brás Cubas and Luis Martins followed in the early 1560s, and the second of these was said to have produced genuine emeralds.

Green stones described as Brazilian emeralds were examined by the Spanish court goldsmith Juan de Arfe y Villafañe by 1572, but he considered them to be of such inferior colour that they went for at most half the price of common amethysts. He described the stones thus: 'The emeralds of Brazil are sad stones (*piedras tristes*), of obscure colour; they used to go for about the same [price] as sapphires, but no longer do with the arrival of Peruvian ones [i.e., Colombian emeralds]. They are so little esteemed that only for their hardness are they appraised. . . .'[18] Since emerald was only loosely identified as beryl in Arfe's time, almost any green crystal could qualify. Such hardness suggests green peridot.

The late Charles Boxer noted that the legend of Brazil's Emerald Range reached England through the travel account of Anthony Knivet, a castaway who survived Elizabethan corsair Thomas Cavendish's failed 1591 South Sea expedition. Knivet, who spent a decade in Brazil, partly as a captive of indigenous Tupi-speakers, said that he participated in an expedition to a 'Mountayne of greene stones' in 1597, and added that he had seen in one Amerindian village, 'Stones as greene as grasse, and great store of white glistering Stones like Christall, but many of them were blew and greene, red and white, wonderfull faire to behold . . .' He had also seen gold nuggets, he said, the size of hazelnuts. Then, '. . . we came into a faire Countrie, and we saw a great glistering Mountaine before us, ten daies before we could come to it . . .'[19]

Knivet, who also said he was saved from poisoned fruit by a Portuguese companion who happened to have a bit of unicorn powder on hand as antidote, is a tricky source. He also believed, as did many sixteenth-century Portuguese explorers, that the great silver mountain of Potosí could be seen 'on a faire day' from the top of the 'great glistering Mountaine'.[20] Boxer and others have noted how the shining mountain story matches the Tupi legend of *Itaberaba-ussu*, one of the markers of the longed-for 'land without evil'.

The sugar planter Ambrósio Fernandes Brandão, in his 1618 *Dialogues of the Great Things of Brazil*, provides more useful details. Not only was he aware of Brazil's legendary Santo Espiritu mines, but he also remarked, through his fictional interlocutors, on how emeralds had lost their value in Europe when those of New Granada flooded the market. Brandão also noted that the 1614 Serra das Esmeraldas expedition of Marcos de Azeredo turned up green stones that were judged 'sun-scorched', and, eventually, false emeralds, by Lisbon court lapidaries.[21]

The existence of Brazilian emerald mines was never doubted, however, and was a central concern of Rio de Janeiro's energetic governor, Salvador Correia de Sá e Benavides, throughout the third quarter of the seventeenth century. Sá organized expeditions to both the Serra das Esmeraldas and the fabled silver mines of Sabarábussú in 1659.[22] As Boxer notes, the *jornada das esmeraldas*, or 'emerald expedition', produced no results, and in fact Sá and his men barely penetrated the interior. Hope did not yet die, however, and in May 1660 King Afonso VI granted the governor's son, João Correia de Sá, monopoly rights to Santo Espiritu's fabled range.[23]

It is unlikely the younger Sá did anything with this grant, because as Boxer notes he was getting into legal trouble by 1661. Others were not dissuaded. As described by the noted Brazilianist Stuart B. Schwartz, interest in this and other mining projects only swelled under Governor Afonso Furtado de Castro (1671–5). Furtado was even more obsessed with Brazil's untapped mineral wealth than his predecessors. Growing Caribbean competition in the sugar industry, and with it the loss of the African slave trade monopoly, were key stimulating factors in the search for riches. It was Governor Afonso Furtado who named Fernão Dias Pais 'governor of the emerald mines'.[24]

Fernão Dias never found the emerald mountains, although he died trying in 1690. Emeralds were soon after all but forgotten in Brazil when Dias's son and several other *paulistas*, aided by African, indigenous and mixed-race auxiliaries, located the great gold mines of the central highlands, soon to be given the oddly restrained name of 'General Mines', or *Minas Gerais*. Around 1725, enslaved African gold washers discovered diamonds in the northern reaches of the Minas district, further overshadowing the once dreamed-of emeralds of the coast range. Green tourmaline crystals turned up from time to time in the course of the colonial period, and the world's best topaz was found just outside the town of Vila Rica do Ouro Prêto. True emeralds were only discovered in Brazil in the 1960s.

Why had these Brazilians been so concerned with finding emeralds, of all things? Why not the gold or diamonds that soon after transformed Brazil from a coast-hugging sugar enclave into a continental colony that dwarfed all other enterprises of the mother country? The hunt for emeralds may have been a peculiar baroque Portuguese obsession akin to Sebastianism, but it may also have been related to the less quixotic East Indian commercial concerns the Portuguese were also famous for pursuing. By the time of Dias's explorations in the 1670s and 1680s, Portuguese merchants, some of them New Christians with ties to Brazil, had been trading New World emeralds to India through their viceregal capital of Goa for more than a century. There, as seen above, a thriving trade in emeralds had been established since the mid-sixteenth century.

❖

Notes

Introduction

1. This narrative relies on Lockhart's classic *Nadir Shah*, Tucker, *Nadir Shah's Quest for Legitimacy*, Axworthy, *Sword of Persia*; Sarkar, *Nadir Shah in India* and Avery, 'Nadir Shah and the Afsharid Legacy'.
2. Published separately as Hodgson, *The Venture of Islam, Volume 3*.
3. Erevan, *History of the Wars*, 77–8.
4. In Fraser's contemporary *History of Nadir Shah*, 155.
5. Lockhart, *Nadir Shah*, 145.
6. Cited in ibid., 152, fn. 5.
7. Sinkankas, *Emerald and Other Beryls*.
8. Morgan, *From Satan's Crown to the Holy Grail*.
9. Otero Muñoz and Barriga Villalba, *Esmeraldas de Colombia*.
10. Domínguez, *Historia de las esmeraldas de Colombia*.
11. Rojas, 'La explotación esmeraldífera de Muzo'. I thank Warwick Bray for bringing this work to my attention and for sending me a copy.
12. Friede, 'Demographic Changes in the Mining Community of Muzo'. This essay was published in Spanish in 1966 (*Boletín Cultural y Bibliográfico* 9, 9, Bogotá). Rodríguez Baquero, *Encomienda y vida diaria*. Rodríguez Baquero was guided by his advisor, Hermes Tovar Pinzón, who briefly discusses the pre-Columbian emerald trade in an introductory essay to a primary source collection he edited in the same year: *Relaciones y visitas a los Andes, siglo XVI, t.III*, 45–50.
13. Winius, 'Jewel Trading in Portuguese India' and 'Portugal, Venice, Genoa, and the Traffic in Precious Stones'. An exception is Teensma, 'De politieke en economische ideeën van de Bruggeling' and 'Jacques de Coutre as Jewel Merchant in India'.
14. Boyajian, *Portuguese Trade in Asia*; Teles e Cunha, 'Hunting Riches'; and Ahmad, *Portuguese Trade and Socio-Economic Changes*.
15. Yogev, *Diamonds and Coral*.

16. Edgar Samuel, *At the End of the Earth*, especially Chapters 16, 17 and 18; Lenman, 'The East India Company and the Trade in Non-Metallic Precious Materials'.
17. Francesca Trivellato, *The Familiarity of Strangers*, especially Chapters 9 and 10.
18. See Moura Carvalho, 'Rarities from Goa'. Emeralds hold pride of place in Keene's *Treasury of the World*.
19. Müller, *Jewels in Spain*. For more illustrations, see Castillo and Elorza Guinea, *El arte de la plata*; Victoria & Albert Museum, *Princely Magnificence* and Hackenbroch, *Renaissance Jewellery*.
20. Otte, *Las perlas del Caribe*.
21. Floor, 'Pearl fishing in the Persian Gulf'; Warsh, 'Adorning Empire'.
22. Studnicki-Gizbert, *A Nation Upon the Ocean Sea*; Boyajian, *Portuguese Trade in Asia*. On the wider trade networks, I rely on Israel, *Diasporas Within a Diaspora* and *Dutch Primacy in World Trade*.

Chapter 1: Sacred Origins

1. Wey Gómez, *The Tropics of Empire*, 140, 343.
2. Szászdi León-Borja, *Los viajes de rescate de Ojeda*, 56–9, and Sauer, *The Early Spanish Main*, 108–14.
3. Garcilaso de la Vega, *Royal Commentaries of the Incas*, 559.
4. Szászdi, 'En torno a la balsa de Salango', 477.
5. Variations on this story include Cieza de León, *The Discovery and Conquest of Peru*, 149, 301.
6. Webster, *Gems*, 103–31.
7. Varthema, *The Travels of Ludorico di Yarthema*, 252, 258, 218. The editor of this volume, Bombay chaplain George Percy Badger, cited Andrea Corsali on emeralds in India: 'I do not know where emeralds are produced: here they are in greater estimation than any other stone.'
8. Barbosa, *The Book of Duarte Barbosa*, 225–6. The translator notes the error, but cites Cosmas Indicopleustes on ancient Indian tastes: 'These people have a great fondness for the emerald stone, and it is worn by their king in his crown. The Ethiopians who obtain this stone from the Blemmyes in Ethiopia, import it into India, and with the price they get are able to invest in wares of the greatest value.'
9. Ibid., 226.
10. The best examples found in Muzo in 1951 and weighing 1,796 and 1,453 carats, respectively, are illustrated in Domínguez, *Historia de las esmeraldas de Colombia*, iv–v.
11. The Egyptian deposits are briefly described by Tifaschi, *Arab Roots of Gemology*, 104.
12. This is my impression based on displayed items at the British Museum, the Metropolitan Museum of Art (New York), the Museum of Fine Arts (Boston), the Calouste Gulbenkian Museum in Lisbon, and many smaller museums in Spain and Italy. Emeralds in this bead-like, drilled crystal form travelled as far afield as Roman Britain (see, for example, the British Museum's exhibits of the so-called Southfleet Hoard and Thetford Treasure).
13. Giuliani et al., 'Oxygen Isotopes'.
14. A brief history of emerald synthesis is in Giuliani et al., *Emeralds of the World*, 84–92.

15. Kazmi and Snee, *Emeralds of Pakistan*, 234.
16. I here interweave conclusions of Earl Irving on the Colombian Andes, in *Structural Evolution of the Northernmost Andes*, and on Muzo specifically, the Colombian Society of Petroleum Geologists and Geophysicists, *Cundinamarca-Boyacá-Muzo Emerald Mines*.
17. D'Elhuyar, 'Informe de un viaje a Muzo', 77. Here and below, all translations from Spanish and Portuguese are mine unless otherwise noted.
18. Cited in Domínguez, *Historia de las esmeraldas de Colombia*, 45.
19. Simón, *Noticias historiales*, 2: 295–300.
20. In Francis, *Invading Columbia*, 79–80.
21. Ibid., 80.
22. Ibid., 99.
23. AGI Contaduría 1300, ff.54v, 77.
24. On the prestation of Aztec greenstones, or *chalchihuites*, see Pagden, *Hernán Cortés*, 40–4, 100. On jade in the earlier Maya context, see Taube, 'The Symbolism of Jade'. On Incas, see Hyland, *The Quito Manuscript*, 38, 142. The Inca Sinchi Roca is said to have adorned himself with gold plates 'with emeralds'.
25. Hearne and Sharer, *River of Gold*.
26. Simón, *Noticias historiales* 2: 241.
27. Ibid., 2: 275.
28. Ibid., 2: 38
29. Francis, 'In the service of God'. Along with having their hair shorn, many of those charged with venerating 'idols' were sentenced to labour in the construction of the new Marian shrine church at Chiquinquirá.
30. Reichel-Dolmatoff, 'Things of Beauty'.
31. Ibid., 28.
32. González de Pérez, *Diccionario y gramática Chibcha*.
33. West, *Colonial Placer Mining*, 54.
34. Francis, *Invading Colombia*, 70–1.
35. Fernández de Oviedo, *Historia General y Natural*, 94.
36. Ibid. Pliny's thoughts on emeralds are collected in Ball, *A Roman Book on Precious Stones*, 140–4.

Chapter 2: Conquistadors

1. McNeill, *The Pursuit of Power*, prefers the example of a uniting France vs. the English in Normandy in the 1450s (83).
2. Wolf, *Geografía y geología del Ecuador*, 329, 641–2. Records of booty picked up by Pizarro's men in Coaque, Manabí, on their way to Peru in 1531 suggest emeralds were either hidden or not as important as later authors claimed. Only a few 'blue stones' in bead form are noted, none described explicitly as emeralds. See Hampe Martínez, 'El reparto de metales, joyas, e indios de Coaque'. See also Navarro Cárdenas, *Investigación histórica de la minería*.
3. JCBL Codex Sp 3 (13 July 1557). The manuscript mentions gold, silver, pearls and emeralds, but only gold and silver are itemized. The gold amounted to an astounding 1,326,039 pesos de buen oro. A 1539 letter to the king sent from Cuzco by Francisco Pizarro mentions his sending a gift of emeralds which he lamented were 'small and poorly worked'. AGI Patronato 90b, 2: 7 (20 Feb. 1539).

4. AGI Lima 565.
5. Captains Juan de San Martín and Antonio de Lebrija, 'Relación del Nuevo Reino', 1539, in Francis, *Invading Colombia*, 93–4.
6. From the anonymous *c.*1545 'Relación de Santa Marta', in Francis, *Invading Colombia*, 104–5.
7. Captains San Martín and Lebrija, 'Relación del Nuevo Reino', 8 July 1539, in Francis, *Invading Colombia*, 61–2.
8. Simón, *Noticias historiales*, 2: 37–8.
9. Ibid., 2: 100, 145, 175. On entries in the royal treasury accounts see, for example, AGI Contaduría 1294b. Here in 1601 the royal fifth was charged on a small black pouch containing several poor-quality emeralds 'understood to be from the sanctuaries of past times'.
10. From a 1539 report of the conquest of the Sabana de Bogotá cited by Tovar Pinzón, *Relaciones y Visitas a los Andes*, 106; discussed in his opening essay, 35.
11. Art historian Helmut Nickel has shown that the Colombian emeralds in host rock from a *c.*1724 Dresden rococo sculpture, 'Moor with Emerald Cluster', were taken from the curiosity cabinet of Elector Augustus (1553–86), who had in turn received them from Emperor Rudolf II in Prague. The figure is also known as the 'Moor with Tray of Emeralds'; see Nickel, 'The Graphic Sources'. The cluster may have derived from a slightly later shipment of stones in host rock from Muzo, however, possibly arriving in Europe in the late 1560s or early 1570s. A similar emerald cluster now in the Natural History Museum of Vienna belonged to Archduke Ferdinand II (1529–95), Habsburg Count of Tyrol (see Plate 5). Both clusters are in fact composites made of loose stones and host minerals from several Colombian mines, including Chivor-Somondoco and Muzo.
12. Simón, *Noticias historiales*, 3: 212–13.
13. Ibid., 3: 266–7; Aguado, *Recopilación Historial*, 2: 205–11.
14. Simón, *Noticias historiales*, 3: 321–5. Aguado tells a much longer and more detailed version of the story, *Recopilación Historial*, 2: 211–19.
15. Aguado, *Recopilación Historial*, 2: 231; 4: 65; Simón, *Noticias historiales*, 4: 9–38.
16. Aguado, *Recopilación Historial*, 2: 235.
17. Ibid., 2: 248.
18. Ibid., 2: 251.
19. Ibid., 2: 260.
20. Ibid., 2: 267.
21. Ibid., 2: 272.
22. AGNC Historia Civil 4: 47 (1559), ff.799–818.
23. Simón, *Noticias historiales*, 4: 190–4.
24. Aguado, *Recopilación Historial*, 2: 286.
25. Simón, *Noticias historiales*, 4: 195–204; See also Tovar Pinzón, *Relaciones y Visitas*, 323–68 and 385–425.
26. Tovar Pinzón, *Relaciones y Visitas*, 416–17; AGNC Minas de Boyacá 3, ff.183–5. In his 1572 *relación* of La Palma and Muzo, conquistador Gutierre de Ovalle noted that, unlike their highland Muisca neighbours, local indigenous peoples universally 'disparaged all things worthy of esteem, holding as precious things of no virtue or value, caring nothing for gold, silver, or precious stones, instead upholding as riches little beads made from the fangs, bones, [and beaks] of animals and birds, plus sets of shells from sea and river and seeds from trees . . .', in Tovar Pinzón, *Relaciones y Visitas*, 342.

27. Aguado, *Recopilación Historial*, 2: 306.
28. Ibid., 2: 307–8.
29. Ibid., 2: 311–12.
30. Ibid., 2: 317–19.
31. Ibid., 2: 320–1.
32. Ibid., 2: 327.
33. AGNC Historia Civil 22, ff.887–972 (1589), AGI Patronato 164, ramo 1.
34. Vargas Machuca, *The Indian Militia*.
35. In his 1582 *relación*, conquistador Diego de Poveda emphasized the possibility of gold mines as Muzo's only hope for salvation. (Tovar Pinzón, *Relaciones y Visitas*, 413–16.) Poveda also related his own *c.*1569 discovery of superior emerald deposits 'three long leagues' from Muzo, perhaps in the neighbourhood of Coscuez or Peñas Blancas, but complained of the lack of water sources (417).

Chapter 3: Emerald City

1. AGI Santa Fe 67, item 38. The signers were Alvaro de Herrán, Juan Ortiz Manosalvas, Benito López de Poveda, Miguel Gómez, Hernán García Patiño, Alonso de Salinas and Pedro Alonso.
2. Rodríguez Baquero, *Encomienda y vida diaria;* Tovar Pinzón, *Relaciones y Visitas*, 406.
3. In Spanish, the technique was known as *desmonte de piedras*. On the history of hushing in Europe, see Craddock, *Early Metal Mining*, 89–91. The method, though widely practised in ancient Spain, is not described in Georgius Agricola's landmark 1556 runing treatise, *De re Metallica*, as Craddock notes.
4. Aguado, *Recopilación Historial* 2: 339–40.
5. Tovar Pinzón, *Relaciones y Visitas*, 420.
6. A rare exception is a local mine owner's mention of several *socavones* chasing veins in the Cerro de Miguel Ruiz beginning around 1656. AGI Escribanía 839c.
7. Vásquez de Epinosa, *Compendio y descripción*, 231.
8. AGNC Minas de Boyacá 1: 6 (ff.730–49) and 2: 24 (ff.895–921). The owner responsible for the disaster was Francisco Vallejo, sued by Juan Ramírez de Poveda y Venero. The project was to develop a mine for Vallejo's partner, Federico Ruisinque. The 1702 suit is in AGNC Minas de Boyacá 2: 12.
9. On colonial-era scarring in Colombia's gold mines, see West, *Colonial Placer Mining*, 13, 30. West does not discuss the emerald districts.
10. AGNC Minas de Boyacá 2: 25 (ff.922–76).
11. Ibid., 2: 7 (1568), 3: 26 (1621), 2: 25 (1633) and 2: 24 (1678).
12. AGI Contaduría 1294b. Juan Ortiz Manosalvas is listed as *mayordomo* of the Rosary brotherhood and Alonso de Salinas *mayordomo* of St Lucy and the Holy Cross. The 1574 *quintos* are in AGI Contaduría 1300, f.135, later ones f.71 (new pagination). The 1567 offering is in AGI Contaduría 1292, f.58. The *redención de cautivos* donation is in AGI Contaduría 1301, f.80. The 1644 donations are noted in AGNC Minas de Boyacá 1: 7 (ff.759–62). The first record I could find of a priest blessing a mine is from 1773, although this practice was probably much older. One Muzo priest was paid in emeralds for administering sacraments as early as 1574. The 1773 blessing (AGNC Minas de Boyacá 2: 1, ff.84–95) was extended to the dam and floodgate, and was said to have been followed by the

discovery of 'a stringer of emerald-bearing crystal [*cardenillo*]'. The priest given emeralds is in AGI Contaduría 1300 (accounts for 12 July 1574). Padre Andrés de Sepúlveda was given 8 pesos, 1 tomín (about 187 carats) of *segunda suerte* emeralds as alms 'for the care of the Holy Sacrament of the City of Muzo'.

13. AGI Contaduría 1300, f.53v.
14. AGNC Minas de Boyacá 3, ff.170–4 (11–viii–1567).
15. Ibid., 3, ff.178–82 (1569), f.187 (17 April 1572).
16. Another stone produced was 'a small one about the size of a hazelnut'. The December 1575 report, by Gabriel de Limpias Feijó, is in AGI Santa Fé 68, and is partially reprinted in Domínguez, *Historia de las esmeraldas de Colombia*, 36–7. The *quintos* are also from 1575, and are listed in AGI Contaduría 1300, ff.140–1.
17. AGNC Minas de Boyacá 1:11. The fact that Ysabel could communicate with local indigenous miners (often called *chontales*, Central American-style) from the Muzo village of Yacopí when she herself was probably of Muisca origin (having been born in Bogotá) suggests that the Muzos and Muiscas had some sort of shared language, perhaps for trade.
18. AGI Santa Fe 51, 3: 50–1.
19. Ibid.
20. Town council records from Tunja include a 1581 petition for freedom by a young woman named Leonor, 'india de Muso'. Local officials prevented her 'master', Juan Ortiz, from taking her back and instead placed her in the protective custody of a local Spanish woman, Catalina Gaitán. ARB (Tunja), Libros de Cabildo (1581, mislabelled 1551). Reference is again made to 'indios chontales'.
21. AGI Santa Fe 18, 2: 4 (2 January 1601).
22. AGNC Minas de Boyacá 2: 20 (ff.749–849).
23. AGI Santa Fe 67, item 46 (25–viii–1598).
24. Ibid., 836. The tax on pearls dropped from one-fifth to one-twelfth, then to one-twentieth.
25. Otero Muñoz and Barriga Villalba, *Esmeraldas de Colombia*, 110.
26. A fragment of *visita* testimony cited by Domínguez, *Historia de las Esmeraldas de Colombia*, 35. See also Ruiz Rivera, *Encomienda y mita*, 69–88.
27. AGNC Negros y Esclavos, Boyacá 1, ff.9–14.
28. Ibid., 1: 22, ff.565v–66.
29. Sandoval, *Treatise on Slavery*, 74–8.
30. Friede, 'Demographic Changes', 340.
31. AGNC Minas de Boyacá 2: 4, ff.522–84. Muzo *cuadrillas* were named for Payme, Tatan, Chaquipay, Pauna, Curipi, Boquipi, Nico, Caquian, Obipi, Bipay, Zarueque, Pinipay, Canipa, Ibama, Zorque, Acoca, Yacupi, Maripi, Atico, Quipama, Tomarca and Topo. The last six were clustered around the Itoco mines.
32. The 1643 Muzo ordinances are partially cited in Domínguez, *Historia de las Esmeraldas de Colombia*, 39, but are fully listed in AGNC Minas de Boyacá 2: 4, ff.522–84. The bridge project is in AGI Escribanía 839c. On Somondoco, see AGNC Real Hacienda t.44, ff.547–8.
33. Juan de Retuerta insisted that he was despoiled of a 'banco rico' worked with three slaves by local *contador* Alonso de Ávila Gaviria. A 1672 suit was brought against Retuerta's son, Francisco, by the priest Pedro Solís de Valenzuela. Solís maintained that among his cattle pastures five leagues from Somondoco he had discovered numerous abandoned diggings. He named the mines 'La Concepción' and petitioned for rights to the waters of several creeks: the Chiblatama, Nía and

Gualomas. Retuerta argued that he had inherited these mines from his father, and had rented them to one Miguel Soriano, who was given three months to 'clean canals' and five years to dig. Soriano had in turn tried to sublet the mines, which prompted a suit from Retuerta, and in the interim Solís had jumped the claim. The documents do not provide a resolution (AGNC Minas de Boyacá 1: 10 f.967). On the Coscuez collapse, see Domínguez, *Historia de las Esmeraldas de Colombia*, 40–1. Miners allegedly found human bones in a blocked adit in 1850, giving rise to this story. I rely on testimonies from the 1640s in AGNC Minas de Boyacá 1: 7, ff.750–87. Mining in Coscuez is again mentioned by Francisco Ovalle in the mid-1650s in AGI Escribanía 839c, f.227.

34. ARB (Tunja), Legajo 41, ff.451–2. The man granted the licence was Juan de Porras Moreno.
35. AGI Santa Fe 51, 3: 67.
36. Ibid., 26, 3: 35.
37. Archivo General de Simancas, Patronato Real, leg. 30, ff. 580–1. Special thanks to Professor Aurelio Espinosa for this reference. He calculated an appraised total of 86,745 ducats.
38. ARB (Tunja), Notaría 1: 11 (12 November 1568), f.181v. In this case a Tunja tailor consigned 'a gold ring set with a fine emerald stone' belonging to his dead wife to a nephew to sell downriver on the Magdalena. Other mentions of emerald jewellery in hock for debts include Notaría 2 (Legajo 31, 1583), f.313; Notaría 2 (Legajo 35, 1585), f.61. The 1583 document lists 'un apretador de oro con esmeraldas y perlas' weighing thirty pesos and in hock for fifty pesos cash, 'a gold medal with emeralds and pearls' weighing seven to eight pesos, and 'a gold eagle with emeralds and pearls', not weighed but in hock with the medal for twelve pesos.
39. AGI Contaduría 1380, ff.10v–11v.
40. The *Leicester Journal*, in Frear Keeler, *Sir Francis Drake's West Indian Voyage*, 167, 178.
41. ANE (Quito), Protocolos Notariales (PN) 1: 2, f. 1449v. The jewels were apparently sold by February 1590. References to emerald jewellery abound in these books.
42. Sotheby & Co., *Sale of the Crown of the Andes*.
43. Haring, *Trade and Navigation*, and Hamilton, *American Treasure*.
44. Haring, *Trade and Navigation*, 330 (appendix IV).
45. Sanz, *Comercio de España con América*, 2: 48–51, 543–57.
46. AGI Contaduría 334, f.576.
47. AGI Contaduría 1380, f.54. See also Tovar Pinzón, who notes collection in 1580 of 551.4 gold pesos' worth of emerald *quintos* in Cartagena (*El imperio y sus colonias*, 93).
48. AGI Contaduría 5.
49. Haring, *Trade and Navigation*, 65, 119.
50. Eugene Lyon described the contents of the manifest in *The Search for the* Atocha, 53–8. For the story of the emeralds' discovery, see Smith, *Fatal Treasure*. Some of the *Atocha* stones are illustrated in Fine, *Treasures of the Spanish Main*.
51. The Bermuda wrecks are described in Peterson, *The Funnel of Gold*, 274–5.
52. The discovery of the *Maravillas* emeralds is best told by Marx, *Robert Marx*, 183–255, and *In the Wake of Galleons*, 281–307. Some of the items found, along with other contemporary pieces, are illustrated in Philips Son and Neale, *A Rare Collection*. See also Marx and Marx, *Treasure Lost at Sea* and *The Search for Sunken Treasure*. Dave Horner published partial translations of *Maravillas*-related documents, including mention of emerald jewels recovered by Spanish salvagers in

Shipwreck, 161. A 1993 Florida find, said to date from the 1760s, yielded even more rough emeralds, one of them weighing more than 1,000 carats, and some emerald jewellery, although the details of this wreck are cloudy. Typical of many in the treasure-hunting business, Victor Benilous and his company A.D. Ventures have made spurious claims linking the stones to Cortés and Moctezuma. Voillot, in *Diamonds and Precious Stones*, 31–40, appears to have swallowed this tall tale whole.

Chapter 4: Empires and Inquisitors

1. Samuel, *At the End of the Earth*, 228. Swetschinski rejects the term 'Sephardim' for Luso-Hispanic Jews and New Christians in this period, but his alternative, 'Portuguese Jews', seems to fit better with the Amsterdam case he examines in *Reluctant Cosmopolitans*, xii. Studnicki-Gizbert's alternative 'Portuguese nation', in *A Nation Upon the Ocean Sea*, is much closer to the documentary usage I found, but I worry that it may confuse in discussions of early Portuguese settlers, such as those sent to Muzo, who may or may not have had Jewish ancestry. I have thus chosen 'Sephardim' by default.
2. See, for example, Glückel of Hameln, *Memoirs*.
3. García-Arenal and Wiegers, *A Man of Three Worlds*. On Pallache's gem dealings: 4, 65, 72, 104–5.
4. Boyajian, *Portuguese Trade in Asia*, especially Chapters 6 and 10. See also Bouchon, *Inde Découverte*.
5. Personal communication. 'Trader Gregory Miguel, son of a Madras merchant with China and Manila connections, left a large inheritance including 1 box with 32 pieces of emerald weighing 10.40 carats, and 14 emeralds and 2 rubies weighing 162.12 carats. He had more.'
6. Royal decrees show attempts to tax or at least monitor the Goa gem trade, especially in the early seventeenth century, but without success. See, for example, Bulhão Pato, *Livros das Monções*, 2: 430.
7. For a recent evaluation of this process, mostly regarding the textile business, see Morineau, 'The Indian Challenge: Seventeenth and Eighteenth Centuries', in Chaudhury and Morineau, *Merchants, Companies, and Trade*, 243–75.
8. Boyajian, *Portuguese Bankers at the Court of Spain*; Disney, *A History of Portugal and the Portuguese Empire*, 1: 206–8, 2: 180. See also Elliott, *Spain and its World*, 114–36.
9. ANTT Inquisition/Lisbon, cases 3594, 10951.
10. Ibid., case 13049.
11. Swetschinski, *Reluctant Cosmopolitans*, 157.
12. ANTT Inquisition/Lisbon, case 11014.
13. Gentil da Silva, *Stratégie des Affaires*. The letters are mostly written in a mix of Portuguese and Spanish.
14. Gentil da Silva, *Lettres de Lisbonne*, 1: 164–5, 182–3. Gomes and his relatives also dealt in salt, spices, sugar and cloth.
15. Ibid, 1: 294, 400.
16. Ibid, 2: 196, 306, 397.
17. 'Cousas de Pedraria', an anonymous late sixteenth-century manuscript in the BNP (Lisbon), Codex 8571 ff.231–9.
18. Boyajian, *Portuguese Trade in Asia*, 137.

19. Ibid., 274, fn. 99. The tables are drawn from data given in Appendix A, 247–55.
20. Ibid., 208.
21. ANTT Inquisition/Lisbon, case 5586.
22. Boyajian, *Portuguese Bankers*, 27. The factor was Manoel Rodrigues do Pôrto, friend and business associate of the diamond-dealing Tinoco clan.
23. Ibid., Appendices A-1 to A-18.
24. Pike, *Linajudos and Conversos*.
25. ANTT Inquisition/Lisbon, cases 7829, 9437.
26. Quiroz, 'The Expropriation of Portuguese New Christians'.
27. This point is clarified in more detail by Daviken Studnicki-Gizbert in Kagan and Morgan, *Atlantic Diasporas*.
28. On Gramaxo and his associates, see Vila Vilar, 'Extranjeros en Cartagena (1593–1630)', reprinted in *Aspectos sociales en América colonial*, 1–41. The Gramaxo ties to India are discussed by Boyajian, *Portuguese Trade in Asia*, 143.
29. AHN, INQ Cartagena de Indias (pleito fiscal) 4816: 3, ff.14–14v (10–v–1638). Special thanks to Daviken Studnicki-Gizbert for pointing out this case to me, and especially to Robert Ferry for alerting me to the India connection quoted here in reference to what Rodrigues calls 'el verde'.
30. Newson and Minchin, *From Capture to Sale*, 40, 150.
31. Araujo's testimony is in Tejado Fernández, *Aspectos de la vida social*, 323–33. On Franco's emeralds, 153.
32. Splendiani et al., *Cincuenta años*.
33. Investigators from several disciplines have examined the Inquisition's persecution of alleged crypto-Jews in Spanish America in precisely this period, including Irene Silverblatt, Nathan Wachtel and Robert Ferry.
34. Splendiani et al., *Cincuenta años*, 3: 63.
35. Ibid., 3: 64.
36. Ibid., 2: 249. Under torture, Rodrigues Mesa named thirty-one practising Cartagena Jews, including his own mother. Fewer than half were pursued by the Inquisition.
37. Ibid., 2: 433, 3: 50. He claimed the leader or the Jews of Angola was Simon Gomez. Members of his group who had come to Cartagena included the *asentista* Fernando Lopes de Acosta, Francisco Pinheiro, Enrique Nunes y Silveira and Sebastião de Acosta. Most important (or vocal) was Manuel Alvarez Prieto.
38. ANTT Inquisition Lisbon item 9609.
39. Splendiani et al., *Cincuenta años*, 2: 451–2, 3: 81–2.
40. Ibid., 2: 453, 458.
41. Newson and Minchin, *From Capture to Sale*, 150.
42. Splendiani et al., *Cincuenta años* 2: 438–43.
43. Ibid., 3: 306–7, 337–44, 392–7.
44. Ibid., 3: 247, 316.
45. Sluiter, 'Dutch-Spanish Rivalry'.
46. See, for example, their essays in Bernardini and Fiering, *The Jews and the Expansion of Europe to the West*, 335–68. See also Kagan and Morgan, *Atlantic Diasporas*.
47. Israel, *Diasporas Within a Diaspora*, 514. For more documentation of the routes used, see Vila Vilar, *Aspectos sociales en América colonial*, 159–64.
48. Bodian, *Hebrews of the Portuguese Nation*.
49. Samuel, *At the End of the Earth*, 227, 241. The document is in Correa, *Livro de Regimentos dos Officiães Mecânicos*.
50. Samuel, *At the End of the Earth*, 203.

51. Splendiani et al., *Cincuenta años*, 3: 235–8.
52. Samuel, *At the End of the Earth*, 245. See also Yogev, *Diamonds and Coral*, 84. The main factor for the Jewish merchants was the Surat factory head Sir George Oxenden.
53. Yogev, *Diamonds and Coral*, 87.
54. Samuel, *At the End of the Earth*, 214. Swetschinski mentions apprenticeship of Portuguese orphans among diamond cutters in these years in *Reluctant Cosmopolitans*, 157.
55. Samuel, *At the End of the Earth*, 223.
56. Bingham, *Elihu Yale*, 198, 314.
57. PA (London), HL/PO/JO/10/1/199. The testimonies are on an unfoliated roll of parchments kept separate from the introductory paper documents.
58. The importance of this takeover in redirecting Asian trade is clarified in Steensgaard, *The Asian Trade Revolution*.
59. I have found no evidence to suggest this document, catalogued around 1877, has been associated with Cheapside by other scholars. There is brief reference to the Polman incident in a Latin document described in the Calendar of Court Minutes for the EIC for 1635–9, but this was published in 1907, and did not contain a copy of the testimonies.
60. Hazel Forsyth has collected a number of references to gems and jewels taken by highwaymen and housebreakers from the 1580s to 1660s recorded in the Middlesex Session records. Though less common than diamonds and pearls, emeralds are mentioned from time to time throughout the period, mostly set in finger rings (personal communication). See also Forsyth, *The Cheapside Hoard*, and Wheeler, *The Cheapside Hoard of Elizabethan and Jacobean Jewellery*. Though writing in the 1920s, Wheeler guessed the watch emerald to be Colombian (p. 5).
61. Lenman, 'The East India Company and the Trade', 104–5.

Chapter 5: Globetrotters

1. Giuliani et al., 'Oxygen Isotopes'. Gemologist Fred Ward had argued this in *Emeralds of the World* (1993, and revised edn, 2001), 40–7.
2. Boyajian, *Portuguese Trade in Asia*, 76–81; Morga, *Sucesos de las islas Filipinas*, 309. Of the Portuguese, Morga said: 'To Malaca they take only gold and money, besides some special trinkets and novelties from Spain, and emeralds. Royal duties are not collected from these vessels.'
3. Bembo, *The Travels and Journal of Ambrosio Bembo*, 233.
4. Matos, *Diário do Conde de Sarzedas*. There are other versions of this story, regarding merchants Lobo da Silva and Baltasar de Veiga. Niccolao Manucci provides a longer version involving conniving Jesuits in his *Storia do Mogor*, 3: 157–9.
5. Bulhão Pato, *Livros das Monções*. See 3: 355 and 4: 37–8 for 1615–17 attempts to tax Ceylonese rubies and sapphires to help raise money to relieve Portugal's West African fort of São Jorge da Mina.
6. Carletti, *My Voyage*; Coverte, *Travels*, 49; Pyrard, *Voyage*, 2 (pt.1): 108. Here Pyrard mentions a Dutch gem merchant he met after a shipwreck on the Maldives. He was imprisoned by the Portuguese at Cochin after being caught trading for pearls off Cape Comorin, converted by the Jesuits, then apparently killed by poison on his way to Goa. In his description of Ceylon (p. 143) Pyrard claimed 'also great

quantities of precious stones, such as rubies, hyacinths, sapphires, topazes, garnets, emeralds, cat's eyes, etc. the best in the Indies; add to that, there is there the finest and greatest fishery of exceeding fine and beautiful pearls; but there are no diamonds'. On p. 175 Pyrard suggests the Goa-Macao run included 'precious stones cut and set in rings, chains, carkanets, tokens, ear-pendants, and bracelets; for the Chinese like vastly to get gems and jewls of all sorts for their wives'.

7. Linschoten, *The Voyage of Jan Huyghen van Linschoten to the East Indies*, 2 vols (London, 1935). 2: 140–1.
8. Lane, *Venice*. Letters of Fitch and Newberrry are in Locke, *The First Englishmen in India*, 74–91, 99, 103.
9. Bulhão Pato, *Livros das Monções*, 3: 495. For a detailed, city-by-city account of the power shift among European and Asian competitors in this region, see Floor, *The Persian Gulf*.
10. Linschoten, *Voyage of Jan Huyghen van Linschoten*, 2: 154–5.
11. AGNC Minas de Boyacá 3, f.223v.
12. Linschoten, *Voyage of Jan Huyghen van Linschoten*, part II, p. 295, mentions substantial West Indian pearls, mostly unregistered, arriving in the Azores with the Spanish treasure fleets. It is likely that emeralds similarly passed into Portuguese hands here. The goods requested in exchange were East Indian spices.
13. Carletti, *My Voyage*, 23, 199–200.
14. Ibid., 220–1.
15. Ibid., 242.
16. Ibid., 245.
17. Coutre, *Andanzas Asiáticas*. The original manuscript is in the BNE (Madrid), Manuscript 2780. See also Teensma, 'Jacques de Coutre as Jewel Merchant'.
18. For the case of another such Fleming caught in the 1605 dragnet, banker Cristóbal Martín of Antwerp, see Lane, *Quito 1599*, 162–3. On the de Coutre brothers' continued resistance to calls to Lisbon, see Bulhão Pato, *Livros das Monções*, 2: 16–17.
19. Coutre, *Andanzas*, 177, my translation here and below.
20. Ibid., 259.
21. Ibid., 261.
22. Ibid.
23. Ibid., 262.
24. Ibid.
25. Linschoten, *Voyage of Jan Huyghen van Linschoten* , pt. II, p. XX; Coutre, *Andanzas*, 262.
26. Coutre, *Andanzas*, 268–9.
27. Ibid., 274–5.
28. Ibid., 279.
29. Ibid., 280.
30. Ibid., 281.
31. For a transcribed Spanish pamphlet relating to Cron's career, see Boxer, 'Uma raridade'.
32. Coutre, *Andanzas*, 309–10.
33. Roe, *The Embassy of Sir Thomas Roe*, 457. The Jesuit priest Josef de Castro, resident in the capital of Agra two decades later, said that Emperor Shah Jahan sent 'one of his agents to Goa with a great quantity of money to buy jewels and precious stones to be presented to the king'. In Hosten, 'The Jesuits at Agra', 500.
34. Teensma, 'Jacques de Coutre as Jewel Merchant', 8.

Chapter 6: Emeralds of the Shahs

1. Jahangir, *The Jahangirnama*, 89.
2. Thackston, *Akbarnama*. For outsiders' views, see Correia-Afonso, *Letters from the Mughal Court*.
3. Jahangir, *The Jahangirnama*. Susan Stronge also notes the seemingly reserved depiction of jewellery in the *Akbarnama* when court inventories list massive 'reserves'. See 'Jewellery of the Mughal Period', in Stronge et al., *A Golden Treasury*, 27–50.
4. Jahangir, *The Jahangirnama*, 96.
5. Ibid., 271.
6. Ibid., 80 (the painting, *The Weighing of Prince Khurram*, is from a manuscript in the British Museum). The al-Sabah emerald rosary is illustrated in Keene, *Treasury of the World*, 131. This may be the same rosary worn by Shah Jahan on the cover of this book.
7. Jahangir, *The Jahangirnama*, 148, 167, 256, 268.
8. Meen, *Crown Jewels of Iran*.
9. Roe, *The Embassy of Sir Thomas Roe*, 283.
10. In Foster, *Early Travels in India*, 102–3.
11. Jahangir, *The Jahangirnama*, 189.
12. Ibid., 231.
13. Tavernier relating a *c*.1648 visit, *Travels in India*, 1: 89.
14. Khan, *The Shah Jahan nama*, 96.
15. Ibid., 208, 212, 266, 371, 474, 528.
16. Tavernier, *Travels in India*, 1: 303–4.
17. Khan, *The Shah Jahan nama*, 154, 494.
18. Ibid., 185, 444, 480, 500.
19. Kolff, *Naukar, Rajput and Sepoy*, 43–54.
20. Mukhia, *The Mughals of India*, 100.
21. Schimmel, *The Empire of the Great Mughals*, 174–88.
22. Tavernier, *Travels in India*, 1: 106.
23. Manucci, *Storia do Mogor*, 2: 316–17.
24. Ibid., 2: 319.
25. Ibid., 2: 319–20, 310–15, 327. Eunuchs were also called Diamond, Ruby, Sapphire, Coral and Ebony.
26. Tavernier, *Travels in India*, 1: 111.
27. Ibid., 1: 111, 114–15.
28. Ibid., 1: 115.
29. Mukhia, *The Mughals of India*, 103.
30. 'God: there is no god but Him, the Living, the Eternal One. Neither slumber nor sleep overtakes Him. His is what the heavens and the earth contain. Who can intercede with Him except by His permission? He knows what is before and behind men. They can grasp only that part of His knowledge which He wills. His throne is as vast as the heavens and the earth, and the preservation of both does not weary Him. He is the Exalted, the Immense One.' *The Koran*, 41.
31. Mukhia, *The Mughals of India*, 104–5.
32. Monshi, *History of Shah Abbas the Great*.
33. Ibid., 2: 837–8; 954–5.
34. Floor, *The Economy of Safavid Persia*. See also Matthee, *The Politics of Trade in Safavid Iran*, and Baghdiantz McCabe, *The Shah's Silk for Europe's Silver*.
35. Raphael du Mans, cited in Baghdiantz McCabe, *The Shah's Silk*, 121.

36. Illustrated in Piotrovsky and Frieze, *Earthly Beauty, Heavenly Art*, 284.
37. Séguy, *The Miraculous Journey of Mahomet*, 13, plate 31. The manuscript is from the late fifteenth century.
38. Bembo, *The Travels and Journal of Ambrosio Bembo*, 394.
39. Ibid., 336, 345.
40. Denny, 'The Palace, Power, and the Arts', 22–3.
41. Best illustrated in Piotrovsky and Frieze, *Earthly Beauty, Heavenly Art*, 276, 287 and frontispiece. See also Köseoglu, *The Topkapi Saray Museum*.
42. The so-called Topkapi Dagger was not the only one of its kind. To celebrate the opening of the Yeni Cami, or New Mosque, in Istanbul in 1663, Turhan Sultan gave an emerald-handled dagger to her son, Mehmed IV (1648–87).

Chapter 7: Tax Dodgers and Smugglers

1. AGI Contaduría 1587.
2. AGI Santa Fe 29, ramo 5: 41, pt. 3.
3. Lane, *Quito 1599*, 79; and Lane, 'El Dorado Negro'.
4. AGI Escribanía 839c, f.142.
5. Ibid., f.37.
6. AGI Contaduría 1587.
7. AGI Contaduría 1588.
8. AGNC Minas de Boyacá 1: 1, f.43.
9. Ibid., ff.234, 293–5.
10. Ibid., f.280v.
11. Ibid., ff.244, 68, 59. Others were found (and similarly sold) by Amerindians held in *encomienda*.
12. Ibid., f.169.
13. Ibid., f.70.
14. Ibid., f.103.
15. Ibid., ff.83–4, 94, 78v–79.
16. Ibid., ff.159v, 172, 194.
17. Ibid., f.180.
18. AGNC Minas de Boyacá 2: 22, ff.857–68, 138.
19. A brief document from 1683 written by Muzo alderman and *quinto* collector Francisco Camero says only mine owners, overseers and workers were allowed in the diggings, and that no children under ten were to be there for any reason. The problem was not child labour, but 'gleaning'. A fine of ten pesos would be charged for breaking these rules. Owners and overseers were also strictly forbidden from staying overnight in the mines themselves. AGNC Minas de Boyacá 2: 8.
20. AGNC Minas de Boyacá 1: 5, ff.644–729.
21. AGNC Minas de Boyacá 2: 6, 3: 17.
22. See Lane, *Blood and Silver* (*Pillaging the Empire* in U.S.), Chapter 4.
23. Zahedieh, 'The Merchants of Port Royal', 575. See also Zahedieh, 'Trade, Plunder, and Economic Development'.
24. Israel, *Diasporas within a Diaspora*, 582; Robles, *América a fines del Siglo XVII*, 38. Robles maintained that there was also an official far upriver on the Magdalena at Carare who inspected canoes for 'contraband merchandise, silver, gold, emeralds, and other things secretly traded'.

25. Robles, *América a fines del Siglo XVII*, 34.
26. For an examination of Port Royal's merchant community, see Meyers, 'Ethnic Distinctions and Wealth among Colonial Jamaican Merchants'.
27. Zahedieh, 'The Merchants of Port Royal', 580; Kayserling, 'The Jews in Jamaica', 711.
28. Ritchie, *Captain Kidd*, 65–6.
29. Yogev, *Diamonds and Coral*. Yogev's main focus was the late seventeenth and eighteenth centuries.
30. Ibid., 88, 100. Hispaniola amber appears not to have been known or exported at this time.
31. Ibid., 290, fn. 30.
32. Ibid., 108–9.
33. Trivellato, 'Juifs de Livourne, Italiens de Lisbonne, hindous de Goa', and *The Familiarity of Strangers*.
34. Yogev, *Diamonds and Coral*, 102–7.
35. Shifts in the Indian diamond trade in this period have also been discussed by Holden Furber, although he makes no mention of emeralds. See Furber, *Rival Empires of the Orient*, 260–2.
36. Chaudhuri, *The Trading World of Asia*. Chaudhuri left analysis of the gem trade to Yogev.

Chapter 8: Twilight of Imperial Emeralds

1. Phillips, *The Treasure of the San José*, 221. The use of appraised values in silver pesos rather than the standard 'gold' weight measures is unusual.
2. The best overall study of this period in English is McFarlane, *Colombia Before Independence*. Spanish visitors Jorge Juan and Antonio Ulloa describe Cartagena contraband in detail *c.*1735 in their 1749 *Noticias Secretas*, available in English as *Discourse and Political Reflections on the Kingdoms of Peru*, 42–8.
3. Santisteban, *Mil leguas por América*, 190.
4. Grahn, *The Political Economy of Smuggling*.
5. AGNC Minas de Boyacá 2: 12; 2: 26.
6. Ibid., f.682. Don Antonio de Tovar's 1633–45 *hoja de servicios*, or knightly 'curriculum vitae', is in AGNC Historia Civil, 12: 2. As a grandson of one of Muzo's conquerors, he held the *encomiendas* of Canipa and Minipi, by 1637 counting only thirty-six 'useful' adult males, only thirteen of whom were said to be working in emerald mines. Tovar collected nearly 800 ducats in tributes, and recognized two *mestizo* children born out of wedlock.
7. AGNC Negros y Esclavos (Colonia), Boyacá item 31. One brawler lived in the *ranchos*, or miners' barrracks, of Agustín de las Barzenas.
8. AGNC Minas de Boyacá 3: 17. The priest was Dr Bernardo Rico, of Mopora, and the mint treasurer an old Muzo hand, Captain José Ricaurte. A 1709–11 case looks at the inter-regional emerald trade in the colony during the War of the Spanish Succession. A Bogotá merchant testified how in 1703 he had gone to Muzo to buy two parcels or bulses of emeralds. A partner on his way to Cartagena promised to pay back their worth with interest on his return. In Cartagena the stones were traded for an assortment of imported textiles, but after five years the Bogotá merchant had still not been reimbursed by his partner. The cloth,

meanwhile, had been sold at great profit. On further investigation it became clear these men had been consigning things back and forth for years without a proper accounting scheme (AGNC Minas de Boyacá 3: 24).

9. AGNC Minas Anexo 1, f.158.
10. Ibid., f.166.
11. AGNC Minas de Boyacá 2: 4.
12. Juan and Ulloa, *A Voyage to South America*.
13. Sinkankas, *Emerald and Other Beryls*, 47–8. The treatise was entitled *Mineralogia, Eller Mineral-Riket*.
14. ANTT Inquisition/Lisbon, maço 26, doc. 257 (mic. roll 4977). The Armenian, a forty-four-year-old single merchant named Pedro Bersan, said he had been born in Eroquia, Armenia. For Cousteau's own account, see Coustos, *The Sufferings of John Coustos*.
15. Sinkankas, *Emerald and Other Beryls*, 48. The book was *Abhandlung von Edelsteinen*, or *Treatise on Precious Stones*.
16. AGI Indiferente 1549. See also Paula De Vos, 'The Rare, the Singular, and the Extraordinary: Natural History and the Collection of Curiosities in the Spanish Empire', in Bleichmar et al., *Science in the Spanish and Portuguese Empires*, 271–89.
17. The story is well documented in AGI Santa Fe 835. These documents were consulted by Segovia Salas in his superb M.A. thesis, 'Crown Policy and the Precious Metals', 93–119.
18. AGNC Minas de Boyacá 2: 1, f.29.
19. Ibid., ff.235, 373–83.
20. AGI Santa Fe 837 (23 Feb. 1790; 18 March 1793).
21. In July 1796 the viceroyalty of New Granada's chief accountant, Martín de Urdaneta, offered King Charles IV (1789–1808) his reflections on Muzo's potential for revival. His plan, to populate Muzo with blasphemers, was not pursued. See Urdaneta, 'Memoria instructiva', 476.
22. AGNC Minas de Boyacá 1: 2.
23. Cited in Domínguez, *Historia de las esmeraldas*, 46.

Conclusion

1. Taussig, *My Cocaine Museum*.

Postscript

1. Arboleda, *Una familia de proceres*, 9. For transcriptions of these early contracts, see Domínguez, *Historia de las esmeraldas*, 47–52.
2. Arboleda, *Una familia*, 80–1.
3. Ibid, 84.
4. Maurice P. Brungardt, 'The Economy of Colombia in the Late Colonial and Early National Periods', in Fisher et al., *Reform and Insurrection*, 186.
5. Domínguez, *Historia de las esmeraldas*, 52–4; Arboleda, *Una familia*, 86–7; and Otero Muñoz and Barriga Villalba, *Esmeraldas de Colombia*, 69–85. Tenerani studied under Antonio Canova, who sculpted a famous statue of George Washington. Using tax records Arboleda estimated Paris must have managed to

sell an annual average of some 11,000 silver pesos' worth of emeralds in Europe between 1831 and 1843. Arboleda gives a 142,000 gold peso figure, whereas García Manjarrés and Vargas Ayala give the same number in *reales* in their *Proyecto minero*, 2.

6. Arboleda, *Una familia*, 100–1. Fallon worked for an English firm, Powles, Illingworth, Wells & Co., that had won rights to mine gold and silver in the old colonial districts of Mariquita and Marmato. They had displaced an earlier company, B.A. Goldsmith, which had bid for Marmato and Supía in 1825.
7. Ancízar, *Peregrinación de Alpha*, 53–62. On the Coscuez tunnel, see Domínguez, *Historia de las esmeraldas*, 39.
8. Ibid., 57.
9. Arboleda, *Una familia*, 103. Rojas gives the datum on Lehmann's 3–6 February 1865 bonanza: Rojas, 'La explotación', 205. See also Domínguez, *Historia de las esmeraldas*, 56–7.
10. García Manjarrés and Vargas Ayala, *Proyecto minero*, 3. The authors add that under Sordo the mine works and related buildings were evaluated at 3,035.5 pesos.
11. Domínguez, *Historia de las esmeraldas*, 68. Arboleda, *Una familia*, 104–5.
12. Domínguez, *Historia de las esmeraldas*, 74.
13. Cited by Ibid., 80–2; Rojas, 'La explotación', 206.
14. Domínguez, *Historia de las esmeraldas*, 101.
15. Montaña, *Renta de esmeraldas*, 1–17. The higher figures are in García Manjarrés and Vargas Ayala, *Proyecto minero*, 6.
16. Henderson, *Modernization in Colombia*, 71, 78.
17. Ibid., 135.
18. Klein, *Smaradge unter dem Urwald*.
19. Domínguez, *Historia de las esmeraldas*, 156–7, 164–8. Rainier, *Green Fire*. Rainier also worked at Muzo and Coscuez.
20. García Manjarrés and Vargas Ayala, *Proyecto minero*, 6. On rising violence, see Bergquist et al., *Violence in Colombia*, 262–3.
21. Cited in Domínguez, *Historia de las esmeraldas*, 134.
22. Ibid., 28.
23. Bergquist et al., *Violence in Colombia*, 263. A gripping, blow-by-blow journalistic account of this period is Téllez, *La guerra verde*.
24. On Carranza's connections to paramilitarism see, for example, Kirk, *More Terrible than Death*, 130–1, and Rangel, *El poder paramilitar*, 53–5. For a more generous assessment based on personal interviews, see Heufelder, *Der Smaragkönig*.

Appendices

1. Citing the same sources (I also looked at Contaduría 1292 and 1300, which he lists), Colombian historian Tovar Pinzón offers somewhat different numbers in his preface to Rodríguez Baquero, *Encomienda y vida diaria*, 6.
2. AGNC Real Hacienda t.37, f.507.
3. Ibid., t.46, ff.401–50. Hernández's testimony is on f.447.
4. In 1571 an indigenous woman named Elvira, 'in the service of Juan Alonso, citizen of Muzo', paid *quintos* in Bogotá on three stones. It is unclear if they belonged to her or her master. AGI Contaduría 1300 (accounts for 24 October 1571).

5. Rojas Gómez, 'Las esmeraldas de Muzo'.
6. AGNC Minas de Boyacá 3: 8, f.186 (1569), 1: 7, f.783 (1614) and 2: 4, ff.522–84 (1643).
7. An early lapidary who paid taxes on stones was Pedro Torres. AGI Contaduría 1301 (accounts for 1582).
8. AGI Contaduría 1587 (accounts of 21 March 1610–20 April 1611).
9. AGNC Minas de Boyacá 1: 1, ff.69–103 (1680). When questioned in December 1677 gem cutters Lorenzo Herrero and Bernardo Clavijo both said it 'has been in style' (*a estado en estilo*) to leave the problem of *quintos* to 'the clients' (*los ynteresados*).
10. Keene, *Treasury of the World*, 18. Cellini describes the European technique *c*.1568 in *The Treatises of Benvenuto Cellini*, 25–7.
11. AGI Contaduría 1587 (accounts 16 June 1629–19 May 1630). One of the merchants was called Hernando Bernal.
12. Arfe y Villafañe, *Quilatador de la plata* (1572 edn), 42, 46, 48.
13. Acosta, *Natural and Moral History of the Indes*, 194–5.
14. Arfe y Villafañe, *Quilatador de la plata* (1598 ed.).
15. Hamilton, *American Treasure*.
16. Arfe y Villafañe, *Quilatador de la plata*, book V (1598 edn), 125v–28.
17. ANTT Corpo Cronologico pt.1, maço 84, no. 109 (20–vii–1550).
18. Arfe y Villafañe, *Quilatador de la plata* (1572 edn), 56, 60.
19. Knivet in Purchas, *Hakluytus Posthumus*, 16: 214, 220.
20. Ibid., 212, 221.
21. Brandão, *Dialogues of the Great Things of Brazil*, 18–19.
22. Boxer, *Salvador de Sá*, 294–306.
23. ANTT Registo Geral de Mercês, D. Afonso VI, liv.4, ff.290–90v.
24. Schwartz, *A Governor and His Image*, 13, 163.

Bibliography

Archives

Archivo Central del Cauca (ACC), Popayán, Colombia: Notariales, Real Hacienda
Archivo General de Indias (AGI), Seville, Spain: Contaduría, Santa Fe, Quito
Archivo General de la Nación, Santafé de Bogotá, Colombia (AGNC), Sección Colonia: Minas de Boyacá, Minas Anexo, Historia Civil, Real Hacienda
Archivo Histórico Nacional, Madrid (AHN): Inquisición de Cartagena de Indias
Archivo Nacional del Ecuador (ANE), Quito, Ecuador: Popayán, Protocolos Notariales
Archivo Nacional do Torre do Tombo (ANTT), Lisbon, Portugal: Inquisición, etc.
Archivo Regional de Boyacá (ARB), Tunja, Colombia; Protocolos Notariales
Biblioteca Nacional de España (BNE), Madrid: Misc. Mss
Biblioteca Nacional de Portugal (BNP), Lisbon: Misc. Mss
British Library (BL), London, East India Company Letterbooks and Court Minutes
John Carter Brown Library (JCBL), Providence, RI, Misc. Mss
Parliamentary Archives (PA), London, Court Transcripts

Published Documents and Contemporary Works

Acosta, José de, *Natural and Moral History of the Indies*, ed. Jane E. Mangan (Durham, NC, 2002)
Agricola, Georgius, *De Natura Fossilium (Texbook of Mineralogy)*, trans. M.C. and J.A. Bandy (New York, 1955)
Aguado, Pedro de, *Recopilación Historial*, ed. Juan Friede, 4 vols (Bogotá, 1956)
Albertus Magnus, *Book of Minerals*, trans. Dorothy Wyckoff (Oxford, 1967)
Amasuno, Marcelino V., ed., *La Materia Médica de Dioscorides en el Lapidario de Alfonso X el Sabio: Literatura y ciencia en la Castilla del siglo XIII* (Madrid, 1987)
Ancízar, Manuel, *Peregrinación de Alpha por las Provincias del Norte de la Nueva Granada, en 1850–1851* (Bogotá, 1956)

Arfe y Villafañe, Juan de, *Quilatador de la plata, oro, y piedras, conforme a las leyes Reales, y para declaración de ellas* (Madrid, 1598)

——, *Quilatador de la plata, oro, y piedras* (1572 ed., Madrid, 1976)

Ball, Sydney H., *A Roman Book on Precious Stones* (Los Angeles, 1950)

Barbosa, Duarte, *The Book of Duarte Barbosa, vol. II*, trans. M.L. Dames (London, 1921)

Bembo, Ambrosio, *The Travels and Journal of Ambrosio Bembo*, ed. Anthony Welch, trans. Clara Bargellini (Berkeley, 2007)

Boxer, Charles R., 'Uma raridade bibliográfica sobre Fernão Cron', *Boletim Internacional de Bibliografia Luso-Brasileira* 12 (1971), 323–64

Brandão, Ambrósio Ferndandes, *Dialogues of the Great Things of Brazil*, trans. Frederick Hall, William F. Harrison, and Dorothy Welkers (Albuquerque, 1987)

Bulhão Pato, Raymundo Antonio de, ed., *Documentos remettidos da Índia, ou Livros das Monções*, 5 vols (Lisbon, 1880)

Carletti, Francesco, *My Voyage Around the World*, trans. Herbert Weinstock (New York, 1964)

Castellanos, Juan de, *Elegías de varones ilustres de Indias* (Bogotá, 1997)

Cellini, Benvenuto, *The Treatises of Benvenuto Cellini on Goldsmithing and Sculpture*, trans. C.R. Ashbee (New York, 1967)

Cieza de León, Pedro de, *The Discovery and Conquest of Peru*, ed. and trans. N.D. Cook and Alexandra Parma Cook (Durham, NC, 1998)

Correa, Virgilio, ed., *Livro de Regimentos dos Officiães Mecânicos da mui nobre e sempre leal cidade de Lixboa* (Coimbra, 1926)

Correia-Afonso, John, ed., *Letters from the Mughal Court: The First Jesuit Mission to Akbar, 1580–1583* (St. Louis, 1981)

Coustos, John, *The Sufferings of John Coustos in the Inquisition at Lisbon* (London, 1746)

Coutre, Jacques de, *Andanzas Asiáticas*, ed. Eddy Stols, Benjamin Teensma, and Johan Verberckmoes (Madrid, 1991)

Coverte, Robert, *The Travels of Captain Robert Coverte*, ed. Boies Penrose (Philadelphia, 1931)

D'Elhuyar, Juan José, 'Informe de un viaje a Muzo', in eds Guillermo Hernández de Alba y Armando Espinosa Baquero, *Tratados de minería y estudios geológicos de la época colonial, 1616–1803*, 63–84 (Bogotá, 1991)

Erevan, Abraham of, *History of the Wars (1721–1738)*, ed. and trans. George A. Bournoutian (Costa Mesa, CA, 1999)

Farah, Caesar, ed. and trans., *An Arab's Journey to Colonial Spanish America: The Travels of Elias al-Mûsili in the Seventeenth Century* (Syracuse, NY, 2003)

Fernández de Oviedo, Gonzalo, *Historia General y Natural de las Indias*, 4 vols, Biblioteca de autores Españoles vol. 119 (Madrid, 1959)

Foster, William, *Early Travels in India, 1583–1619* (London, 1921)

Francis, J. Michael, ' "In the service of God, I order that these temples of idolatrous worship be razed to the ground": Extirpation of Idolatry and the Search for the *Santuario Grande* of Iguaque', in eds Richard Boyer and Geoffrey Spurling, *Colonial Lives: Documents in Latin American History, 1550–1850*, 39–53 (New York, 2000)

——, ed. and trans., *Invading Colombia: Spanish Accounts of the Gonzalo Jiménez de Quesada Expedition of Conquest* (University Park, PA, 2007)

Fraser, James, *History of Nadir Shah* (London, 1742)

Frear Keeler, Mary, ed., *Sir Francis Drake's West Indian Voyage, 1585–1586* (London, 1981)

Garcés, Jorge A., ed., *Plan del camino de Quito al Río Esmeraldas, según las observaciones astronómicas de Jorge Juan y de Antonio de Ulloa, 1736–1742* (Quito, 1942)

Garcilaso de la Vega, El Inca, *Royal Commentaries of the Incas*, trans. Harold Livermore (Austin, 1966)

Gentil da Silva, José, ed., *Stratégie des Affaires à Lisbonne entre 1595 et 1607: Lettres marchandes des Rodrigues d'Evora et Veiga* (Paris, 1956)

——, *Lettres de Lisbonne: Les Gomes, 1564–1578*, 2 vols (Paris, 1959)

Glückel of Hameln, *The Memoirs of Glückel of Hameln*, ed. Robert Rosen, trans. Marvin Lowenthal, (New York, 1977)

González, Enrique, *Esmeraldas de las minas de Muzo y Coscuez: Colección de artículos publicados en La Fusión contra los últimos contratos de explotación* (Bogotá, 1911)

González de Pérez, María Stella, ed., *Diccionario y gramática Chibcha: manuscrito anónimo de la Biblioteca Nacional de Colombia* (Bogotá, 1987)

Hosten, H., ed., 'The Jesuits at Agra in 1635–1637', *Journal of the Royal Asiatic Society* 4, 21 (1938): 479–501

Hyland, Sabine, ed., *The Quito Manuscript: An Inca History Preserved by Fernando de Montesinos* (New Haven, CT, 2007)

Jahangir, Emperor, *The Jahangirnama: Memoirs of Jahangir, Emperor of India*, ed. and trans. Wheeler M. Thackston (New York, 1999)

Juan, Jorge, and Antonio Ulloa, *A Voyage to South America*, ed. Irving Leonard, trans. John Adams (New York, 1964)

——, *Discourse and Political Reflections on the Kingdoms of Peru*, ed. John J. TePaske, trans. Besse A. Clement (Norman, OK, 1978)

Khan, Inayat, *The Shah Jahan nama of Inayat Khan*, eds W.E. Begley and Z.A. Desai, trans. A.R. Fuller (Delhi, 1990)

Klein, Fritz, *Smaradge unter dem Urwald: Meine Entdeckungs- und Erlebnisreisen in Lateinamerika* (Berlin, 1941)

The Koran, trans. N.J. Dawood (London, 1995)

Linschoten, Jan Huyghen van, *The Voyage of Jan Huyghen van Linschoten to the East Indies*, 2 vols (London, 1935)

Locke, John C., ed, *The First Englishmen in India* (London, 1930)

Manucci, Niccolao, *Storia do Mogor*, trans. William Irvine, 4 vols (London, 1907)

Matos, Artur Teodoro, ed., *Diário do Conde de Sarzedas, vice-rei do Estado da Índia, 1655–1656* (Lisbon, 2001)

Monshi, Eskandar Beg, *History of Shah Abbas the Great*, trans. Roger M. Savory, 2 vols (Boulder, 1978)

Montaña, Francisco, *Renta de esmeraldas: apuntes fiscales* (London, 1915)

Morga, Antonio de, *Sucesos de las islas Filipinas*, trans. J.S. Cummins (Cambridge, 1971)

Pagden, Anthony, ed. and trans., *Hernán Cortés: Letters from Mexico* (New Haven, CT, 1986)

Purchas, Samuel, *Hakluytus Posthumus or Purchas His Pilgrimes* (New York, 1906)

Pyrard, François, *The Voyage of François Pyrard of Laval to the East Indies*, ed. and trans. Albert Gray, 2 vols (London, 1887–90)

Rainier, Peter W., *Green Fire* (New York, 1942)

Robles, Gregorio de, *América a fines del Siglo XVII: Noticia de los lugares de contrabando* (Valladolid, 1980)

Roe, Thomas, *The Embassy of Sir Thomas Roe to India, 1615–19, as Narrated in his Journal and Correspondence*, ed. William Foster (London, 1926)

Rojas Gómez, Roberto, 'Las esmeraldas de Muzo en el Siglo XVI', *Boletín de Historia y Antigüedades* (Bogotá) 227 (1933): 69–80

Sandoval, Alonso de, *Treatise on Slavery*, abridged, ed. and trans. Nicole Von Germeten (Indianapolis, IN, 2008)

Santisteban, Miguel de, *Mil leguas por América: diario de Miguel de Santisteban*, ed. David J. Robinson (Bogotá, 1992)

Schwartz, Stuart B., ed., *A Governor and His Image in Baroque Brazil: The Funeral Eulogy of Afonso Furtado de Castro do Rio de Mendonça, by Juan Lopes Sierra*, trans. Ruth E. Jones (Minneapolis, MN, 1979)

Séguy, Marie-Rose, ed., *The Miraculous Journey of Mahomet: Mirâj Nâmeh* (Manuscript Supplément Turc 190, Bibliothèque Nationale, Paris) (New York, 1977)

Simón, Pedro, *Noticias historiales de las conquistas de Tierra Firme en las Indias Occidentales*, 9 vols (Bogotá, 1953)

Splendiani, Anna María, José Enrique Sánchez Bohórquez, Emma Cecilia Luque de Salazar, eds, *Cincuenta años de la inquisición en el Tribunal de Cartagena de Indias, 1610–1660*, 3 vols (Bogotá, 1997)

Tavernier, Jean-Baptiste, *Travels in India*, ed. William Crooke, trans. Valentine Ball, 2 vols, 2nd edn (New Delhi, 1977)

Thackston, Wheeler, ed. and trans., *Akbarnama* (Washington, D.C., 1998)

Tifaschi, Ahmad ibn Yusuf Al, *Arab Roots of Gemology: Ahmad ibn Yusuf Al Tifaschi's Best Thoughts on the Best of Stones (c.1240)*, ed. and trans. Samar Najm Abul Huda (London, 1998)

Tovar Pinzón, Hermes, ed., *Relaciones y Visitas a los Andes, Siglo XVI, vol. III: Región Centro-Oriental* (Bogotá, 1996)

Urdaneta, Martín de, 'Memoria instructiva de la Provincia de los Muzos y Colimas', *Boletín de Historia y Antigüedades* (Bogotá) XIV (1924): 467–82

Vargas Machuca, Bernardo, *The Indian Militia and Description of the Indies*, ed. Kris Lane, trans. Timothy F. Johnson (Durham, NC, 2008)

Varthema, Ludovico di, *The Travels of Ludovico di Varthema in Egypt, Syria, Arabia, etc., A.D. 1503–1508*, trans. J. Winter Jones (London, 1863)

Vásquez de Epinosa, Antonio, *Compendio y descripción de las Indias Occidentales*, Biblioteca de autores Españoles vol. 231 (Madrid, 1969)

Zapata, Julio, *El ignominioso contrato de Muzo* (Bogotá, 1910)

Published Secondary Sources

Ahmad, Afzal, *Portuguese Trade and Socio-Economic Changes on the Western Coast of India, 1600–1663* (Delhi, 2000)

Andrade Reimers, Luis, *Las esmeraldas de Esmeraldas durante el siglo XVI* (Quito, 1978)

Arboleda, Gustavo, *Una familia de proceres: Los Parises* (Bogotá, 1919)

Avery, Peter, 'Nadir Shah and the Afsharid Legacy', in Peter Avery, Gavin Hambly and Charles Melville, eds, *The Cambridge History of Iran, vol. 7: From Nadir Shah to the Islamic Republic*, 3–62 (Cambridge, 1991)

Axworthy, Michael, *Sword of Persia: Nader Shah, from Tribal Warrior to Conquering Tyrant* (London, 2006)

Baghdiantz McCabe, Ina, *The Shah's Silk for Europe's Silver: The Eurasian Trade of the Julfa Armenians in Safavid Iran and India, 1530–1750* (Atlanta, 1999)

Bergquist, Charles, Ricardo Peñaranda and Gonzalo Sánchez, eds, *Violence in Colombia: The Contemporary Crisis in Historical Perspective* (Wilmington, DE, 1992)

Bernardini, Paolo, and Norman Fiering, eds, *The Jews and the Expansion of Europe to the West, 1450–1800* (New York, 2001)

Bingham, Hiram, *Elihu Yale: The American Nabob of Queen Square* (New York, 1939)

Bleichmar, Daniela, Paula De Vos, Kristin Huffine and Kevin Sheehan, eds, *Science in the Spanish and Portuguese Empires, 1500–1800* (Stanford, CA, 2009)

Bodian, Miriam, *Hebrews of the Portuguese Nation: Conversos and Community in Early Modern Amsterdam* (Bloomington, IN, 1997)

Bouchon, Geneviève, *Inde Découverte, Inde Retrouvée, 1498–1630: Études d'histoire indo-portugaise* (Lisbon, 1999)

Boxer, Charles R., *Salvador de Sá and the Struggle for Brazil and Angola, 1602–1686* (London, 1952)

Boyajian, James C., *Portuguese Bankers at the Court of Spain, 1626–1650* (New Brunswick, NJ, 1983)

——, *Portuguese Trade in Asia under the Habsburgs, 1580–1640* (Baltimore, 1993)

Castillo, Pilar del, and Juan Carlos Elorza Guinea, eds, *El arte de la plata y de las joyas en la España de Carlos V* (La Coruña, 2000)

Chaudhuri, K.N., *The Trading World of Asia and the English East India Company, 1660–1760* (Cambridge, 1978)

Chaudhury, Sushil, and Michel Morineau, eds, *Merchants, Companies, and Trade: Europe and Asia in the Early Modern Era* (Cambridge, 1999)

Colombian Society of Petroleum Geologists and Geophysicists, *Cundinamarca-Boyacá-Muzo Emerald Mines* (2nd annual field conference guide, mimeograph, 1961)

Craddock, Paul T., *Early Metal Mining and Production* (Washington, D.C., 1995)

Denny, Walter B., 'The Palace, Power, and the Arts', in *Palace of Gold and Light: Treasures from the Topkapi, Istanbul*, 16–25 (Istanbul, 2000)

Disney, Anthony R., *A History of Portugal and the Portuguese Empire*, 2 vols (Cambridge, 2009)

Domínguez, Rafael, *Historia de las esmeraldas de Colombia* (Bogotá, 1965)

Elliott, John H., *Spain and its World, 1500–1700* (New Haven, CT, 1989)

Eschwege, Wilhelm Ludwig von, *Pluto Brasiliensis*, trans. Domício de Figueredo Murta, 2 vols (São Paulo, 1944)

Ferry, Robert J., 'Don't Drink the Chocolate: Domestic Slavery and the Exigencies of Fasting for Crypto-Jews in Seventeenth-Century Mexico', *Nuevo Mundo/Mundos Nuevos* (2005). Online: http://nuevomundo.revues.org/index934

Fine, John C., *Treasures of the Spanish Main: Shipwrecked Galleons in the New World* (Guilford, CT, 2006)

Fisher, John R., Allan J. Kuethe and Anthony McFarlane, eds, *Reform and Insurrection in Bourbon New Granada and Peru* (Baton Rouge, LA, 1990)

Floor, Willem, 'Pearl fishing in the Persian Gulf in the 18th Century', *Persica* 10 (1982): 1–69

——, *The Economy of Safavid Persia* (Wiesbaden, 2000)

——, *The Persian Gulf: A Political and Economic History of Five Port Cities, 1500–1730* (Washington, D.C., 2006)

Forsyth, Hazel, *The Cheapside Hoard* (London, 2003)

Francis, J. Michael, 'Población, enfermedad y cambio demográfico, 1537–1636: Demografía histórica de Tunja, una mirada crítica', *Fronteras de la Historia* 7 (2002): 15–95

Friede, Juan, 'Demographic Changes in the Mining Community of Muzo after the Plague of 1629', *Hispanic American Historical Review* (August 1967): 338–43

Furber, Holden, *Rival Empires of the Orient, 1600–1800* (Minneapolis, MN, 1976)

García-Arenal, Mercedes, and Gerard Wiegers, *A Man of Three Worlds: Samuel Pallache, a Moroccan Jew in Catholic and Protestant Europe*, trans. Martin Beagles (Baltimore, MD, 1999)

García Manjarrés, Carlos, and Carlos Arturo Vargas Ayala, *Proyecto minero para las minas de Muzo y Coscuez (Colombia-Suramerica)* (Bogotá, 1970)

Girard, Albert, *Le commerce français a Séville e Cadix au temps des Habsbourg: contribution a l'étude du commerce etranger en Espagne au XVIe et XVIIe siècles* (New York, 1967)

Giuliani, Gaston, et al., 'Oxygen Isotopes and Emerald Trade Routes Since Antiquity', *Science* 287 (28 January 2000): 631–3

——, eds, *Emeralds of the World* (Munich, 2002)

Gommans, Jos, *Mughal Warfare: Indian Frontiers and High Roads to Empire, 1500–1700* (London, 2002)

Goslinga, Cornelis, *The Dutch in the Caribbean and on the Wild Coast, 1580–1680* (Gainesville, FL, 1971)

Grahn, Lance, *The Political Economy of Smuggling: Regional Informal Economies in Early Bourbon New Granada* (Boulder, CO, 1997)

Greenfield, Amy Butler, *A Perfect Red: Empire, Espionage, and the Quest for the Color of Desire* (New York, 2005)

Hackenbroch, Yvonne, *Renaissance Jewellery* (London, 1979)

Hamilton, Earl J., *American Treasure and the Price Revolution in Spain, 1501–1650* (Cambridge, MA, 1934)

Hampe Martínez, Teodoro, 'El reparto de metales, joyas, e indios de Coaque: un episodio fundamental en la expedición de conquista del Perú', *Quinto Centenario* 15 (1989): 77–94

Haring, Clarence H., *Trade and Navigation Between Spain and the Indies in the Time of the Habsburgs* (Cambridge, MA, 1918)

Hearne, Pamela, and Robert J. Sharer, eds, *River of Gold: Precolumbian Treasures from Sitio Conte* (Philadelphia, PA, 1992)

Henderson, James D., *Modernization in Colombia: The Laureano Gómez Years, 1889–1965* (Gainesville, FL, 2001)

Heufelder, Jeanette Erazo, *Der Smaragdkönig: Victor Carranza und das grüne Gold der Anden* (Munich, 2005)

Hodgson, Marshall G.S., *The Venture of Islam, Volume 3: The Gunpowder Empires and Modern Times* (Chicago, 1977)

Horner, Dave, *Shipwreck: A Saga of Sea Tragedy and Sunken Treasure* (Dobbs Ferry, NY, 1999)

Irving, Earl M., *Structural Evolution of the Northernmost Andes, Colombia* (Washington, D.C., 1975)

Israel, Jonathan I., *Dutch Primacy in World Trade, 1585–1740* (Oxford, 1989)

——, *Diasporas Within a Diaspora: Jews, Crypto-Jews and the World Maritime Empires, 1540–1740* (Leiden, 2002)

Kagan, Richard L., and Philip D. Morgan, eds, *Atlantic Diasporas: Jews, Conversos, and Crypto-Jews in the Age of Mercantilism, 1500–1800* (Baltimore, MD, 2009)

Kayserling, Meyer, 'The Jews in Jamaica and Daniel Israel Lopez Laguna', *The Jewish Quarterly Review* 12, 4 (July 1900): 708–17

Kazmi, Ali H. and Lawrence W. Snee, eds, *Emeralds of Pakistan: Geology, Gemology, and Genesis* (New York, 1989)

Keene, Manuel, *Treasury of the World: Jewelled Arts of India in the Age of the Mughals* (London, 2001)

Kirk, Robin, *More Terrible than Death: Violence, Drugs, and America's War in Colombia* (New York, 2003)

Kolff, Dirk H.A., *Naukar, Rajput and Sepoy: the Ethnohistory of the Military Labour Market in Hindustan, 1450–1850* (Cambridge, 1990)

Köseoglu, Cengiz, *The Topkapi Saray Museum: the Treasury*, ed. and trans. J.M. Rogers (London, 1987)

Lane, Frederic, *Venice: A Maritime Republic* (Baltimore, MD, 1973)

Lane, Kris, *Blood and Silver: A History of Piracy in the Caribbean and Central America* (Oxford, 1999). Published in the U.S. as *Pillaging the Empire: Piracy in the Americas, 1500–1750* (Armonk, NY, 1998)

——, *Quito 1599: City and Colony in Transition* (Albuquerque, 2002)

——, 'El Dorado Negro, o el verdadero precio del oro Neogradino', in eds Claudia Mosquera and Luiz Barcelos, *Afro-reparaciones: Memorias de la esclavitud y justicia reparativa para negros, afrocolombianos y raizales*, 281–94 (Bogotá, 2007)

Lenman, Bruce P., 'The East India Company and the Trade in Non-Metallic Precious Materials from Sir Thomas Roe to Diamond Pitt', in eds H.V. Bowen, Margarette Lincoln and Nigel Rigby, *The Worlds of the East India Company*, 97–110 (Suffolk, 2002)

Lleras Codazzi, Ricardo, *Catálogo descriptivo de los minerales de Muzo* (Bogotá, 1925)

Lockhart, Laurence, *Nadir Shah: A Critical Study Based Mainly on Contemporary Sources* (London, 1938)

Lorenzo Sanz, Eufemio, *Comercio de España con América en la época de Felipe II*, 2 vols (Valladolid, 1979)

Lyon, Eugene, *The Search for the* Atocha (New York, 1974)

Maclagan, Edward, *The Jesuits and the Great Mogul* (London, 1932)

Markovits, Claude, *Merchants, Traders, Entrepreneurs: Indian Business in the Colonial Era* (New York, 2008)

Marx, Robert F., *The Lure of Sunken Treasure: Under the Sea with Marine Archeologists and Treasure Hunters* (New York, 1973)

——, *Robert Marx: Author, Archeologist, Treasure Hunter, Quest for Treasure* (Dallas, 1982)

——, *In the Wake of Galleons* (Flagstaff, AZ, 2001)

Marx, Robert F., and Jennifer Marx, *The Search for Sunken Treasure: Exploring the World's Great Shipwrecks* (Toronto, 1993)

——, *Treasure Lost at Sea: Diving to the World's Great Shipwrecks* (Buffalo, NY, 2003)

Matthee, Rudolph, *The Politics of Trade in Safavid Iran: Silk for Silver, 1600–1730* (Cambridge, 2006)

McFarlane, Anthony, *Colombia Before Independence* (Cambridge, 1993)

McNeill, William H., *The Pursuit of Power: Technology, Armed Force, and Society since A.D. 1000* (Chicago, 1982)

Meen, V.B., *Crown Jewels of Iran* (Toronto, 1968)

Meyers, Allan D., 'Ethnic Distinctions and Wealth among Colonial Jamaican Merchants, 1685–1716', *Social Science History* 22, 1 (Spring 1998): 47–81

Morgan, Diane, *From Satan's Crown to the Holy Grail: Emeralds in Myth, Magic, and History* (Westport, CT, 2007)

Moura Carvalho, Pedro, ' "Rarities from Goa" at the Courts of Humayun, Akbar, and Jahangir (1530–1627)', in eds Jorge Flores and Nuno Vassallo y Silva, *Goa and the Great Mughal*, 98–115 (Lisbon, London, 2004)

Mukhia, Harbans, *The Mughals of India* (London, 2004)

Müller, Priscilla E., *Jewels in Spain, 1500–1800* (New York, 1972)

Navarro Cárdenas, Maximina, *Investigación histórica de la minería en el Ecuador*. 2nd edn (Quito, 1990)

Newson, Linda A., and Susie Minchin, *From Capture to Sale: The Portuguese Slave Trade to Spanish South America in the Early Seventeenth Century* (Leiden, 2007)

Nickel, Helmut, 'The Graphic Sources for the "Moor with the Emerald Cluster"', *Metropolitan Museum Journal* 15 (1981): 203–10

O'Neil, Paul, *Gemstones* (Alexandria, VA, 1983)

Otero Muñoz, Gustavo, and Antonio M. Barriga Villalba, *Esmeraldas de Colombia* (Bogotá, 1948)

Ottaway, T.L., et al., 'Formation of the Hydrothermal Emerald Deposit in Colombia', *Nature* 369 (16 June 1994): 552–4

Otte, Enrique, *Las perlas del Caribe: Nueva Cádiz de Cubagua* (Caracas, 1977)

Parra Morales, Trinidad, *Los Muzos: un pueblo extinguido* (Bogotá, 1985)

Pearson, Michael N., *The Portuguese in India* (Cambridge, 1987)

Peralta Barrera, Napoleón, *El País de los Muzos* (Tunja, 1998)

Pérez de Barradas, José, *Los Muiscas antes de la Conquista*, 2 vols (Madrid, 1951)

Peterson, Mendel, *The Funnel of Gold* (Boston, MA, 1975)

Philips Son and Neale, Inc., *A Rare Collection of Early Spanish and Colonial Jewelry and Religious Artifacts: A Private Collection to be Sold at Auction on Wednesday, October 26, 1983* (New York, 1983)

Phillips, Carla Rahn, *The Treasure of the* San José: *Death at Sea in the War of the Spanish Succession* (Baltimore, MD, 2007)

Pike, Ruth, *Aristocrats and Traders: Sevillian Society in the Sixteenth Century* (Ithaca, NY, 1972)

——, *Linajudos and Conversos in Seville: Greed and Prejudice in Sixteenth- and Seventeenth-Century Spain* (New York, 2000)

Piotrovsky, Mikhail, and John Frieze, eds, *Earthly Beauty, Heavenly Art: Art of Islam* (Amsterdam, 2000)

Pogue, Joseph E., 'The Emerald Deposits of Muzo, Colombia', *Transactions of the American Institute of Mining Engineering*, 799–822 (Arizona Mtg., AZ, Sept. 1916)

Prior, Katherine, *The Maharaja's Jewels* (Paris, 2000)

Quiroz, Alfonso W., 'The Expropriation of Portuguese New Christians in Spanish America, 1635–1649', *Ibero-Amerikanisches Archiv* 11, 4 (1985): 407–65

Rangel, Alfredo, ed., *El poder paramilitar* (Bogotá, 2005)

Reichel-Dolmatoff, Gerardo, 'Things of Beauty Replete with Meaning – Metals and Crystals in Colombian Indian Cosmology', in *Sweat of the Sun, Tears of the Moon: Gold and Emerald Treasures of Colombia*, 17–33 (Los Angeles, 1981)

Ritchie, Robert C., *Captain Kidd and the War against the Pirates* (Cambridge, MA, 1986).

Rodríguez Baquero, Luis Enrique, *Encomienda y vida diaria entre los indios de Muzo, 1550–1620* (Bogotá, 1995)

Ruiz Rivera, Julian B., *Encomienda y mita en Nueva Granada* (Sevilla, 1975)

Russell-Wood, A.J.R., *The Portuguese Empire: A World on the Move* (Baltimore, MD, 1998)

Samuel, Edgar R., *The Portuguese Jewish Community of London* (London, 1992)

——, *At the End of the Earth: Essays on the History of the Jews of England and Portugal* (London, 2004)

Sanz, Eufemio Lorenzo, *Comercio de España con América en la época de Felipe II*. 2 vols (Valladolid, 1979)

Sarkar, Jadunath, *Nadir Shah in India* (Calcutta, 1973)

Sauer, Carl O., *The Early Spanish Main* (Berkeley, CA, 1966)

Sauer, Jules Roger, *Emeralds Around the World* (n.p., 1992)

——, *Emeralds and Other Gemstones of Brazil.* (n.p., 1992)

Schimmel, Annemarie, *The Empire of the Great Mughals: History, Art, and Culture*, trans. Corinne Attwood (London, 2004)

Sinkankas, John, *Emerald and Other Beryls* (Radnor, PA, 1981)

Sluiter, Engel, 'Dutch-Spanish Rivalry in the Caribbean Area, 1594–1609', *Hispanic American Historical Review* 28, 2 (May 1948): 165–96

Smith, Jedwin, *Fatal Treasure: Greed and Death, Emeralds and Gold, and the Obsessive Search for the Legendary Ghost Galleon* Atocha (New York, 2003)

Sotheby & Co., *Sale of the Crown of the Andes: A Magnificent Devotional Crown in Gold and Emeralds Sold on the Order of an American Syndicate, 21 November 1963* (London, 1963)

Steensgaard, Niels, *The Asian Trade Revolution of the Seventeenth Century: The East India Companies and the Decline of the Caravan Trade* (Chicago, 1974)

Stein, Burton, *A History of India* (London, 1998)

Stronge, Susan, ed., *The Jewels of India* (Bombay, 1995)

——, *Painting for the Mughal Emperor* (London, 2002)

Stronge, Susan, Nima Smith and J.C. Harle, *A Golden Treasury: Jewellery from the Indian Subcontinent* (New York, 1988)

Studnicki-Gizbert, Daviken, *A Nation Upon the Ocean Sea: Portugal's Atlantic Diaspora and the Crisis of the Spanish Empire, 1492–1640* (New York, 2007)

Subrahmanyam, Sanjay, *The Portuguese Empire in Asia, 1500–1700* (London, 1993)

——, *Penumbral Visions: Making Polities in Early Modern South India* (Ann Arbor, MI, 2001)

——, *Explorations in Connected History: Mughals and Franks* (Delhi, 2004)

Swetschinski, Daniel M., *Reluctant Cosmopolitans: The Portuguese Jews of Seventeenth-Century Amsterdam* (Portland, OR, 2000)

Szászdi, Ádám, 'En torno a la balsa de Salango (Ecuador) que capturó Bartolomé Ruiz', *Anuario de Estudios Americanos* 35 (1978): 453–554

Szászdi León-Borja, István, *Los viajes de rescate de Ojeda* (Santo Domingo, 2001)

Taube, Karl A., 'The Symbolism of Jade in Classic Maya Religion', *Ancient Mesoamerica* 16 (2005): 23–50

Taussig, Michael, *My Cocaine Museum* (Chicago, 2005)

Teensma, Benjamin N., 'De politieke en economische ideeën van de Bruggeling: Jacques de Coutre (1575–1640), alsmede enige tekstkritiek' (Leiden, 1994)

——, 'Jacques de Coutre as Jewel Merchant in India', Amsterdam: *Proceedings of the 11th European Conference on Modern South Asian Studies*, (1990) 1–12

Tejado Fernández, Manuel, *Aspectos de la vida social en Cartagena de Indias durante el seiscientos* (Sevilla, 1954)

Teles e Cunha, João, 'Hunting Riches: Goa's Gem Trade in the Early Modern Age', in eds Pius Malekandathil and T. Jamal Mohammed, *The Portuguese, Indian Ocean, and European Bridgeheads, 1500–1800: Festschrift in Honour of Prof. K.S. Mathew*, 269–304 (Tellicherry, Kerala, 2001)

Téllez, Pedro Claver, *La guerra verde: treinta años de conflicto entre los esmeralderos* (Bogotá, 1993)

Topik, Steven, Carlos Marichal and Zephyr Frank, eds, *From Silver to Cocaine: Latin American Commodity Chains and the Building of the World Economy, 1500–2000* (Durham, NC, 2006)

Tovar Pinzón, Hermes, *El imperio y sus colonias: las cajas reales de la Nueva Granada en el Siglo XVI* (Bogotá, 1999)

Trivellato, Francesca, 'Juifs de Livourne, Italiens de Lisbonne, hindous de Goa. Réseaux marchands et échanges interculturels à l'époque moderne', *Annales* 58: 3 (May–June 2003): 581–604

——, *The Familiarity of Strangers: The Sephardic Diaspora, Livorno, and Cross-Cultural Trade in the Early Modern Period* (New Haven, CT, London, 2009)

Tucker, Ernest S., *Nadir Shah's Quest for Legitimacy in Post-Safavid Iran* (Gainesville, FL, 2006)

Vassallo e Silva, Nuno, 'Jewels and Gems in Goa from the Sixteenth to Eighteenth Century', in ed. Susan Stronge, *The Jewels of India*, 53–62 (Bombay, 1995)

Victoria and Albert Museum (exhibition catalogue). *Princely Magnificence: Court Jewels of the Renaissance, 1500–1630* (London, 1981)

Vieira de Castro, Filipe, *The Pepper Wreck: A Portuguese Indiaman at the Mouth of the Tagus River* (College Station, TX, 2005)

Vila Vilar, Enriqueta, *Aspectos sociales en América colonial: de extranjeros, contrabando, y esclavos* (Bogotá, 2001)

Voillot, Patrick, *Diamonds and Precious Stones*, trans. Jack Hawkes (New York, 1998)

Ward, Fred, *Emeralds* (Baltimore, MD, 1993)

Webster, Robert, *Gems: Their Sources, Descriptions, and Identification*, 5th rev. ed. by Peter G. Read (London, 1994)

Weinstein, Michael, *The World of Jewel Stones* (New York, 1967)

West, Robert C., *Colonial Placer Mining in Colombia* (Baton Rouge, LA, 1952)

Wey Gómez, Nicolás, *The Tropics of Empire: Why Columbus Sailed South to the Indies* (Cambridge, MA, 2008)

Wheeler, R.E. Mortimer, *The Cheapside Hoard of Elizabethan and Jacobean Jewellery* (London, 1928)

Winius, George D., 'Jewel Trading in Portuguese India in the XVI and XVII centuries', *Indica* 25, 1 (Bombay, 1988): 15–34

——, 'Portugal, Venice, Genoa, and the Traffic in Precious Stones at the Beginning of the Modern Age' (English version of a paper published in Genoa, *Atti del III Congresso Internazionale di Studi Sorici VII*, 1989), reprinted in G.D. Winius, *Studies in Portuguese Asia, 1495–1689* (Aldershot, 2001)

Wise, Richard W., *Secrets of the Gem Trade: The Connoisseur's Guide to Precious Gemstones* (Lenox, MA, 2003)

Wolf, Theodor, *Geografía y Geología del Ecuador* (Leipzig, 1892)

Yogev, Gedalia, *Diamonds and Coral: Anglo-Dutch Jews and Eighteenth-Century Trade* (Leicester, 1978)

Zahedieh, Nuala, 'The Merchants of Port Royal, Jamaica, and the Spanish Contraband Trade, 1655–92', *William & Mary Quarterly*, 3rd ser. 43, 4 (Oct. 1986): 570–93

——, 'Trade, Plunder, and Economic Development in Early English Jamaica, 1655–89', *Economic History Review* 2nd ser. 39, 2 (1986), 205–22

Unpublished Theses

Rojas A., Martha, 'La explotación esmeraldífera de Muzo a través del tiempo: su orígen precolombino, cambios y supervivencias en los distintos períodos históricos', Licenciate thesis in Anthropology, Universidad de los Andes, Bogotá, Colombia, 1974

Segovia Salas, Rodolfo, 'Crown Policy and the Precious Metals in New Granada, 1760–1810', Master of Arts thesis, History, University of California, Berkeley, 1960

Warsh, Molly, 'Adorning Empire: The History of the Early Modern Pearl Trade, 1492–1688', PhD dissertation, History, The Johns Hopkins University, 2009

Index